Perl
Programming
for the Absolute
Beginner

JERRY LEE FORD, JR.

THOMSON

COURSE TECHNOLOGY

Professional ■ Technical ■ Reference

ISBN-10: 1-59863-222-1

ISBN-13: 978-1-59863-222-4

Library of Congress Catalog Card Number: 2006923266

Printed in the United States of America

07 08 09 10 11 TW 10 9 8 7 6 5 4 3 2 1

Publisher and General Manager, Thomson Course Technology PTR:
Stacy L. Hiquet

Associate Director of Marketing:
Sarah O'Donnell

Manager of Editorial Services:
Heather Talbot

Marketing Manager:
Mark Hughes

Senior Acquisitions Editor:
Todd Jensen

Marketing Coordinator:
Meg Dunkerly

Project Editor:
Jenny Davidson

Technical Reviewer:
Rob Kinyon

PTR Editorial Services Coordinator:
Elizabeth Furbish

Interior Layout Tech:
Digital Publishing Solutions

Cover Designer:
Mike Tanamachi

Indexer:
Sharon Shock

Proofreader:
Sara Gullion

THOMSON

™

COURSE TECHNOLOGY

Professional ■ Technical ■ Reference

Thomson Course Technology PTR,
a division of Thomson Learning Inc.
25 Thomson Place
Boston, MA 02210
http://www.courseptr.com

*To my wonderful children Alexander, William, and Molly,
and my beautiful wife Mary.*

ACKNOWLEDGMENTS

This book represents the hard work and effort of many individuals. I would like to thank Todd Jensen, this book's acquisitions editor, for working with me on our seventh writing project. Thanks also go out to Rob Kinyon, who as the book's technical editor helped keep me on track by providing valuable advice and guidance. I'd also be remiss if I did not thank Jenny Davidson for lending her considerable copy editing services. Finally, I'd like to thank everyone else at Thomson Course Technology PTR for all their hard work.

ABOUT THE AUTHOR

Jerry Lee Ford, Jr. is an author, educator, and IT professional with over 17 years of experience in information technology, including roles as an automation analyst, technical manager, technical support analyst, automation engineer, and security analyst. Jerry has a master's degree in Business Administration from Virginia Commonwealth University in Richmond, Virginia. He is the author of 16 books and co-author of 2 additional books. His published works include *Microsoft Visual Basic 2005 Express Edition Programming for the Absolute Beginner, VBScript Professional Projects, Microsoft Windows Shell Scripting and WSH Administrator's Guide, Learn VBScript in a Weekend, Microsoft Windows Shell Scripting for the Absolute Beginner, Learn JavaScript in a Weekend,* and *Microsoft Windows XP Professional Administrator's Guide.* He has over five years' experience as an adjunct instructor teaching networking courses in Information Technology. Jerry lives in Richmond, Virginia, with his wife, Mary, and their children William, Alexander, and Molly.

TABLE OF CONTENTS

Part III   **ADVANCED TOPICS**...**225**

Chapter 7   **REGULAR EXPRESSIONS**...............................**227**

Chapter 8   **DEBUGGING**...**267**

Introduction

Welcome to *Perl Programming for the Absolute Beginner.* Perl is an enormously popular scripting language that runs on many different operating systems, including Windows, Linux, Unix, and Mac OS X. Perl is a general purpose programming language that can be used to do just about anything. Perl is a favorite programming language for many system administrators who need a fast, flexible, and reliable tool for creating and running administrative scripts. Perl is also used on web servers throughout the Internet to provide the glue that ties together the software run inside web browsers with the software and data stored on web servers in order to create interactive online commerce.

In short, Perl is everywhere. Perl can be used to write small scripts that can perform repetitive tasks over and over again many times faster than can be done manually. Perl scripts can be made up of as few as 10 to 20 lines of code. As such, Perl scripts can be developed many times faster than traditional software programs, allowing Perl programmers to be more productive and efficient. This helps to make Perl a great choice for most small scripting tasks. It helps make Perl a great first programming language to learn. Perl scripts can also be quite large and complicated and perform the most complicated of tasks when need be. Still, you will find that Perl scripts can be developed in only a fraction of the time that it takes to develop programs using other programming languages like C++ and Visual Basic.

Perl does not require that you first learn how to interact with and master a complicated development environment in order to become productive. Perl provides you with a robust and powerful programming language that is easy to learn, yet sufficiently complex to tackle just about any job. Perl allows beginner programmers to focus on the basic steps involved in programming without having to worry about many of the complexities that other programming languages impose on programmers.

Because Perl runs just about everywhere, you can often take your Perl scripts with you from one operating system to another and run them with little if any changes. This ease of portability is one of the strengths that has helped to make Perl one of the most popular programming languages in the world.

As this book will show you, Perl is relatively easy to learn, even though it may take years to fully master. Perl is also a great starter language from which you can jump off and learn other programming languages. It can be used to tackle the most simple and complex programming tasks. It can be used to create just about any type of computer programs that you can think of, including computer games, as this book will demonstrate.

WHO SHOULD READ THIS BOOK?

This book has been designed to teach you how to develop Perl scripts and to help you become an effective programmer. Previous programming experience is not a prerequisite. This book does not assume that you have experience with other programming languages or that you are already a technical guru. Still, you do need to have a good general understanding of computers and how they work. In addition, you need to have some experience with your computing platform of choice. In other words, if you want to learn Perl so that you can eventually start developing Windows or Unix administrative scripts, then you need to have previous Windows or Unix experience. Likewise, if you want to take what you learn in this book and apply it to web development, then you need to bring with you a basic understanding of how the Internet works, how to work with HTML, and so on.

Regardless of whether you are an experienced programmer looking to learn a second programming language or you are reading this book as the first step in your programming career, you will find that this book's games-based teaching approach is both effective and fun and that it makes the learning process a lot more enjoyable. You will also find that the knowledge you'll gain from developing Perl-based games will provide you with a strong foundation from which you can branch out and tackle even more complex challenges.

WHAT YOU NEED TO BEGIN

As has already been stated, Perl runs on many different operating systems and in many different environments. When developing this book, I worked with Perl on computers running Windows XP, SuSe Linux 9.2, and Max OS X 10.4. You will see examples of scripts demonstrated on each of these operating systems. However, the scripts that this book will teach you how to create won't be tied to a specific operating system, meaning you should be able to run them on any computer on which Perl has been installed.

So, while you do not need to have access to all of these different operating systems, you do need access to a computer where Perl is installed or where you can install and run it. Regardless of which operating system you choose, you should still be able to follow along with all the examples demonstrated in this book without any problem.

In order to create your Perl scripts, you will need access to a text editor. A *text editor* is a software application that saves text without any additional formatting. If you are going to be working with Windows, you can use Notepad when writing your Perl scripts. If you are using Linux or Unix, you can use vi. If your Linux or Unix operating system provides a graphical interface, you probably have access to a plain text editor as well. If you are working with Mac OS X, you can use the TextEdit program. Just make sure that you select the Make Plain Text option on the Format menu prior to saving your first script.

Over time you may find yourself yearning for more features than those provided by these basic text editors. For example, you may want to look for custom script editors that provide advanced features like syntax color-coding, automatic indenting, and syntax checking. You'll find links to a number of exceptional Perl editors on this book's companion website (www.courseptr.com/downloads). To learn more about these Perl editors, check out Appendix B, "What's on the Companion Website?".

How This Book Is Organized

I have written this book based on the assumption that you will read it sequentially from cover to cover. However, if you already have a strong programming background with a different programming language, you might prefer to jump around and pick topics that are of the most interest to you.

Perl Programming for the Absolute Beginner is organized into four parts. Part I consists of two chapters that provide you with a gentle introduction to Perl and get you started on creating your first Perl scripts. Part II is made up of four chapters that are designed to provide you with a solid overview of the programming statements that make up the Perl programming language and provide instruction on how to organize and structure your Perl scripts. Part III consists of two advanced chapters that cover regular expression and debugging. Part IV is made up of appendices that provide you with additional sample scripts, information about the book's website, other resources that you may find helpful, as well as a glossary of terms used throughout the book.

A detailed overview of the information that you will find in this book is outlined below.

- **Chapter 1, "Perl Basics."** This chapter provides you with an overview of Perl. This includes an examination of Perl's capabilities and a little background information. You will learn the basic steps involved in creating and running Perl scripts on various operating systems. This will include learning how to execute both Perl one-liners and Perl scripts. You will also learn how to develop your first Perl script game.

- **Chapter 2, "Working with Strings, Numbers, and Operators."** This chapter teaches you how to work with strings and numbers and how to store and manipulate information in variables. You will be introduced to Perl's operators and will learn how to process input and control the display script output. In addition, you will learn how to create your second Perl script game, the Story of William the Great.

- **Chapter 3, "Controlling Program Flow."** In this chapter you will learn how to apply conditional logic in your scripts. You will also learn how to set up different kinds of programming loops in order to repeatedly process large amounts of data. You will then take everything that you have learned and apply it to the chapter's game project, the Perl Fortune Teller.

- **Chapter 4, "Working with Collections of Data."** In this chapter you will learn how to more efficiently work with collections of related data. You will learn how to create and sort lists. You will learn how to store and manage data in arrays. You will also learn how to create hashes and to add, delete, and process hash contents. This chapter will wrap up by teaching you how to apply what you have learned to the development of the Star Wars Jedi Master Quiz.

- **Chapter 5, "Improving Script Organization and Structure."** The primary focus of this chapter is to show you how to enhance the overall organization of your scripts using subroutines and functions. This will include learning how to pass arguments and return results back to calling statements. This chapter wraps up by showing you how to apply the information presented in the chapter through the development of the What's My Number game.

- **Chapter 6, "Scope and Modules."** This chapter covers a number of different topics. You will learn how to limit access to variables and to define and wrap up variables in packages. You will also learn how to speed up script development time and enhance your scripts using Perl modules. This chapter wraps up by teaching you how to create the Perl Lottery Number Picker and by introducing pseudocode as a script development tool.

- **Chapter 7, "Regular Expressions."** This chapter will expound on one of Perl's primary strengths, regular expressions. You will learn how to set up pattern matches and then to find, extract, and replace text strings and numbers. You will then learn how to develop the chapter game project, the Rock, Paper, Scissors game. You will also be introduced to flowcharting and learn how to use it to plan out the logical flow of your Perl scripts.

- **Chapter 8, "Debugging."** In this chapter you will learn how to find and fix errors that may occur in your Perl scripts. This will include learning how to track down and fix syntax and logical errors. You will learn how to use Perl's built-in debugger in order to trace logic flow, debug commands, and set up breakpoints that allow you to pause script execution at predefined points. The chapter then wraps up by showing you how to develop the Perl Tic Tac Toe game.

- **Appendix A, "Perl Scripting Examples."** This appendix provides you with a sample collection of Perl scripts that will provide you with ideas of how you can apply your Perl programming knowledge and experience to performing real-world tasks like system administration and CGI scripting.

- **Appendix B, "What's on the Companion Website?"** This appendix reviews the materials that you will find on the book's companion website (www.courseptr.com/downloads). This includes copies of all the Perl game scripts that are presented in this book as well as links to trial and freeware copies of various Perl editors that you may want to experiment with.

- **Appendix C, "What Next?"** In this appendix, I will present you with some closing thoughts and a few tips on how to further your Perl programming education. This will include additional recommended reading and links to some especially helpful websites dedicated to Perl.

- **Glossary.** This appendix provides a glossary of key terms that are used throughout the book.

CONVENTIONS USED IN THIS BOOK

I have used a number of different conventions in order to make this book as easy as possible to read and understand. These conventions are described below.

As you read along, I'll provides suggestions and point out different ways of doing things in order to help make you a better and more efficient Perl programmer.

I will point out areas where mistakes are likely to occur and provide you with advice on how to avoid these types of situations.

I will provide you with shortcuts and programming tips that can help you to work faster and more efficiently.

IN THE REAL WORLD

In addition to teaching you the basics of Perl programming, I will pause at various places in the book to explain how certain programming techniques can be applied to specific real-world situations.

CHALLENGES

I will close out each chapter by teaching you how to create a new computer game. I will then wrap things up by providing you with a series of suggestions that you can follow up on in order to enhance and improve the chapter's game project and to further advance your Perl programming skills.

Part

I

Introducing Perl

PERL BASICS

Perl is an extremely popular computer language that runs on many operating systems, including Windows, Linux, and Mac OS X. Large and small companies around the world in just about any industry you can think of utilize Perl to develop or tie together mission critical software programs. In this chapter, I will introduce you to Perl scripting and provide you with a little background information, laying the foundation that you will need to read the rest of this book. This will include learning how to create, edit, and execute Perl scripts on various operating systems, including Windows, Linux, and Mac OS X. By the end of this chapter, you will have created your first Perl script game and will have a good understanding of the mechanics of script creation.

Specifically, you will learn:

- What Perl is and the kinds of tasks that Perl scripts can automate
- A little bit about Perl's history
- How to access Perl documentation
- The mechanics of creating, editing, and running Perl scripts on different operating systems

PROJECT PREVIEW: THE PERL HUMOR SCRIPT

In this chapter and in all chapters that follow, you will learn how to create a new computer game using Perl. This chapter's game, the Perl Humor Script, is a text-based script that is run from the operating system's Command Prompt.

 Although it may seem funny to begin writing Perl scripts before you have had a complete review of the language, I think you will find it both helpful and informative to learn by jumping right in to things. But don't worry if you do not understand everything that you see right away; just try to absorb what you can and keep going. By the time you have finished this book, everything covered should make sense to you.

By completing this chapter's game project, you will learn the basic steps required to create and execute Perl scripts. The Perl Humor Script is relatively simple as far as Perl scripts go. Still, it demonstrates a number of important Perl programming concepts. Although this script will run just fine on Linux and Mac OS X, I'll demonstrate how to create and run it on Windows XP.

To run the Perl Humor Script, you will need to open the Windows Command Prompt, type in the name of the script, and then press Enter. The Perl script will respond by displaying a text message that asks the player if he or she would like to hear a joke, as shown in Figure 1.1. If the player responds with anything other than an answer of yes, the script will stubbornly keep asking the player the same question repeatedly (as shown in Figure 1.2) until the player replies yes. The Perl script then sets up its joke by asking the player to answer a trick

FIGURE 1.1

The Perl Humor Script prompts the player for permission to tell a joke.

question, as shown in Figure 1.3. If the player guesses incorrectly, the game prompts the player to rethink his or her answer before guessing again, as shown in Figure 1.4. If the player guesses correctly, the Perl script congratulates the player, as shown in Figure 1.5.

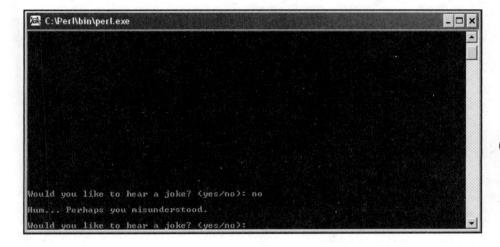

FIGURE 1.2

The Perl script stubbornly keeps asking until the player responds with an answer of yes.

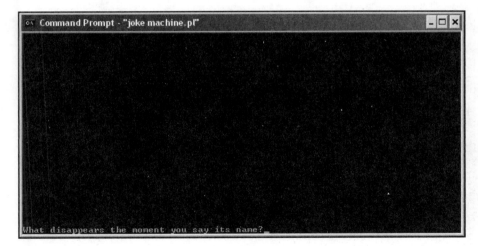

FIGURE 1.3

Once given permission, the Perl script asks the player to try and guess the answer to a trick question.

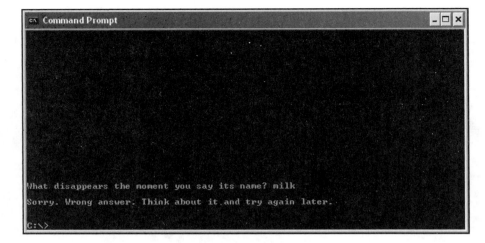

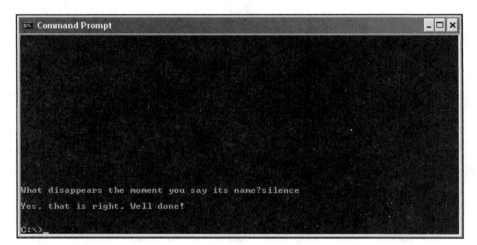

PERL SCRIPTING OVERVIEW

Perl is an interpreted programming language, often referred to as a scripting language, that was created by Larry Wall in 1987. Perl is sometimes referred to as the Practical Extraction and Report Language, which in fact is a backronym and not an acronym, meaning that this extended name was associated with Perl long after the language was originally given the name Perl.

Perl is free. You do not have to go out and buy a copy of it from your local computer superstore. You do not have to purchase a Perl compiler or a Perl editor to create scripts. You only need the perl interpreter. If it is not already installed on your computer, you can download and install a copy of it at no charge. You can also create and sell Perl scripts without having to pay any royalty fees.

Perl's syntax is based very heavily on the syntax used by the C programming language. However, Perl also incorporates syntactical features borrowed from Unix shell scripting, sed, awk, and List. In addition, Perl is written in C, so it is relatively fast.

Perl is a general purpose scripting language. It is sometimes referred to as the Swiss Army Knife of Programming Languages, meaning that it can be implemented anywhere in order to perform just about any task. Often, you can create Perl scripts in just a fraction of the time that it might take for you to do so using another programming language. Perl can parse text files, generate reports, interact with databases, work with CGI to develop web scripts, and execute built-in network functions. Perl has also been called the Duct Tape of the Internet because it is so versatile that it is often used to tie together different software applications that were never intended to work together.

A Little Perl History

Perl was created in 1987 by Larry Wall and made available to the general public when Larry published on comp.sources.misc.newsgroup. According to the documentation that was included with Perl, it was intended to be a practical programming language that combined the best features of C, sed, sh, and awk, using a syntax that closely resembled the C programming language. Perl was optimized for processing and extracting information from text files and for printing reports. Larry also envisioned Perl as a good language to use when creating system management scripts.

In 1988 Perl 2 was released. New features included better support for regular expressions, the ability to localize variables, the ability to run scripts using warnings, the addition of the sort operator, and optimization improvements that made Perl run faster. In 1989 Perl 3 was released. New features included debugger enhancements, support for binary data, and a host of new built-in functions. In 1991 the first Perl programming book was published. In response, Perl's version number increased to 4 as an acknowledgement of this event. No major changes were introduced with the version jump to Perl 4.

In 1994 Perl 5 was released. It was a complete rewrite of the language. New features included a limited support of objects (object-oriented programming), more extensive documentation, and support for modules. Modules are add-on extensions developed for Perl that allow its capabilities to be extended without requiring any changes to the perl interpreter.

Note the difference in capitalization of the word Perl in the previous paragraph. By convention, you should capitalize the word Perl when referring to the programming language and use all lowercase spelling when referring to perl interpreter, which is responsible for reading and executing Perl scripts.

In 1995 Perl and CGI were combined and embedded into HTML for the first time, opening up a whole new world of opportunity for Perl programmers and paving the way for Perl to become a major programming language for web application developers.

In 2000 a new initiative was begun at the annual Perl Conference to begin work on a redesign of the language. Under Larry Hall's guidance, Perl community feedback was solicited. Hundreds of RFCs (Request for Comments) were received. By 2001 a framework was outlined for Perl 6. Among other things, Perl 6 will significantly increase the language's object-oriented capabilities.

The new plans for Perl 6 require a complete reworking of the language. As a result, Perl 6 is not being designed with backward compatibility as a requirement. Even though a compatibility mode has been promised, some older Perl scripts may require modification in order to run under Perl 6.

Where's Perl 6?

As of the publishing of this book in 2006, Perl 6 was still under development, and Perl 5.8.7 was the current version. Perl 6 has been under development for years and there is still no official release date in site.

Why the delay? Perl does not have the backing of a major software development corporation like Microsoft behind it to move it along. Instead, a volunteer community is developing Perl. Few are paid anything for their work, and no one is paid full-time.

What Can Perl Scripts Do?

Perl's initial mission was to read and parse files, process data that was gathered, and then generate reports. Using Perl, you can write scripts to extract data from text, binary, and even database files; process and sort it in any way that suits; and then save it or use it to generate new reports or to create HTML documents. Over the years Perl's capabilities have been constantly expanded.

Perl scripts run on many different platforms. This includes running on over 100 different operating systems and a number of different computing environments, including the Internet, local area networks, and with databases. Today, Perl can be used just about anywhere computing is done. Perl is so powerful and flexible that the possible number of applications to which it could be applied is endless. Still, it is possible to generalize and list broad categories where Perl is being applied today, as outlined in the following list.

- **Server Administration.** Computer administrators use Perl to create Perl scripts that automate all kinds of tasks, such as performing disk administration, service management, and performance tuning. It is especially adept at performing tasks that are highly repetitive, mundane, or subject to human error.

- **Desktop Administration.** Desktop administrators use Perl to develop scripts that perform an assortment of tasks, including configuring network access, synchronizing local and network files, software installation, and account management.

- **Network Administration.** Network administrators use Perl to develop scripts that help to configure, diagnose, and administer networks. This category also includes scripts that interact with and control network devices.

- **Application Development.** Applications programmers use Perl every day to create all kinds of software. Perl is a key component in software applications running in corporate, government, and military applications all around the world.

- **Database Administration.** Database administrators use Perl to automate database administration tasks such as database setup, backup, account administration, problem diagnosis, and performance tuning.

- **Web Development.** Web developers use Perl in conjunction with CGI to develop applications that allow software run in user browsers to interact with software run on back-end corporate web and database servers, thus facilitating true interactive web commerce.

One of Perl's major strengths is that it is portable, meaning that a script written on one operating system will in many cases run on another operating system with little if any modification, so long as the script does not contain any platform-specific features.

THE PROGRAMMING LANGUAGE, THE INTERPRETER, AND SCRIPTS

Perl is a robust programming language made up of a large collection of language statements, operators, functions, and so on. Using the Perl language, you create Perl scripts. To run these scripts, they must be submitted to the perl interpreter, which is responsible for translating statements inside Perl scripts into a format that the operating system understands and can execute. The perl interpreter is written in C, which is an extremely powerful and efficient programming language. As a result, the perl interpreter is relatively fast.

Another component of Perl is Perl modules. A *module* is an add-on component that provides Perl with capabilities not built into the perl interpreter. Perl programmers around the world create Perl modules. Chances are that if you run into a situation where you want to use Perl to do something but cannot figure out how to do it with the core language, somebody else has run into this same problem and solved it by creating a new Perl module. You can find thousands of modules for free download at www.cpan.org/modules/. To learn more about modules, check out Chapter 6, "Scope and Modules."

As has already been stated, Perl scripts are interpreted programs. What this means is that unlike C++ or Visual Basic, Perl scripts are not precompiled and made ready for immediate execution. Instead, Perl programs are processed by the perl interpreter at run-time. When called, the first thing the perl interpreter does is parse the script into a syntax tree. If any syntax errors are detected, they are flagged and script execution stops. Otherwise, the perl interpreter executes the script line-by-line by stepping through the syntax tree.

WORKING FROM THE COMMAND PROMPT

Unlike many modern programming languages, Perl does not support the development of applications that have a graphical user interface or GUI. Instead, Perl scripts are text based and run from the Command Prompt. In order to become an effective Perl programmer, you must become comfortable working with the Command Prompt.

The Command Prompt is a text-based interface to the operating system that accepts commands and submits them for processing and then displays any results or errors that are returned.

Every modern operating system provides access to a Command Prompt. For some Unix and Linux systems, the Command Prompt may be the default user interface displayed at startup. However, if you are using a Unix or Linux system with a graphical user interface or are running Windows or Mac OS X, you will need to seek out the Command Prompt.

Accessing the Command Prompt on Windows XP

Access to the Command Prompt in Windows XP is provided through the Windows command console. To open a new command console and display the Command Prompt, click Start > All Programs > Accessories > Command Prompt, as demonstrated in Figure 1.6.

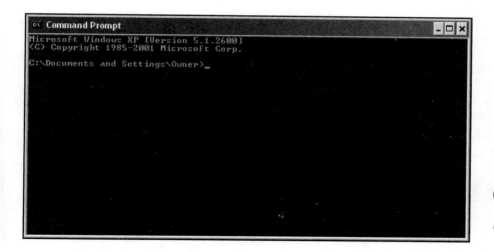

FIGURE 1.6

Accessing the
Command Prompt
in Windows XP.

 TRICK The Windows Command Prompt can also be accessed by clicking Start > Run and then typing CMD and clicking OK.

Accessing the Command Prompt on Mac OS X

To access the Command Prompt in Mac OS X, you need to open a Terminal window. To do so, double-click on the Macintosh HD icon, which by default is located on the Mac OS X desktop. Next, double-click on the Applications folder and scroll down to the bottom. You should see a folder named Utilities. Double-click on it. You will be presented with a collection of Mac OS X utility programs, one of which is named Terminal. Double-click on it to access the Mac OS X Command Prompt, as demonstrated in Figure 1.7.

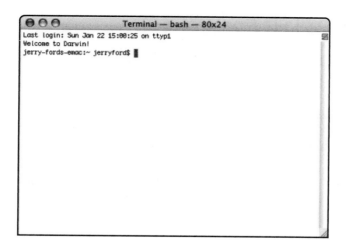

FIGURE 1.7

Accessing the
Command Prompt
in Mac OS X.

TRICK   The Mac OS X Command Prompt can also be accessed by clicking on the Spotlight icon in the upper-right-hand corner of the desktop and typing **Terminal** in the Spotlight field. When you do this, Mac OS X responds by displaying an icon representing the Terminal utility. Click on the Terminal icon to open it.

Accessing the Command Prompt in Unix and Linux

As has been stated, some Unix and Linux implementations boot up to the Command Prompt. Other Unix and Linux implementations boot up to a graphical desktop. For these operating systems, you will have to track down the location of a terminal application and open it. For example, Figure 1.8 shows the xterm terminal console found on many Unix and Linux systems.

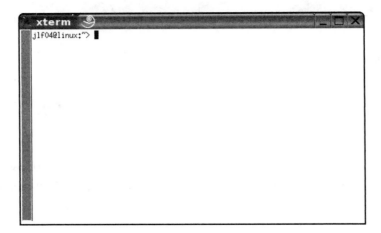

FIGURE 1.8

Accessing the
Command Prompt
on Linux and Unix
systems using the
xterm console.

NOT EVERYTHING SMELLS LIKE ROSES

Just like every other programming language that has even been developed, Perl has its pros and cons. This chapter has already expounded on many of Perl's finer features. But to present a fair and balanced view of Perl, it is important to point out a few things that people sometimes complain about.

For starters, Perl is an extremely flexible programming language. Some critics say that it is too flexible. Perl does not provide mechanisms for enforcing data security like other modern programs do. This means that unless you are disciplined enough to follow good programming practices in how you set up your scripts, you can do some really sloppy and unconventional things in Perl. For example, Perl does not prevent you from accessing an object created in one part of your scripts from any other part of your scripts. There are no built-in mechanisms for preventing the accidental modification or deletion of object attributes or data. In short, Perl lets you manipulate objects any time and in any way you wish. Other modern programming languages are far more disciplined in their implementation of objects and have rules as to when and how objects and their data can be manipulated. To some, Perl's wide-open approach is everything they have always wanted in a programming language. However, others cringe at the mere thought of the lack of structure imposed by Perl and worry about the number of different ways that Perl potentially allows programmers to shoot themselves in the foot.

Another drawback to Perl is that it is not as efficient as other programming languages such as C and C++ when it comes to certain processor bound tasks, resulting in slower execution and greater memory consumption. Still, most Perl advocates think that Perl's flexibility, ease of use, and reduced script development time more than offset any such disadvantages.

Perl is generally regarded as a programming language that is easy to learn. While this is certainly true, the programming language is so flexible and freewheeling that it can be made very complex depending on how it is used. For example, one of Perl's strengths is its flexibility. It provides you with many different ways to perform the same task. Because of this, things get complicated when different programmers use different techniques for solving the same problem. By and large Perl programmers love Perl's flexibility. However, it is this very strength that turns off some programmers who see Perl's wide-open nature as lending itself to complexity and anarchy.

DETERMINING IF PERL IS INSTALLED ON YOUR COMPUTER

Obviously, before you can start working with Perl, you must determine if it is installed on your computer, and if it is not, you must download and install it. To see if Perl is installed on your computer, enter the following command at the Command Prompt:

```
perl -v
```

If Perl is installed, it will respond by printing out its version number, as demonstrated in Figure 1.9.

If the version of Perl installed on your computer is not at least version 5.0, you should install a newer version of Perl. Compared to Perl 5.X, previous versions of Perl have more bugs and fewer capabilities.

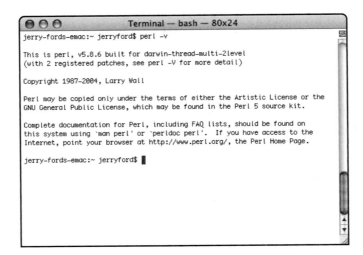

WHERE TO FIND PERL

If you don't have Perl installed on your computer, you can download and install it from a number of different distribution sites found on the Internet. If, for example, you plan on running your Perl scripts on a computer running Mac OS X, then Perl 5.8.X should be installed. In the event that it is not, you can download a Perl installation package from Apple at www.apple.com/downloads/macosx/unix_open_source/perl.html, as shown in Figure 1.10.

If you are using the older Mac Classic operating system, then you may have a copy of MacPerl installed on the computer. If it is not installed or if you want to install a newer version of Perl, you can do so by downloading a new distribution of MacPerl at www.cpan.org/ports/mac/.

Another very popular source for downloading Perl distribution is ActiveState's ActivePerl. ActiveState provides download Perl installation packages for a number of popular operating systems, including:

- AIX
- HP-UX
- Linux
- Mac OS X
- Solaris
- Windows

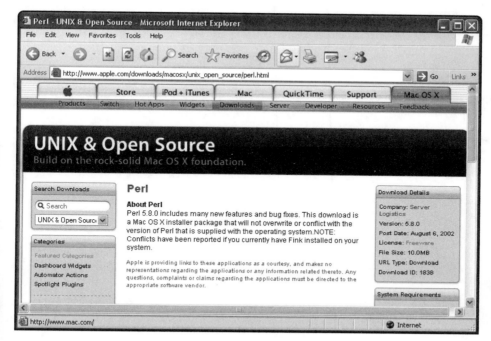

FIGURE 1.10

Downloading Perl
for Mac OS X from
the Apple website.

ActiveState's website can be found at www.activestate.com, as demonstrated in Figure 1.11. In addition to downloading a free copy of Perl from ActiveState, you can also purchase commercial support for Perl. The advantage of acquiring Perl in this manner is that you can get assistance and technical support from ActiveState in the event that you have problems installing Perl or run into trouble later on.

Another major source of Perl distributions is the CPAN Perl Ports page found at www.cpan.org/ports/. The Comprehensive Perl Archive Network or CPAN is the primary repository of Perl distributions, documentation, scripts, and modules. Perl has been ported to hundreds of different platforms. From here, you can download and install Perl distribution packages for any of the platforms listed in Table 1.1.

TRICK Many Linux and Unix software distributions automatically install Perl as part of the operating systems' install process. In addition, many Linux and Unix vendors provide pre-built software installation packages that they bundle with the operating system which can be installed optionally during operating system installation or after the fact. Therefore, you may be able to install Perl using a package installation utility provided by the Linux or Unix vendor.

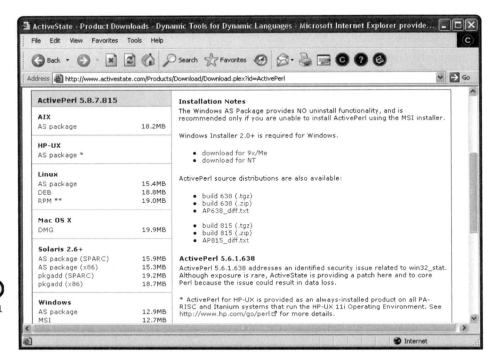

FIGURE 1.11

Downloading Perl from the ActiveState website.

TABLE 1.1	PERL PORTS THAT CAN BE DOWNLOADED FROM CPAN		
Acorn	Digital	IRIX	NetBSD
AIX	Digital	Japanese	NetWare
Amiga	DEC OSF/1	Jperl	NEWS-OS
Apollo	Domain/OS	Linux	NextStep
Apple	Dragon	LynxOS	NonStop
Atari	DYNIX/ptx	Mac OS	NonStop-UX
AtheOS	Embedix	Mac OS X	Novell
BeOS	EMC	Macintosh	ODT
BSD	EPOC	MachTen	Open
BSD/OS	FreeBSD	MinGW	OpenBSD
Coherent	Fujitsu	Minix	OpenVMS
Compaq	GNU Darwin	MiNT	OS/2
Concurrent	Guardian	MorphOS	OS/390
Cygwin	HP	MPE/iX	OS/400
Darwin	HP-UX	FlyBSD	OSF/1
DG/UX	IBM	MVS	OSR

Plan 9	Sharp	Tivo	Windows 3.1
Pocket PC	Siemens	Tru64	Windows 95/98/Me/NT/2000/XP
PowerMAX	SINIX	Ultrix	z/OS
Psion	Solaris		
QNX	SONY	Unixware	Sequent
Reliant	Stratus	U/WIN	
RISCOS	Sun	VMS	
SCO	Syllable	VOS	
MS-DOS	Symbian	Win32	
SGI	Tandem	WinCE	

WHERE TO FIND PERL'S DOCUMENTATION

Every Perl distribution ships with a full copy of Perl's documentation, which covers both the Perl language and its interpreter. This documentation consists of:

- Perl's Reference or Manual pages
- Frequently Asked Questions or FAQs pages
- Perl tutorials
- Perl history documentation

Perldoc

There are a number of different ways to get at Perl's documentation, depending on which type of operating system you are using. For example, if you are running Linux, Unix, or Windows, you can run a Perl utility named perldoc. This utility program provides you with the ability to search through Perl's documentation for specific topics. For example, to get information about Perl on a computer running Windows XP, you would open the Windows Command Prompt by clicking on Start > All Programs > Accessories > Command Prompt and then entering the following command.

```
Perldoc perl
```

Figure 1.12 shows the output returned by this command. Because the output is too large to be viewed at one time, it is displayed a page at a time. To move forward a page at a time press the Enter key.

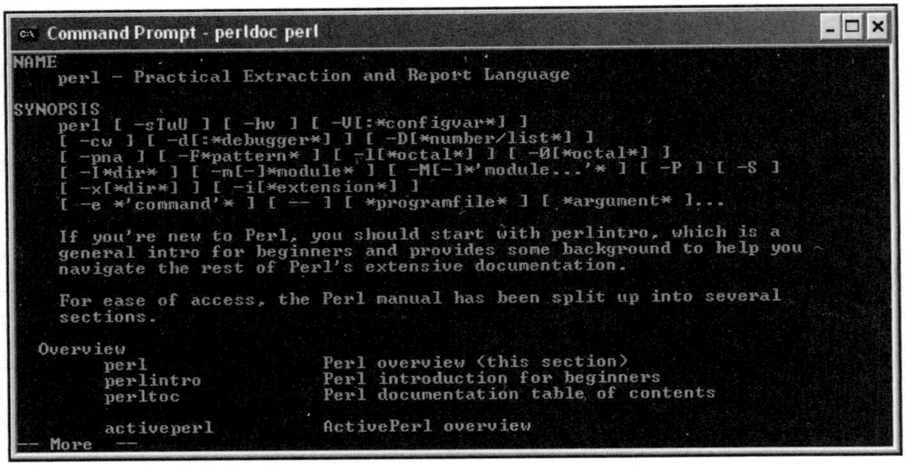

FIGURE 1.12

Using perldoc to
access Perl
documentation on
Windows XP.

Information in Perl's manual pages is organized into different areas. For example, there are sections named perlfaq, perlfunc, perldiag, and perldebug where you will find information about FAQs, Perl functions, Perl diagnostics, and Perl debugging. You can access these sections by typing in `perldoc` followed by the name of a section. Alternatively, if there is a specific topic you which to search on, you can do so by typing perldoc follow by `-tf` and then the name of the topic to be searched for, as demonstrated in Figure 1.13.

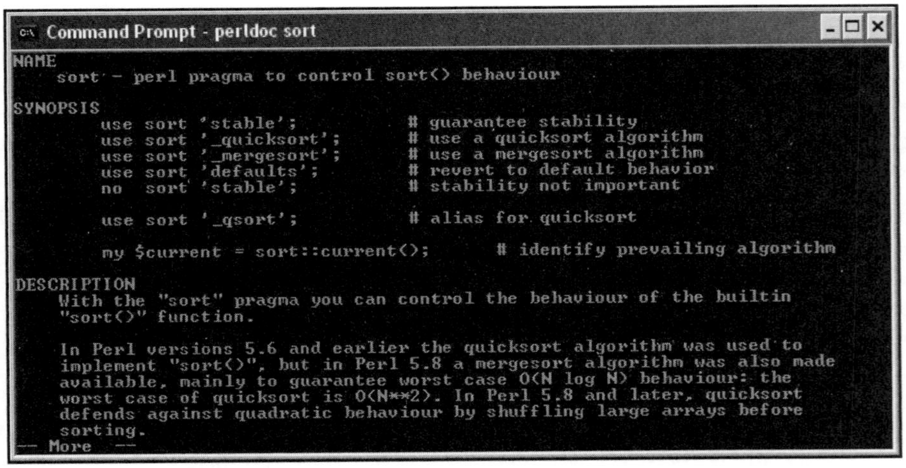

FIGURE 1.13

Using perldoc to
search for
information about
the sort function
on Windows XP.

Man Pages

If you are working with Linux, Unix, or Mac OS X, you can use the man program to access Perl manual pages. To do so, just open up a Command Prompt and type man followed by the topic you want information on. Information about the specified topic, if available, is then displayed as demonstrated in Figure 1.14.

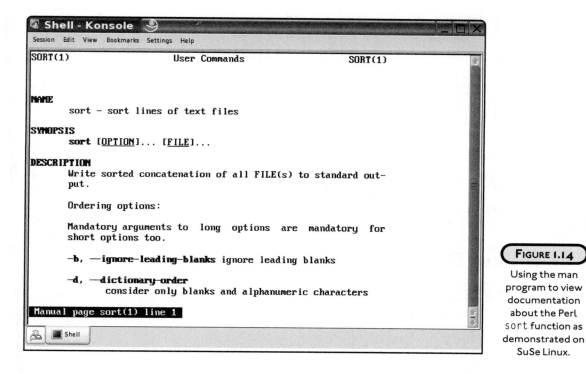

FIGURE 1.14

Using the man program to view documentation about the Perl sort function as demonstrated on SuSe Linux.

ActiveState Documentation

If you are using a Windows distribution of Perl downloaded from ActiveState, you can view manual pages as HTML pages by opening your web browser and pointing it to C:\perl\html\index.html, as demonstrated in Figure 1.15.

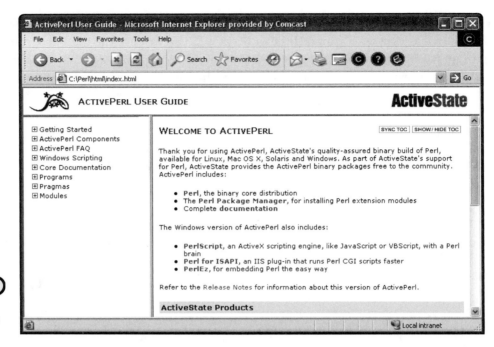

Figure 1.15

Viewing Perl's
manual pages as
HTML pages.

Writing Your First Perl Scripts

Perl lets you run Perl scripts in either of two ways. First off, its lets you execute small one-line Perl scripts directly from the Command Prompt. These types of scripts are often referred to as one-liners. The second way to run your Perl scripts is as files, which can then be saved and repeatedly executed.

Creating Perl One-liners

One reason that so many server and desktop administrators like Perl is that it provides the ability to write and execute one-liner Perl scripts that can be executed on the fly from the Command Prompt.

Perl one-liners are perfect for performing one-time tasks like renaming all the files in a directory and then displaying a sorted file listing showing the results. To run a Perl one-liner, you must first get to the Command Prompt. Once there, you can key in your script and press Enter to run it. For example, if you are working with Windows, try entering the following one-liner.

```
perl -e "print \"Hello, World!\n\";"
```

This simple Perl script calls on the perl interpreter passing it a script for processing. The -e switch tells the perl interpreter that a one-liner follows. The rest of the statement contains the actual Perl script to be executed. When executed, the text string Hello, World! is displayed.

If you tried running this example on a Unix-, Linux-, or Mac OS X-based system, you most likely ran into trouble. This is because there are some small differences in the way Perl works on different operating systems.

To get this example to run on a Unix-, Linux-, or Mac OS X-based operating system, you would need to rewrite the previous statement as shown here.

```
perl -e 'print "Hello, World!\n";'
```

Writing Your First Perl Script File

Now is a good time to spend a few minutes learning how to create and run Perl script files. As you will see, it is a surprisingly simple process. Begin by opening your preferred text or Perl editor. If necessary, create a new plain text file. Next add the following code statements.

```
#!/usr/bin/perl -w
print "Hello, World!\n";
```

These two statements make up the entire Perl script. Now, save your Perl script and assign it a name of Hello.pl. Although you are not required to include the .pl file extension as part of your Perl script's name, it is a good idea to do so. Doing so explicitly identifies the Perl script. Adding the .pl file extension also makes things work better on Windows and Mac OS X, which use file extensions to associate file types with applications. Another popular file extension that you will sometimes see used when naming Perl scripts is .plx.

Now that you have written your first Perl script, let's run it. Begin by accessing the Command Prompt for your particular operating system. Then, using the cd command, change to the directory where you saved your Perl script, type the name of the Perl script, and press Enter, as demonstrated in Figure 1.16.

TRAP   If you are unable to execute the Perl script on Unix or Linux, you may need to make the script file executable before you can run it. To do so, execute the following command and then try running your script again.

```
chmod +x hello.pl
```

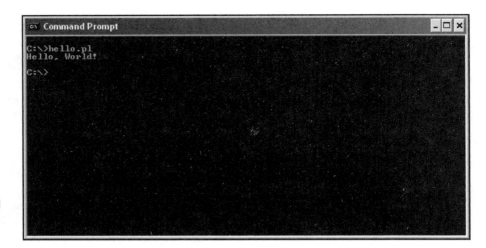

Figure 1.16

Executing your
first Perl script.

Dissecting Hello.pl

Assuming that you did not make a typo when keying in either of the two lines that make up the Perl script, you should see the sentence Hello, Word! displayed when the script runs. While this example may not be the most exciting script ever written, it does provide a framework for analyzing the construction of Perl scripts. So, let's take a few minutes to dissect this Perl script and see what makes it tick.

In Perl, you can help document your scripts by embedding comments directly inside your scripts. You do so by preceding any text that you want to be treated as a comment with the # character. The first statement in the script is actually a special type of comment, often referred to as the *shebang*. On Unix- and Linux-based operating systems, the shebang is used to invoke the perl interpreter. However, on Windows and Mac OS X operating systems, the shebang is ignored when you save your Perl scripts using the optional .pl file extension. These two operating systems use file extensions to associate files with applications. So on Linux and Unix systems, unless Perl was installed using something other than the default directory structure, Perl is installed in the /usr/bin/. On Windows and Mac OS X, where file extensions are used to associate files with applications, the shebang comment statement is ignored.

HINT   Even if you use Unix or Linux and don't ever anticipate running your scripts on Windows or Mac OS X, I recommend that you go ahead and add a .pl file extension to all your Perl scripts. This will help make your scripts more portable and is considered a good programming practice.

The -w switch located at the end of the first line is optional. When added, it tells the perl interpreter to enable warnings when processing the script. This way if any errors occur, you'll see error messages that hopefully will help you track down what went wrong.

IN THE REAL WORLD

Today, many modern programming languages require that you learn how to work with and master a complex integrated development environment or IDE as a prerequisite for developing application programs. Perl does not. Instead, Perl allows you to create Perl scripts using any plain text editor. Despite this, you may want to spend a little time investigating some of the Perl editors that are currently available. They provide you with a number of features that you won't get from your text editor. The features include:

- Syntax color coding of Perl keywords
- Line numbering
- Advanced find and replace commands
- Automatic code indention
- Support for editing multiple scripts at the same time

If you are interested in finding a Perl editor that best fits your needs, read Appendix B, "What's on the Companion Website?" where you will find information about a number of Perl editors that are included on this book's companion website.

 Under the covers, Mac OS X is really just a Unix operating system. Therefore, whenever this book refers to a specific Perl feature on Unix, the information presented also applies to Mac OS X.

The second statement in the Perl script executes a Perl function named print. In this script, the print function's job is to print the text string embedded inside the matching pair of double quotation marks. Note the \n characters that are also included inside the double quotation marks. These two characters have a special meaning to Perl, telling it to print a newline character at the end of the text string. Perl does not display the \n formatting characters. The last thing that you should take note of from the second statement is that it ends with a ; character. The ; character is used to identify the end of a statement in Perl scripts. As such, you should always remember to add it to the end of every statement in your Perl scripts, except for comment statements where it wouldn't serve any purpose.

How Perl Executes Your Script

When you typed in `hello.pl` and pressed the Enter key at the Command Prompt, the perl interpreter was called and passed your script for execution. The perl interpreter's job is to convert the statements that make up your Perl script into a format that the operating system can execute. As mentioned earlier, the perl interpreter performs this task by developing a syntax tree. In doing so it checks and validates each statement that makes up the script to ensure that there are no errors. Assuming that no syntactical errors are discovered, the perl interpreter begins running your script, and once the script finishes executing, the perl interpreter stops running and returns control back to the Command Prompt.

BACK TO THE PERL HUMOR SCRIPT

Okay, it is time to turn your attention back to the chapter's main game project, Perl Humor Script. The development of this game will demonstrate how to create a script that can interact with the player by displaying messages, retrieving command-line input, and applying simple programming logic to control the operation of the script.

Designing the Game

Before writing the first line of code, it is important to spend a little time planning the script's overall design. The Perl Humor Script will begin by prompting the player for permission to tell a joke. If the player responds by typing in anything other than `yes`, the script will simply repeat its request over and over again. Once the player finally enters `yes`, the script will display its trick question and wait for the player to make his or her guess. If the guess entered by the player is wrong, the script advises the player to rethink the answer and to come back and try again later. If the player's guess is correct, he or she is congratulated.

TRICK You can usually terminate the execution of interactive Perl script on Windows, Unix, and Linux by pressing Ctrl + C or by pressing Control + C on Mac OS X.

As you can see, the overall logical flow of the Perl script is fairly simple. To set it up, we will complete its development in six steps, as outlined below:

1. Create a new script file and add opening comment statements.
2. Clear the screen and prepare to collect the player's responses.
3. Prompt the player for permission to tell the joke and process the player's response.
4. Clear the screen and display the trick question.
5. Analyze the player's guess in order to determine whether it is correct.
6. Develop programming logic to clear the screen.

Creating a New Perl Script

Begin by opening your text or Perl editor in order to create a new file. Save the file and assign it a name of JokeMachine.pl. Next, add the following code statements to the file.

```
#!/usr/bin/perl -w
#
# JokeMachine.pl
```

These statements are just comments. The first statement is the shebang. The next line is an empty comment that was added for aesthetic reasons in order to visually separate the first and third lines. The third line is simply the name of the script embedded in a comment. Other information that you might want to add to this line includes your name and the creation date of the script.

Prepping the Screen and Game

Next, add the following pair of statements to the script just under the previous statements.

```
clear_the_screen();

$reply = "";
```

The first statement calls a subroutine called clear_the_screen() located at the bottom of the script. In order to give the script a clean presentation, it is a good idea to clear the console area of any other text that may already be displayed. To accomplish this we'll write a small subroutine a little later that performs this task. A *subroutine* is a collection of code statements that can be called and executed as a unit. We'll call this subroutine when needed throughout the script in order to clear the screen before displaying text strings on the screen. The second statement defines a variable that the script will use to store player input. A *variable* is a reference to a location in memory where data can be stored and retrieved.

TRAP

Don't worry if all this doesn't make a lot of sense just yet. For now you should try and focus your attention on the overall process that you are going through and attempt to absorb as much of what is going on as possible. In later chapters you will learn everything you need in order to be able to come back and make sense out of what each of these individual programming statements is actually doing.

Prompting the Player

Next, add the following programming statements to the script. These statements are responsible for prompting the player for permission to tell the joke. This is accomplished by setting up a while loop that iterates over and over again until the script gets the response it wants from the player (e.g. a reply of yes).

```
while ( $reply ne 'yes') {
  print 'Would you like to hear a joke? (yes/no): ';
  chomp($reply = <STDIN>);

  if( $reply ne 'yes') {
    print "\nHum... Perhaps you misunderstood.\n\n";

  }
}
```

The above statements are controlled by a while statement. The while statement is covered in great detail Chapter 3, "Controlling Program Flow."

Displaying the Trick Question

Once the player finally gives the Perl script permission to tell its joke, the screen has to be cleared again and the script's trick question needs to be presented to the player. The script then collects the player's guess. To accomplish all this, add the following statements to your script.

```
clear_the_screen();

print "\nWhat disappears the moment you say its name?";
chomp($reply = <STDIN>);
```

Notice that the first statement executes the clear_the_screen() subroutine again before printing the trick question. The last statement listed above is responsible for capturing the player's response and assigning it to the variable set up earlier in the script.

Analyzing the Player Guess

Next, add the following statements to the Perl script. These statements analyze the player's response (which is stored in the $reply variable) to see what it is equal to. Based on this analysis, either of two text strings is printed.

```
if( $reply ne 'silence') {
  print "\nSorry. Wrong answer. Think about it and try again later.\n\n";
} else {
  print "\nYes, that is right. Well done!\n\n";
}
```

The above statements are controlled by an if...else statement. You will learn all about if...else statements in Chapter 3.

Controlling the Display

To wrap things up, add the following Perl statements to the end of the script.

```perl
sub clear_the_screen {

  for ($i=0; $i < 25; ++$i){
    print "\n";
  }
}
```

These code statements define the clear_the_screen subroutine. By grouping statements into subroutines, you enable them to be called whenever necessary from any point in a script. You will learn how to work with subroutines in Chapter 5, "Improving Script Organization and Structure."

 HINT This chapter has demonstrated the execution of this Perl script in Windows XP. By default, the Windows command console displays text in a window that is 80 characters wide and 25 lines tall. If you run this script in an operating system other than Windows, you may need to change the number of blank lines that the clear_the_screen subroutine prints.

The Final Result

Okay, that's it. At this point the Perl script should be complete. To help document the construction of this script and make it easier to understand, you may want to go back and embed comments in it that explain what is occurring at key locations within the script. To demonstrate how this is done, look at the following version of the script, which now includes embedded comments.

```perl
#!/usr/bin/perl -w
#
# JokeMachine.pl

clear_the_screen(); #Call subroutine that clears the screen

$reply = "";  #Initialize variable that stores player reply

#Continue to ask the player for permission to tell the joke until
```

```perl
#the player replies with an answer of yes
while ( $reply ne 'yes') {
  print 'Would you like to hear a joke? (yes/no): ';
  chomp($reply = <STDIN>);

  if( $reply ne 'yes') {
    print "\nHum... Perhaps you misunderstood.\n\n";

  }
}


clear_the_screen(); #Call subroutine that clears the screen

#Display the trick question and prompt the player for a response
print "\nWhat disappears the moment you say its name?";

chomp($reply = <STDIN>); #Capture the player's response

#Determine whether the player guessed the right answer
if( $reply ne 'silence') {
  print "\nSorry. Wrong answer. Think about it and try again later.\n\n";
} else {
  print "\nYes, that is right. Well done!\n\n";
}

#This subroutine loops and adds 25 blank lines to the screen when called
sub clear_the_screen {

  for ($i=0; $i < 25; ++$i){
    print "\n";
  }
}
```

Other than improving script readability and helping to document what is going on, the comments added to the script have no impact on how it runs. Once you have finished keying in the code statements for this script, save and run it. If it fails to run and an error is displayed, you've most likely made a typo. Look at the text of the error message. It may provide you with enough information to quickly track down where the error is. If the error message doesn't help, then go back and double-check the text of each statement in the script and look for typos.

SUMMARY

This chapter has covered a lot of material. You learned what Perl is and what it can be used for. You learned how to install Perl on your computer. You learned about Perl's portability and compatibility with various operating systems. This chapter showed where to look for Perl documentation. You learned how to execute Perl one-liners and to develop your own Perl scripts.

The Perl Humor Script is a pretty simple and straightforward example of a Perl script. The thing to take away from completing this script is an understanding of the steps involved in creating, editing, and executing Perl scripts on whatever operating system you are using. Now, when it comes to computer programs and scripts, there is always room for improvement or enhancement. I suggest you set aside a few extra minutes to review the following challenges and see if you can spice up the Perl Humor Script just a bit.

CHALLENGES

1. At present, the Perl Humor Script only tells one joke. Try modifying it to tell additional jokes.
2. Currently the text that provides users with instruction on how to interact with the script is a little dry. See if you can spice things up a bit by making it a little more humorous and witty.

WORKING WITH STRINGS, NUMBERS, AND OPERATORS

Like any programming language, Perl provides you with the ability to store and retrieve data. It also provides you with all the tools you need to manipulate and compare this data. In this chapter you will learn how Perl handles numbers and strings. This will include learning how to set up expressions and manipulate strings. You will also learn how to collect user input and display text output. On top of all this you will learn how to create your second computer game, the Story of William the Great. In doing so you will get to put to work much of what you'll learn in this chapter.

Specifically, you will learn:

- How to store and retrieve data using variables
- How to build mathematical expressions
- How to concatenate strings
- How to collect user input and control script output

PROJECT PREVIEW: THE STORY OF WILLIAM THE GREAT

In this chapter, you will learn how to create a new Perl script that tells the Story of William the Great. This story is told by plugging in key story elements provided by the user. These elements are collected when the game first begins executing.

Specifically, story elements are collected in the form of five questions posed to the user. The user answers each question without knowing in advance the context in which her answers will be used in telling the story, like you would find done in any mad lib-style game. This interactive method of story telling will, of course, lead to unpredictable results.

The Story of William the Great begins by displaying an opening message. To continue with the story, the user is required to press the Enter key, as shown in Figure 2.1.

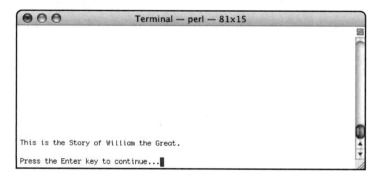

FIGURE 2.1

The story begins with an introductory message.

Next, the user is told that in order for the story to be told, some information must first be collected, as shown in Figure 2.2.

FIGURE 2.2

Information must be collected from the user to tell the story.

The user is then presented with a series of five questions, as demonstrated in Figure 2.3.

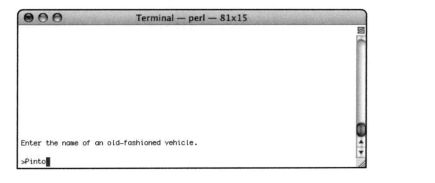

FIGURE 2.3

The user is asked to provide answers to a series of five questions.

Each question is presented without informing the user of the context in which the answers will be used. Once the necessary information has been collected, the user is prompted to begin the telling of the story, as demonstrated in Figure 2.4.

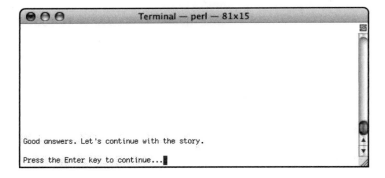

FIGURE 2.4

Once the user has answered all questions, the story can be told.

The story is told a page at a time. As each page is displayed, the information previously collected from the user is plugged into predefined locations in the story to provide an unpredictable and humorous touch, as demonstrated in Figure 2.5.

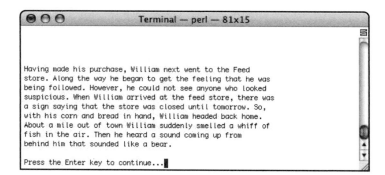

FIGURE 2.5

The story is told a
page at a time.

Finally, the story ends and the user is returned to the Command Prompt, as shown in Figure 2.6.

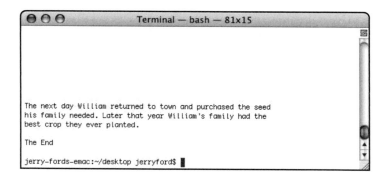

FIGURE 2.6

The story
continues until
the happy ending is
told.

The demonstration of the execution of the Story of William the Great was done on a computer running Mac OS X. However, it will run just as effectively on other operating systems such as Windows, Linux, and Unix.

PERL'S FREE-WHEELING APPROACH TO CODE STRUCTURE

All of the sample Perl scripts that you will see demonstrated throughout this book will be formatted and presented in a structured manner, using statement indentation and the logical grouping of related programming statements. However, there is no rule or requirement in Perl that says that code must be written this way.

Perl code is free form, meaning that Perl is extremely flexible in what it accepts as a valid program statement. Perl lets you insert blank spaces, tabs, and even blank lines at just about any point you want. In fact, about the only places you cannot insert white space are in the middle of keywords, variable names, and function names.

For many, this level of flexibility is just part of what makes Perl a fun and easy to work with programming language. To others, this type of flexibility is seen as a negative feature, because it provides undisciplined programmers the ability to create some really sloppy code. Really, this aspect of Perl is just a matter of personal preference. Certainly, professional Perl programmers understand the value of developing clear, well-formatted Perl scripts and will self-impose a disciplined code structure.

To give you a better idea of the free-form nature of Perl, consider the following sample script.

```perl
#!/usr/bin/perl -w
#
# JokeMachine.pl

clear_the_screen(); #Call subroutine that clears the screen

$reply = "";  #Initialize variable that stores player's reply

#Continue to ask the player for permission to tell the joke until
#the player replies with an answer of yes
while ( $reply ne 'yes') {
  print 'Would you like to hear a joke? (yes/no): ';
  chomp($reply = <STDIN>);

  if( $reply ne 'yes') {
    print "\nHum... Perhaps you misunderstood.\n\n";

  }
}


clear_the_screen(); #Call subroutine that clears the screen

#Display the trick question and prompt the player for a response
print "\nWhat disappears the moment you say its name?";

chomp($reply = <STDIN>); #Capture the player's response

#Determine whether the player guesses the right answer
if( $reply ne 'silence') {
```

```
  print "\nSorry. Wrong answer. Think about it and try again later.\n\n";
} else {
  print "\nYes, that is right. Well done!\n\n";
}


#This subroutine loops and adds 25 blank lines to the screen when called
sub clear_the_screen {

  for ($i=0; $i < 25; ++$i){
    print "\n";
  }
}
```

You should recognize this sample code as being the Perl Humor Script that you developed in the previous chapter. As you can see, it is pretty structured. Indented code statements visually improve code appearance and make it easy to follow along. Rather than follow this structured approach to code layout, a more creative programmer might instead restructure the scripts as shown below.

```
#!/usr/bin/perl

                                  #
                               # Joke
                             #  Machine
                        clear_the_screen() ;
                      $reply  = "";  while (
                      $reply ne 'yes')  {print
              'Would you like to hear a joke? (yes/no): ';
          chomp ($reply = <STDIN>); if( $reply ne 'yes') {
        print  "\nHum... Perhaps your misunderstood.\n\n";}}
       clear_the_screen()                                    ;
     print       "\nWhat disappears the moment you say its name?" ;
   chomp($reply = <STDIN>);                  if ( $reply ne 'silence') {
print "\nSorry. Wrong answer. Think about it and try again later.\n\n";
       } else    {    print "\nYes, that is right. Well done!
                 \n\n" ;} sub clear_the_screen {
                      for($i=0;$i<25;++$i){
                           print "\n";
                              }}
```

Other than the manner in which white space has been manipulated, there is no difference between this script and the previous one.

 While Perl's free-form support for code layout is certainly interesting, I highly recommend that you follow a structured approach in your script development. This will make your Perl scripts easier to read and understand. Any programmers that come along behind you will greatly appreciate your discipline.

PERL'S FLEXIBLE VIEW OF DATA

Like any programming language, Perl must have a way of working with data. Compared to other programming languages, Perl has an extremely flexible view of what data is. Whereas programming languages like C++, Visual Basic, and Java all require the strict definition of data types, Perl views all data as just being one of two types: scalar data and list data.

Scalar data, also referred to as a *scalar,* is a single piece of data made up of a number or a string, whereas *list data* is a collection of different pieces of data. Scalars represent either of two fundamental types of data: numbers and strings. A *number* is just that, a number. Numbers can be integers, floating point numbers, hexadecimal, octal, and so on. Perl does not make any actually distinctions between different types of numbers. A *string* is just a sequence of characters. You will learn about list data in Chapter 4, "Working with Collections of Data."

In Perl scripts, scalar data is used to represent things like a file, a text string, a number, or a piece of user input.

Working with Strings

To Perl, a string is a sequence of characters treated as a single thing. A string can contain any type of ASCII data, including letters, numbers, and special characters. Strings can even be empty (""). There is no preset limit to how long a string can be. The only practical limit is that imposed by the computer's available memory. To create a string, you must enclose zero or more characters within a matching pair of quotes. Perl allows you to use either single or double quotes. For example, each of the following is an example of a string.

```
'Alexander'
'February usually has 28 days.'
"123456789"
"32 degrees"
```

TRAP Perl also allows strings to be created without placing them inside quotes. This type of string is referred to as a *bareword*. Any time Perl comes across a bareword, it makes the assumption that it is a string. The creation of strings in this manner is a poor programming practice that you should always avoid if for no other reason than barewords make Perl scripts difficult to read.

A bareword made up of entirely lowercase letters creates the risk in the future that an unquoted string may clash with a Perl future reserved word. *Reserved words* are keywords that make up the Perl programming language and can only be used in accordance with the rules of Perl. If you enable warnings (-w), Perl will display a warning message about barewords.

Differences in Single- and Double-Quoted Strings

There are a number of differences in how Perl works with strings enclosed within single and double quotes. You need to be aware of these differences to properly apply the correct type of quotation marks based on different situations.

For starters, only a string placed inside double quotes can perform variable interpolation. *Variable interpolation* is the process in which Perl replaces a variable's name with its value. Therefore, if a Perl script has a variable named $name that had a value of William assigned to it, and the following two statements were executed, the first statement would result in the display of a string that displayed the value William, whereas the second statement would instead display $name.

HINT A *variable* is a reference to a piece of data stored in memory. More information on variables is available later in this chapter.

```
print "His name is $name";   #Displays His name is William
print 'His name is $name';   #Displays His name is $name
```

As you can see, when a variable is placed inside a single-quoted string, Perl treats it as a literal data and does not replace it. When a variable is placed inside a double-quoted string, Perl recognizes it as a variable and replaces it with its assigned value.

TRICK As you will learn a little later in the chapter, Perl variable names begin with a $ character. Therefore, any time Perl sees a $ character in a string, it assumes that it belongs to a variable name. However, if you do not want the $ character to be interpreted as the beginning of a variable name, you must precede it with a \ character. This is a technique sometimes referred to as *escaping*, as demonstrated in the following statement.

```
print "His name is \$name";  # Displays His name is $name
```

Another difference between single- and double-quoted strings is that double-quoted strings can contain escape characters, whereas, for the most part, single-quoted strings do not. In Chapter 1's Perl Humor Script, you saw examples where \n escape characters were embedded inside strings. These escape characters are used to tell Perl to execute a newline operation. For example, when executed, the following statement displays a string and the cursor is left positioned at the end of the string.

```
print "His name is $name";  #Displays His name is William
```

However, by embedding the \n escape character at the end of the string, as shown below, you tell Perl to display the string and then execute a newline operation. The end result is that the cursor is displayed on a new line, immediately following the display of the string.

```
print "His name is $name\n";  #Displays His name is William
```

Perl Escape Characters

Perl provides you with access to a large number of string escape characters. Some of the more commonly used escape characters are shown in Table 2.1.

 HINT To see a listing of all the escape characters supported by Perl, enter perldoc perlop and look for the Quote and Quote-like Operators.

TABLE 2.1 PERL STRING ESCAPE CHARACTERS

Characters	Description
\n	Newline
\r	Carriage return
\t	Tab
\f	Formfeed
\b	Backspace
\u	Converts the next letter to uppercase
\l	Converts the next letter to lowercase
\U	Converts any text that follows to uppercase
\L	Converts any text that follows to lowercase
\E	Terminates a \U or \L sequence
\\	Allows for the display of a backward slash
\'	Allows for the display of a single-quote character
\"	Allows for the display of a double-quote character

There are two exceptions to the rule that single-quoted strings do not support escape characters. Single-quoted strings do allow you to embed the \' and \" escape characters as a means of allowing the ' and " characters to be taken literally in strings. For example, the following statement allows the single quote to be displayed.

```
print 'Molly\'s favorite toy is Barbie';  #Displays Molly's favorite
toy is Barbie
```

Other Ways to Define Strings

So, as you can see, although single- and double-quoted strings are quite similar, there are distinct differences between the two. Most of the time that you need to embed variables inside strings, you'll want to use double quotes. In situations where you have one or more dollar signs that you want represented as dollar signs within your string, use single quotes.

If you find yourself needing to escape a number of characters in a statement, things can get a little ugly, as demonstrated in the following example.

```
print "\"When you see Joe\", Sue said, \"Say Hi for me!.""";
```

To help make things easier to understand, Perl provides you with the q// and qq// operators. Using these operators, you can build the equivalent of single- and double-quoted strings without having to add in all the escape characters. For example, using the q// operator you can rewrite the previous statement to produce a statement that is the equivalent of a single-quoted string as shown below.

```
print q/"When you see Joe", Sue said, "Say Hi for me!"/;
```

As you can see, this statement is easier to read. Similarly, you could rewrite the example again to be the equivalent of a double-quoted string as shown below.

```
print qq/"When you see Joe", Sue said, "Say Hi for me!"/;
```

The q// and qq// operators also allow you to replace the opening and trailing / delimiter characters with any non-numeric or non-alphabetic character. For example, the following statement swaps the # character with the / character as the delimiter for the previous example.

```
print qq#"When you see Joe", Sue said, "Say Hi for me!"#;
```

The ability to change the delimiter character is helpful in situations where you want to avoid using a particular delimiter character because you plan to use it inside the string.

Working with Numbers

Perl allows you to work with numbers in many different formats, although the language itself does not make any distinction between different types of numbers. This convenience is strictly for your benefit. For example, Table 2.2 demonstrates a number of different ways that you can work with numbers in your Perl scripts.

Perl does not differentiate the various types of numbers shown in Table 2.2. Perl simply views any representation of a number as a scalar number and automatically converts between numbers as required.

 Perl does not allow you to insert commas into numbers in order to make them easier to read. Therefore, attempting to define a number as 1,000,000 will result in an error. However, if you want, Perl will allow you to substitute the underscore character in place of a comma for readability. You could therefore rewrite 1,000,000 as 1_000_000. This helps to make the number easier for people to view. Perl, on the other hand, ignores the underscore characters when processing the number.

Converting Scalar Data

Perl does not enforce a strict distinction between scalar strings and scalar numbers. As a result, Perl can easily convert data between these two data types when necessary. In most other modern programmer languages, you must explicitly convert data from one data type to another; otherwise, an error will occur. Perl, on the other hand, converts data to whatever type it thinks is required based on the current situation. For example, Perl will allow you to add "5" and 5 together and give you a result of 10, even though the "5" is a string and 5 is a number. This flexibility in Perl is a double-edged sword. On the one hand it provides the programmer with a lot of flexibility when it comes to manipulating data. On the other hand, it also allows programmers to write error-prone code. For example, Perl will happily attempt

Type	Example	Description
Integer	5	Whole numbers
Floating Point	5.5	A real number containing a fractional part
Scientific Notation	2e10	A number based on the power of 10
Hexadecimal	0xb	A numeric system with a base of 16 that is identified by a leading 0X
Octal	01	A numeric system with a base of 8 that is identified by a leading 0

TABLE 2.2   PERL STRING ESCAPE CHARACTERS

to add "five" to 5 and will give you a result of 5. It does this because, not knowing what else to do, Perl assigns a value of 0 to the string and then adds that number to 5. Clearly a computation like this serves little purpose, yet Perl will allow you to get away with it without generating an error. However, if you turn warnings (-w) on, Perl will alert you to the situation.

STORING DATA IN SCALAR VARIABLES

In order to store and work with a piece of data, you need a means of referencing it. Perl provides this capability in the form of scalar variables. Scalar variables begin with the $ sign followed by a name. Examples of scalar variable names include:

```
$name
$total_count
$date
$pin_number
```

There are a number of rules that you must follow when creating scalar variable names; these rules are outlined in the following list.

- Scalar variable names can only consist of alphanumeric characters or underscore characters.
- The first character (after the $ sign) cannot be a number.
- Scalar variable names cannot exceed 255 characters.

Scalar variable names are case sensitive. This means that Perl would consider $name and $Name to be two different scalar variables. Perl treats scalar variables without an assigned value as being undefined. If Perl comes across an undefined scalar string variable, it will assign a value of "" (an empty string) to it. If Perl comes across an undefined scalar numeric variable, it will assign a value of 0 to it.

TRAP

Unlike many other modern programming languages, Perl does not require you to declare and initialize scalar variables in advance of using them within your Perl scripts. However, this is sloppy programming and should be avoided.

It is best to always define and assign a starting value to any variable that your script will use at the beginning of the script or at the beginning of the subroutine that uses them. If warnings (-w) have been turned on when your script executes, Perl will display a message warning you of the "use of uninitialized value".

Variable Scope

By default, Perl scalar variables have a global scope with Perl scripts. The term scope means that the scalar variable can be accessed from any point within the script. However, Perl will let you localize the accessibility of a variable to within a loop or subroutine, provided you define it in a special way.

Additional information about subroutines and loops is available in Chapter 5, "Improving Script Organization and Structure," and Chapter 3, "Controlling Program Flow." More information on variable scope is available in Chapter 6, "Scope and Modules."

Assigning Data to Scalar Variables

To assign a value to a scalar variable you use the = (equals) operator as demonstrated below.

```
$name = "Molly";
$age = 4;
```

In the first example, a scalar string variable named $name has been defined and assigned an initial value of Molly. In the second example, a scalar numeric variable named $age has been defined and assigned an initial value of 4. As you can see, the name of the value is on the left-hand side of the = operator and the value that is assigned is on the right-hand side. The value assigned can be any valid expression. An *expression* is something that has, or evaluates to, a value. For example, both "Molly" and 4 are expressions. So is 4 + 5 and $height + $width.

In Perl, expressions cascade from right to left, allowing you to chain together multiple expressions as demonstrated below.

```
$x = $y = $z = 1;
```

In this example, the value of the scalar variable $z is assigned a value of 1. The value assigned to $z is then assigned to the value stored in $y. Finally, the value of $x is assigned the value currently stored by $y, which is 1

Variable Interpolation

One of the major strengths of variables is that you can use them to substitute data into expressions through an automatic process known as *interpolation*. For example, take a look at the following statements.

```
$text = "there was a land called OZ.";
$message = "Once upon a time $text ";
```

When executed, Perl assigns a scalar string to $text in the first statement and then substitutes the value assigned to that scalar variable by inserting it into the string located in the second statement. The end result is a total new string with a value of Once upon a time there was a land called OZ that is assigned to $message.

TRICK

If you want, you can block variable interpolation by escaping it (e.g. by preceding it with a \ character as demonstrated below).

```
$message = "Once upon a time \$text ";
```

In this example, the string that is assigned to $message is "Once upon a time \$part2 ".

Understanding How to Work with Perl Operators

As you have already seen, expressions are a key building block for Perl statements. In order to help you build expressions, Perl provides you with access to a large collection of built-in operators. A couple of these operators apply to scalar strings but most are applicable only to scalar numbers.

String Operators

Perl only provides two operators for manipulating strings. The first is the concatenation operator, and the second is the x operator, which is used to build strings made up of a sequence of repeated characters. Both of these operators are demonstrated in the sections that follow.

The Concatenation (.) Operator

The first string operator is the concatenation operator, which is specified using the . character (period). Its application is straightforward, just place it between two strings or scalar string variables that you want to join together, as demonstrated in the following example.

```
$message = "Once upon a time " . "there was a land called OZ.";
```

When executed, a string whose value is Once upon a time there was a land called OZ is assigned to the $message scalar string variable. You can just as easily use the value assigned to scalar string variables to concatenate and assign a new string value as demonstrated below.

```
$part1 = "Once upon a time ";
$part2 = "there was a land called OZ.";

$message = $part1 . $part2;
```

When executed, the exact same string is created as was created in the previous example and is assigned to the $message scalar string variable.

TRICK

Another way to concatenate the contents of two scalar string variables together is to include both of them in a double-quoted string, as demonstrated below. In doing so, Perl automatically concatenates them and assigns the results to the $message scalar string variable.

```
$message = "$part1 $part2";
```

As has already been stated, Perl is an extremely flexible programming language that allows you to do all kinds of neat little tricks. One such trick is Perl's ability to let you concatenate together a string by simply embedding a variable inside a string. However, in order for this to work, you must give Perl a little extra help by identifying the beginning and ending to the variable name, so that Perl can distinguish it from the text it has been embedded inside of. To accomplish this, you enclose the variable, less the $ character, inside a pair of { } braces as follows.

```
$name = "Super";
$message = "It's a bird, it's a plane, no it's ${name}man!";
```

In this example, the scalar string assigned to $message is

```
It's a bird, it's a plane, no it's Superman!
```

The x Operator

The second operator that Perl provides for concatenation operations is the x operator, which is useful for building strings that consist of a sequence of repeated characters, such as when reports are generated that have rows of lines to separate sections of the report or lines of data. This operator takes two arguments. The first argument is a string that is to be repeated. The second argument specifies the number of times the string is to be repeated.

As an example of how to use the x operator, consider the following example.

```
$row = "_" x 75;

print "$row\n\n";
print "Monthly Accounting Receivables and Inventory Report\n\n";
print "$row\n";
```

When executed, this example displays the following output. The first statement uses the x operator to assign a scalar variable a text string made up of 75 underscore characters. This variable is then embedded in the second and fourth statements.

```
Monthly Accounting Receivables and Inventory Report
```

Obviously, the x operator provides you with a shorthand way to create long strings and can be a big help when formatting reports.

Arithmetic Operators

As Table 2.3 shows, Perl provides support for performing a host of mathematical operations.

Using these operators you can create expressions to solve any type of numeric calculation, as demonstrated by the following statements.

```
print 5 + 5
print 99 - 5
print 4 + 8 - 4 * 7 / 3
```

Operator Precedence

In Perl, like all other programming languages, mathematic operations are executed according to a specific order of precedence. Specifically, exponentiation occurs first, then multiplication and division followed by modulus and finally addition and subtraction. For example consider the following expression.

```
$result = 5 ** 2 / 5 * 5 - 5 + 5;
```

When executed by Perl, the value assigned to $result is 25, which is computed as follows:

1. Exponentiation occurs first, so 5 ** 2 = 25.
2. Multiplication and division are then performed from left to right, so 25 / 5 = 5 and that result is then multiplied by 5 to get 25.
3. Addition and subtraction are performed last, so 25 - 5 is 20 and then 5 is added to that result to get 25.

Operator	Example	Description
+	5 + 5	Addition
-	5 - 1	Subtraction
*	5 * 5	Multiplication
/	10 / 5	Division
%	50 % 2	Modulus
**	5 ** 2	Exponentiation

TABLE 2.3   PERL'S ARITHMETIC OPERATORS

Perl allows you to modify the order in which mathematical computations are made using parentheses, which override the order of precedence. Take for example, the following statement:

```
$result = 5 ** 2 / (5 * 5) - 5 + 5;
```

As you can see, it is very nearly identical to the previous statement, except that parentheses have been added that enclose the multiplication of 5 times 5. As a result of this small change, an entirely new result is calculated as outlined below.

When executed by Perl the value assigned to $result is 1, which is computed as follows:

1. The multiplication of 5 * 5 occurs first, resulting in a value of 25.
2. Exponentiation occurs next, so 5 ** 2 = 25.
3. Next, division is processed and 25 divided by 25 yields a value of 1.
4. Addition and subtraction are performed last, so 1 - 5 is -4, which is then added to 5, resulting in a final value of 1.

Refining Mathematical Precision

While mathematical calculations in Perl may seem straightforward, there is a small glitch that you need to be aware of when it comes to precision. Specifically, Perl will not always provide you with the appropriate level of precision that you are looking for. For example, consider the following calculation.

```
$result = 10 / 3;
```

Depending on what your application is designed to accomplish and the level of accuracy required, you might want Perl to return a whole number without any fractional remainder (e.g. an answer of 3). However, Perl will return a value of 3.33333333333333, which is not so bad as long as you know to expect it. Perl gives you the ability to format numbers into integers using the int function. As demonstrated below, you can format the result of a division using int to produce an integer result.

```
$result = int 10 / 3;
```

Perl also provides you with the ability to round fractional results down to a specific decimal position using the sprintf function. This function accepts two arguments. The first argument tells the function the number of decimals to return and the second argument supplies the function with the number to be converted.

```
$result = sprintf("%.3f", 10 / 3);
```

%.3f tells Perl to format the supplied number using three decimal positions. As a result, a value of 3.333 is assigned to $result.

Perl also lets you visually format numbers using the printf function, which accepts two arguments just like the sprintf function.

```
printf("%.3f", 10 / 3);  #Displays 3.333
```

Increment and Decrement Operators

In Chapter 3, you will learn how to set up loops to process large amounts of data. One of the controlling mechanisms used in certain types of loops is a counter. A counter provides you with a means of keeping track of the number of times a loop iterates. To create a counter, you can use the addition operator as demonstrated below.

```
$counter = $counter + 1;  #Add one to the value of $counter
```

However, counting like this is so common in Perl scripts that Perl has a special operator called the autoincrement operator (++) to assist you. The use of this operator is demonstrated below.

```
$counter++;  #Add one to the value of $counter
```

This example is functionally identical to the previous example, adding one to the value of $counter when the statement executes. Perl also provides an autodecrement operator (- -) that provides a shorthand way of subtracting one from the value of a scalar numeric variable, as demonstrated below.

```
$counter--;  #Subtract one from the value of $counter
```

Assignment Operators

As you have already seen many times already, you can assign values to scalar variables using the equals (=) operator. Perl also supports a number of shortcut assignment operators. Table 2.4 lists a number of common assignment operators.

TRICK In addition to the numeric operators listed in Table 2.3, Perl also provides a shortcut operator for the concatenation operator as demonstrated below.

```
$name = "Lee"
$name .= "Man"
```

When executed the value of $name is set equal to LeeMan.

TABLE 2.4	PERL ASSIGNMENT OPERATORS	
Operator	**Example**	**Description**
=	$a = 5	Sets $a equal to 5
+=	$a += 5	Same as $a = $a + 5
-=	$a -= 5	Same as $a = $a - 5
*=	$a *= 5	Same as $a = $a * 5
/=	$a /= 5	Same as $a = $a / 5
%=	$a %= 5	Same as $a = $a % 5
**=	$a **= 5	Same as $a = $a ** 5

Relational Operators

Perl provides you with access to two sets of operators that can be used to determine the relationship between two values. The first set of relationship operators, shown in Table 2.5, is for numeric comparisons.

As an example of how to use the operators, consider the following statements.

```
5 < 10
3 <= 5
5 > 10
5 > $x
```

The first two examples will return a value of true because 5 is less than 10 and 3 is less than or equal to 5. The third example will return a value of false since 5 is not greater than 10. The value returned by the last example will vary, depending on the value assigned to the $x scalar variable.

TABLE 2.5	PERL NUMERIC RELATIONAL OPERATORS
Operator	**Description**
==	Equal to
!=	Not equal to
<	Less than
>	Greater than
<=	Less than or equal to
>=	Greater than or equal to

The second set of relationship operators, shown in Table 2.6, are used for performing string comparisons.

TABLE 2.6	PERL STRING RELATIONAL OPERATORS
Operator	**Description**
eq	Equal to
ne	Not equal to
lt	Less than
gt	Greater than
le	Less than or equal to
ge	Greater than or equal to

As an example of how to use these operators, consider the following statements.

```
a lt b
bob gt ann
x gt X
```

All evaluations are performed based on the ASCII character order. The first example will return a value of true because a is less than b. Likewise, the second example also returns a value of true because bob is greater than ann (each side of this comparison is evaluated from left to right, with b being greater than a). The third example also returns a value of true because in the ASCII character order, lowercase characters occur before uppercase characters.

Logical Operators

Another useful set of operators is Perl logical operators, which perform tests of other comparison operations. These operators are outlined in Table 2.7.

As an example of how to work with these operators, consider the following statements.

```
(5 > 4 ) and (5 < 10)
(5 > 4) or (4 > 5 )
5 not 4
```

TABLE 2.7 PERL LOGICAL OPERATORS	
Operator	**Description**
and	Returns true when both X and Y are true
or	Returns true when either X or Y are true
not	Returns true when X is false

The first example evaluates to true since 5 is greater than 4 and 5 is less than 10. The second example also evaluates to true since one of the two tests being evaluated is true (5 is greater than 4). In the third example, a value of true is returned since 5 is not equal to 4.

 Perl also provides a second set of logical operators, borrowed from the C programming language. These operators are && (and), || (or), and ! (not). These three C-style operators work exactly like their Perl-style equivalents.

INPUT AND OUTPUT

You have already seen a number of examples of how to collect user input. This has been accomplished in previous examples using the angle operator (<>). The operator's purpose is to provide you with a means to read from and write to files.

Working with Standard Input

So far, each time you have seen the angle operator used in this book, it has been wrapped around the STDIN file handle, which is a default handle provided by Perl for retrieving data from the standard input. As you saw when developing the Perl Humor Script in Chapter 1, <STDIN> by default is keyboard input. For example, the following statement can be used to tell Perl to pause script execution and wait until the user types something and presses the Enter key.

```
$result = <STDIN>
```

Any text typed by the user, including the newline character is assigned to the $result scalar variable. Typically, you will not want to include the newline character when storing data retrieved from the STDIN. To remove the newline character, you can use the chomp function, as demonstrated below.

```
$result = <STDIN>
chomp $size
```

In this example, the chomp function strips off the newline character, if present, from the value assigned to the $result scalar variable. If you prefer, you can combine the chomp function with <STDIN> to retrieve user input and strip off the newline character in a single statement as demonstrated below.

```
chomp($result = <STDIN>);
```

Working with Standard Output

Like STDIN, Perl also provides you with a means of writing to standard output or STDOUT. By default STDOUT is your computer's display. You may be thinking right now that you have seen plenty of examples where text has been displayed on the screen and yet you have not seen the STDOUT used even once. This is because, by default, Perl assumes that when you display output using a function like print that you want the output sent to SDTOUT, as demonstrated below.

```
print "Once upon a time";
```

Functionally, this statement is identical to the following.

```
print STDOUT "Once upon a time…";
```

BACK TO THE STORY OF WILLIAM THE GREAT

Okay, it is time to turn your attention back to the development of this chapter's game project, the Story of William the Great. Completing this Perl script should help to reinforce your understanding of how to work with scalar variables, collect user input, and control the display of output. As you create this script, try to take a few extra minutes to make sure that you understand the overall logic being implemented. Hopefully, you'll be able to follow along and understand most of the programming logic and statements that make up the script, although a 100 percent understanding is not necessary at this point in the book.

Designing the Game

As the Story of William the Great will demonstrate, many Perl scripts are just collections of statements that execute sequentially from beginning to end, unless statement flow is altered by flow-control statements. The Story of William the Great will be developed in a number of separate steps, as outlined below.

1. Creating and documenting a new Perl script.
2. Prepping for data collection and introducing the story.
3. Providing the user with instructions.
4. Collecting user input.

5. Beginning the story.
6. Telling the story.
7. Ending the story.
8. Creating a subroutine to clear the screen.

Each of these steps is covered in greater detail in the sections that follow.

Creating a New Perl Script

Let's begin the script by opening your preferred text or script editor and entering the following statements.

```
#!/usr/bin/perl
#
# The Story of William the Great (WilliamTheGreat.pl)

clear_the_screen();
```

The first statement is the shebang. It is followed by a blank comment statement (added for aesthetics) and a comment statement that identifies the script and its filename. The last line is a statement that executes a subroutine named clear_the_screen(). When executed, this subroutine clears the screen in order to prepare it for additional display text.

 HINT If the name of the clear_the_screen() subroutine looks familiar to you, it should. This same subroutine was added to the Perl Humor Script that you created in Chapter 1.

Beginning the Story

Next, let's continue work on the script by appending the following statements to the end of the script file.

```
$reply   = "";
$vehicle = "";
$dessert = "";
$food    = "";
$smell   = "";
$animal  = "";

print "This is the Story of William the Great.\n\n";
print "Press the Enter key to continue...";
chomp($reply = <STDIN>);
```

The first six statements define variables that will be used to store information collected from the user. The next two `print` statements introduce the story and prompt the user to press a key when he or she is ready to continue. The last statement is used to pause script execution by arbitrarily telling Perl to wait for the user to press the Enter key in order to continue.

 HINT Although the user can enter text prior to pressing the Enter key, and this text is assigned to the `$reply` variable, the script does not do anything with this data.

Giving the Player Instructions

Next, append the following statements to the end of the script file.

```perl
clear_the_screen();

print "To hear this story, you must provide some information.\n\n";
print "Press the Enter key to continue...";
$reply = <STDIN>;
```

The first statement calls the `clear_the_screen()` subroutine. The two `print` statements that follow inform the user that his or her input is required in order for the story to be told. The last statement pauses script execution until the user presses the Enter key.

Collecting User Input

Let's continue work on the script by appending the following statements to the end of the script file.

```perl
clear_the_screen();

print "Enter the name of an old-fashioned vehicle.\n\n";
print ">";  #Display an input prompt
chomp($vehicle = <STDIN>);

clear_the_screen();

print "What is your favorite type of dessert?\n\n";
print ">";
chomp($dessert = <STDIN>);

clear_the_screen();

print "What tastes best with jelly or jam?\n\n";
```

```
print ">";
chomp($food = <STDIN>);

clear_the_screen();

print "Name a type of smell that reminds you of your grandmother.\n\n";
print ">";
chomp($smell = <STDIN>);
clear_the_screen();

print "Name a large wild animal.\n\n";
print ">";
chomp($animal = <STDIN>);

clear_the_screen();

print "Good answers. Let's continue with the story.\n\n";
print "Press the Enter key to continue...";
$reply = <STDIN>;
```

As you can see, these statements follow a simple pattern. First the screen is cleared by calling the clear_the_screen() subroutine and then a pair of print statements are used to display a question which is then assigned to a scalar variable. The actual value assigned to each scalar variable has the newline character removed from it using the chomp function.

Telling the Beginning of the Story

At this point the script has collected all the input that is needed to tell the Story of William the Great. To begin the story, append the following statements to the end of the script file.

```
clear_the_screen();

print "Once upon a time, there was a little boy named William.\n";
print "William was a young man just 7 years of age. One day,\n";
print "William's mother asked him to go to the market and by some\n";
print "corn, bread, and seed in order to plant this year's crops.\n";
print "To pay, his mother gave him the last of the family's\n";
print "money.\n\n";
print "Press the Enter key to continue...";
$reply = <STDIN>;
```

The first statement calls the `clear_the_screen()` subroutine. The next seven `print` statements display the opening portion of the story and prompt the user to press the Enter key to continue. The last statement pauses script execution until the user presses the Enter key.

Telling the Rest of the Story

To tell the rest of the story, append the following script statement to the end of the script file.

```perl
clear_the_screen();

print "William knew that he must be careful on his way to the\n";
print "market for recently there had been a number of stories of\n";
print "bandits hiding behind trees along the road in to town\n";
print "waiting to jump out and rob travelers. As William headed\n";
print "down the road with the last of his family's money, he knew\n";
print "that he could not let them down, otherwise everyone would\n";
print "surely starve.\n\n";
print "Press the Enter key to continue...";
$reply = <STDIN>;

clear_the_screen();

print "William's trip into town was a safe one. While he did\n";
print "notice a broken down $vehicle on the side of the road about\n";
print "a mile out from the town, he saw no other travelers along\n";
print "the way.\n\n";
print "Press the Enter key to continue...";
$reply = <STDIN>;

clear_the_screen();

print "Once in town William headed straight for the baker, where he\n";
print "saw freshly baked $dessert and $food. As tempting as the\n";
print "$dessert and $food were, William knew that he could not\n";
print "buy them, for his family needed the corn and bread his mother\n";
print "asked for in order to have enough food to eat until the new\n";
print "crops finally came in.\n\n";
print "Press the Enter key to continue...";
$reply = <STDIN>;
```

```
clear_the_screen();

print "Having made his purchase, William next went to the Feed\n";
print "store. Along the way he began to get the feeling that he was\n";
print "being followed. However, he could not see anyone who looked\n";
print "suspicious. When William arrived at the feed store, there was\n";
print "a sign saying that the store was closed until tomorrow. So,\n";
print "with his corn and bread in hand, William headed back home.\n";
print "About a mile out of town William suddenly smelled a whiff of\n";
print "$smell in the air. Then he heard a sound coming up from\n";
print "behind him that sounded like a $animal.\n\n";
print "Press the Enter key to continue...";
$reply = <STDIN>;

clear_the_screen();

print "In horror William started to take off running. But then he\n";
print "stopped, fearing that whatever was after him might follow him\n";
print "all the way home. Instead, William decided to turn and stand\n";
print "up to whatever was behind him. To William's surprise, the\n";
print "source of all his fears and the origin of that $smell smell\n";
print "and the $animal noise was his mother. She had forgotten to\n";
print "ask William to also buy some flour and she had tried\n";
print "to catch him on his way into town but had gotten tired and\n";
print "decided to rest and wait for his return when she reached\n";
print "the $vehicle.\n\n";
print "Press the Enter key to continue...";
$reply = <STDIN>;
```

As you can see, these statements are organized into groups that follow a pattern, first clearing the screen, then displaying a portion of the story before pausing and waiting on the user to press the Enter key.

Ending the Story

To end the telling of the story, append the following script statement to the end of the script file.

```
clear_the_screen();

print "The next day William returned to town and purchased the seed\n";
print "his family needed. Later that year William's family had the\n";
print "best crop they ever planted.\n\n";
print "The End\n\n";
```

The first statement calls the `clear_the_screen()` subroutine and then displays the end of the story.

Clearing the Screen

At this point, only one task remains, adding the program code that makes up the `clear_the_screen()` subroutine. Do so by appending the following statements to the end of the script file.

```
sub clear_the_screen {

  for ($i=0; $i < 25; ++$i){
    print "\n";
  }
}
```

More information is available about subroutines in Chapter 5, "Improving Script Organization and Structure." For now, just understand that subroutines are used to define and execute a collection of statements and facilitate code reuse by allowing the statements to be called for execution over and over again as many times as necessary.

The Final Result

Once you have finished keying in the Story of William the Great, save your Perl script as WilliamTheGreat.pl. Through the creation of this script, you have demonstrated your understanding of a number of important Perl programming concepts. The concepts include the use of scalar variables to store and retrieve data, the ability to collect user input, and the use of the `chomp` function to remove the `newline` character from collected input.

As a review, a fully assembled version of the script is provided below. To help make this script easier to understand, comments have been embedded that document key script statements.

```
#!/usr/bin/perl
#
# The Story of William the Great (WilliamTheGreat.pl)
```

```
clear_the_screen(); #Call subroutine that clears the screen

#Define a variable to hold user input
$reply   = "";
$vehicle = "";
$dessert  = "";
$food    = "";
$smell   = "";
$animal  = "";

#Display an introductory message and format display using carriage returns
print "This is the Story of William the Great.\n\n";
print "Press the Enter key to continue...";  #Prompt user before continuing
#Set variable equal to standard input and remove any trailing newline
chomp($reply = <STDIN>);

clear_the_screen();  #Call subroutine that clears the screen

print "To hear this story, you must provide some information.\n\n";
print "Press the Enter key to continue...";  #Prompt user before continuing
chomp($reply = <STDIN>);

clear_the_screen();  #Clear the screen

print "Enter the name of an old-fashioned vehicle.\n\n";
print ">";  #Display an input prompt
chomp($vehicle = <STDIN>);  #Capture the user's answer

clear_the_screen();  #Clear the screen

print "What is your favorite type of dessert?\n\n";
print ">";  #Display an input prompt
chomp($dessert = <STDIN>); #Capture the user's answer

clear_the_screen();  #Clear the screen

print "What tastes best with jelly or jam?\n\n";
print ">";  #Display an input prompt
```

```
chomp($food = <STDIN>);   #Capture the user's answer

clear_the_screen();   #Clear the screen

print "Name a type of smell that reminds you of your grandmother.\n\n";
print ">";   #Display an input prompt
chomp($smell = <STDIN>);   #Capture the user's answer

clear_the_screen();   #Clear the screen

print "Name a large wild animal.\n\n";
print ">";   #Display an input prompt
chomp($animal = <STDIN>);   #Capture the user's answer

clear_the_screen();   #Clear the screen

print "Good answers. Let's continue with the story.\n\n";
print "Press the Enter key to continue...";   #Prompt user before continuing
chomp($reply = <STDIN>);

clear_the_screen();   #Clear the screen

print "Once upon a time, there was a little boy named William.\n";
print "William was a young man, just 7 years of age. One day,\n";
print "William's mother asked him to go to the market to by some\n";
print "corn, bread, and seed in order to plant this year's crops.\n";
print "To pay, his mother gave him the last of the family's\n";
print "money.\n\n";
print "Press the Enter key to continue...";   #Prompt user before continuing
chomp($reply = <STDIN>);

clear_the_screen();   #Clear the screen

print "William knew that he must be careful on his way to the\n";
print "market for recently there had been a number of stories of\n";
print "bandits hiding behinds trees along the road in to town\n";
print "waiting to jump out and rob travelers. As William headed\n";
print "down the road with the last of his family's money, he knew\n";
```

```
print "that he could not let them down, otherwise everyone would\n";
print "surely starve.\n\n";
print "Press the Enter key to continue...";   #Prompt user before continuing
chomp($reply = <STDIN>);

clear_the_screen();   #Clear the screen

print "William's trip into town was a safe one. While he did\n";
print "notice a broken down $vehicle on the side of the road about\n";
print "a mile out from the town, he saw no other travelers along\n";
print "the way.\n\n";
print "Press the Enter key to continue...";   #Prompt user before continuing
chomp($reply = <STDIN>);

clear_the_screen();   #Clear the screen

print "Once in town William headed straight for the bakery, where he\n";
print "saw freshly baked $dessert and $food. As tempting as the\n";
print "$dessert and $food were, William knew that he could not\n";
print "buy them, for his family needed the corn and bread his mother\n";
print "asked for in order to have enough food to eat until the new\n";
print "crops finally came in.\n\n";
print "Press the Enter key to continue...";   #Prompt user before continuing
chomp($reply = <STDIN>);

clear_the_screen();   #Clear the screen

print "Having made his purchase, William next went to the Feed\n";
print "store. Along the way he began to get the feeling that he was\n";
print "being followed. However, he could not see anyone who looked\n";
print "suspicious. When William arrived at the feed store, there was\n";
print "a sign saying that the store was closed until tomorrow. So,\n";
print "with his corn and bread in hand, William headed back home.\n";
print "About a mile out of town William suddenly smelled a whiff of\n";
print "$smell in the air. Then he heard a sound coming up from\n";
print "behind him that sounded like a $animal.\n\n";
print "Press the Enter key to continue...";   #Prompt user before continuing
chomp($reply = <STDIN>);
```

```
clear_the_screen();  #Clear the screen

print "In horror William started to take off running. But then he\n";
print "stopped, fearing that whatever was after him might follow him\n";
print "all the way home. Instead, William decided to turn and stand\n";
print "up to whatever was behind him. To William's surprise, the\n";
print "source of all his fears and the origin of that $smell smell\n";
print "and the $animal noise was his mother. She had forgotten to\n";
print "ask William to also buy some flour and she had tried\n";
print "to catch him on his way into town but had gotten tired and\n";
print "decided to rest and wait for his return when she reached\n";
print "the $vehicle.\n\n";
print "Press the Enter key to continue...";  #Prompt user before continuing
chomp($reply = <STDIN>);

clear_the_screen();  #Clear the screen

print "The next day William returned to town and purchased the seed\n";
print "his family needed. Later that year William\'s family had the\n";
print "best crop they ever planted.\n\n";
print "The End\n\n";

#This subroutine clears the screen by adding 25 blank lines
sub clear_the_screen {

  for ($i=0; $i < 25; ++$i){
    print "\n";
  }
}
```

Now, go ahead and run the script. Assuming that you have not made any typing mistakes when keying in the script, everything should work as expected. If on the other hand you receive one or more error messages, read those messages for clues as to where the locations of errors within the script might be and then go back and double-check the code for typos.

HINT   You will find the source code for the Story of William the great as well as the source code for all the other Perl scripts presented in this book on the book's companion website at http://www.courseptr.com/downloads.

SUMMARY

In this chapter you learned how Perl works with scalar data, including how to store and retrieve data stored in scalar variables. You learned how to work with scalar data by creating expressions that used operators to mathematically manipulate numeric data or to concatenate string data. You learned how to perform comparison operations and examined different ways in which Perl converts numeric and string data, based on the context in which it is used. You also learned how to collect user input and display output using STDIN and STDOUT. Finally, you created the Story of William the Great, demonstrating your understanding of a number of the key concepts covered in this chapter.

Before you move on to Chapter 3, why don't you take a few extra minutes to review the following list of challenges and see if you can improve on the Story of William the Great.

CHALLENGES

1. Expand upon the Story of William the Great sending William on another adventure. As you do so, remember to go back and prompt the user for additional information that you can use to help tell the new adventure.

2. Make the telling of the story more interesting by looking for additional opportunities to integrate more user-supplied information.

Part

II

Mastering Key Perl Programming Constructs

CHAPTER 3

CONTROLLING
PROGRAM FLOW

By default, Perl scripts are processed in a top-down fashion, with each code statement read and processed in the order written. In some cases this is all that you need to write an effective script. However, most of the time you need the ability to perform conditional logic or create loops in order to develop really useful Perl scripts. Using conditional logic, you can create scripts that alter their logical flow based on tested conditions. Using loops, you can develop scripts that can execute indefinitely, allowing them to process huge amounts of data. You can also create loops that repeatedly execute the same series of statements as many times as required. As this chapter will show, Perl has strong support for conditional logic and loops, offering you many different options for getting things done.

Specifically, you will learn

- How to create and execute code blocks
- How Perl interprets true and false conditions
- How to create conditional logic using variations of the if statement and the unless statement
- How to create for, foreach, do...while, while, and until loops
- How to use different Perl statements to control loop processing

PROJECT PREVIEW: THE PERL FORTUNE TELLER GAME

This chapter's game project is the Perl Fortune Teller script. This game will help to tie together the material covered in this chapter. Specifically, you'll get the chance to set up `for` and `while` loops and to develop conditional logic using `if` code blocks. This game begins by setting up the story line for the game, displaying a welcome message, and prompting the user for permission to continue as demonstrated in Figure 3.1.

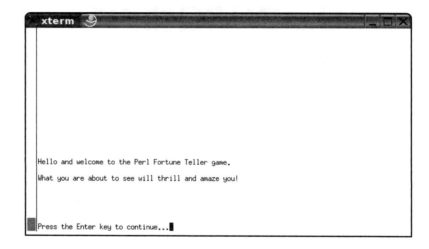

FIGURE 3.1

Running the Perl Fortune Teller script on a computer running Linux.

The script continues by displaying text that lays the foundation of the story line for the game, as shown in Figure 3.2.

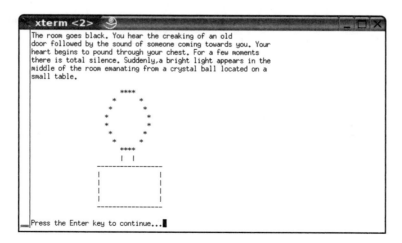

FIGURE 3.2

The user is presented with background information required to set up the game's story line.

The fortune teller then addresses the user, inviting her to ask any question that she would like to have answered, as shown in Figure 3.3.

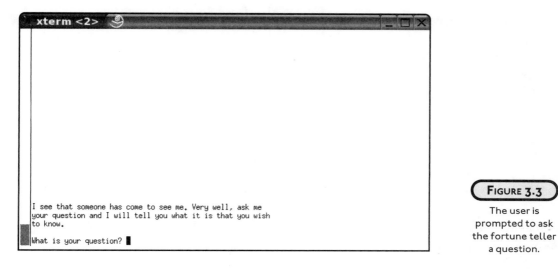

```
I see that someone has come to see me. Very well, ask me
your question and I will tell you what it is that you wish
to know.
What is your question? █
```

FIGURE 3.3

The user is prompted to ask the fortune teller a question.

The player can ask the fortune teller as many additional questions as she wishes, as demonstrated in Figure 3.4.

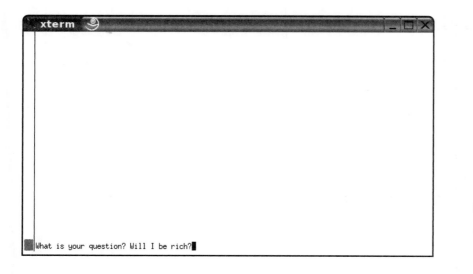

```
What is your question? Will I be rich?█
```

FIGURE 3.4

Asking the fortune teller another question.

The fortune teller responds by displaying any of six different randomly selected answers, as demonstrated in Figure 3.5.

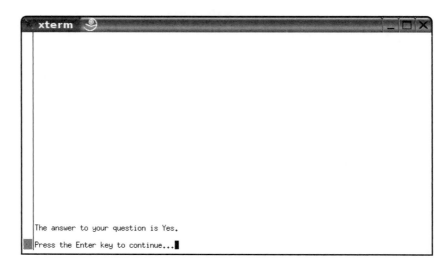

FIGURE 3.5

The fortune teller
answers the user's
every question.

When the user is done asking questions, she can enter quit to terminate the script. Before
stopping, the script invites the user to return and play again, as shown in Figure 3.6.

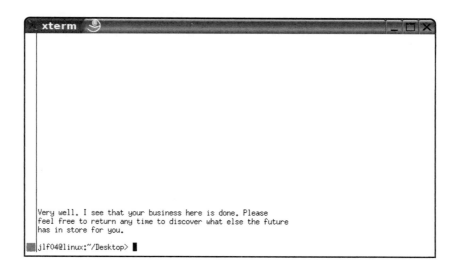

FIGURE 3.6

The Perl Fortune
Teller game ends
by inviting the
player to come
back and play
again.

CODE BLOCKS

By default, Perl processes code statements in the order they are typed and each statement is
taken individually. As an alternative to this approach, Perl provides you with the ability to
organize related statements into blocks of code. *Code blocks* consist of one or more code statements that are called and executed as a unit. To define a code block, all you have to do is

surround the statements that will make up the block with curly braces ({}), as demonstrated next.

```
{
  print "Number of wins: $wins\n";
  print "Number of losses: $losses\n";
  print "Your total score is: $score\n";
}
```

Using code blocks, you can organize groups of related code statements. A code block can also contain embedded code blocks, which, as you will see in examples throughout this chapter, is important when developing complex programming logic. By default, any code statements located within a code block are executed by default in a top-down manner.

 TRICK

The last statement in any code block does not require an ending semicolon character. Therefore, the previous example could be rewritten as shown here:

```
{
  print "Number of wins: $wins\n";
  print "Number of losses: $losses\n";
  print "Your total score is: $score\n"
}
```

However, you should include the ending semicolon on the last code statement in your code blocks anyway. This way, if you ever come back and add additional statements to the end of your code blocks, you do not have to worry about remembering to add the semicolon to the end of the statement that used to be the last code statement in the code block.

Code blocks not associated with conditional or looping statements are sometimes referred to as bare blocks. A *bare block* can be placed anywhere within a Perl script. However, code blocks are most commonly used when working with conditional and looping statements. For example, the following statements show a small if statement containing a code block made up of a single statement.

```
if ($x == $y) {
  print "We have a match!";
}
```

In similar fashion, the following statements demonstrate how a code block is used in the formation of a small while loop.

```
while ($intCounter <= 5) {
  print "$intCounter";
  $intCounter++;
}
```

TRICK

Statement layout within code blocks is free form. This means that you can indent code statements and add blank lines as necessary to visually improve the presentation of code statements. This will make your Perl scripts easier to read and will help to ensure that you remember to include both the opening and closing curly braces.

Applying Conditional Logic

In every example that you have seen so far in this book, code statements were, for the most part, listed and processed sequentially. However, using Perl's conditional statements, you can modify this behavior.

In Perl, conditional logic involves the programmatic analysis of two or more conditions, the result of which alters the logical execution of code statements. Perl supports a number of conditional statements, each of which are designed to control the execution of code blocks. These statements allow you to pick and choose when certain code blocks execute, allowing you to dynamically alter the logical flow of your Perl scripts based on the current situation. When executed, a conditional statement executes its embedded code block one time.

Conditional statements execute based on the value of a tested expression. If the value of the expression is evaluated as being true, the code block embedded within the if statement is executed. If the value of the expression is evaluated as being false, the code block is not executed and script execution continues on with either an alternative code block or with the next code statement following the conditional statement.

Conditional statements (and loop statements which are covered later in this chapter) are also known as complex statements. A *complex statement* is one that is designed to control the execution of code blocks. Complex statements do not end with semicolons, although the statements inside the embedded code block still require the semicolon character.

Perl's View of What's True and False

Before beginning a review of each of Perl's conditional statements, it is important that you first understand how Perl evaluates expressions and arrives upon a determination of true or false. For starters, Perl fully resolves the value of an expression prior to performing conditional logic. Perl then takes the resulting scalar value and performs a conditional evaluation, making a determination of whether the scalar value is true or false. It is therefore important that you understand just how Perl views the idea of true and false.

In Perl's view, the following values are evaluated as being false.

- An empty string ("")
- A string with a value of "0"
- The number zero (0)
- An undefined value (undef)

In Perl, any scalar data can be tested to determine if it is a true or false value. Any scalar variable that has not been assigned a value is assigned a default value of undef. If Perl comes across an undefined scalar variable, it substitutes a value of 0 for it. As you can see, this meets the criteria for an evaluation of false. If a scalar value evaluates to anything other than the values specified above, Perl views it as being true.

Variations of the if Statement

Perl's primary means of implementing conditional logic is through the if statement. Perl supports a number of different variations, including:

- if
- if…else
- if…elsif
- unless

Each of these variations of the if statement are examined in detail in the sections that follow.

if

The if statement is used to control the conditional execution of code blocks. It is almost impossible to develop useful Perl scripts without using the if statement or one of its variations. You have already seen the if statement in action in Chapter 1, "Perl Basics," where you used the if statement when creating the Perl Humor Script, as demonstrated by the following:

```
if ($reply ne 'yes') {
    print "\nHum... Perhaps you misunderstood.\n\n";
}
```

Here, an if statement was used to evaluate the response collected from the user and stored in a scalar variable named $reply to determine whether the user wanted to hear the script's joke.

The if statement tests the value of a specified expression to determine if it evaluates to a value of true. The syntax of the if statement is outlined here.

```
if (expression) {
  code block
}
```

To better understand how the if statement works, consider the following example.

```
$playerscore = 10;
$computerscore = 5;
if ($playerscore > $computerscore) {print "Congratulations! You have won."}
```

Here the expression being tested is whether $playerscore is greater than $computerscore. Perl will evaluate this expression as being true. As a result, the code block embedded within the if statement will execute, resulting in a text string being printed on the screen. In this example, the expression that was evaluated was relatively short and the accompanying code block was made up of a single statement. As a result, everything fit on a single line. However, in most instances, statements are typically spread across multiple lines as demonstrated below.

```
$playerscore = 10;
$computerscore = 5;
if ($playerscore > $computerscore) {
  print "Congratulations! You have won.";
}
```

From Perl's perspective, the two previous examples are identical and both result in the code block being executed. If, on the other hand, the previous example was modified as shown below, Perl will evaluate the expression as being false and will skip the execution of any code statements located in the embedded code block. Program flow will then continue on with the next code statement following the if statement's closing curly brace (}).

```
$playerscore = 10;
$computerscore = 50;
if ($playerscore > $computerscore) {
  print "Congratulations! You have won.";
}
```

Note that to set up conditional tests using the if statement, you need to build expressions using Perl's numeric and string operators, which were covered previously in Chapter 2 "Working with Strings, Numbers, and Operators." Also, make sure that you don't mix up numeric and string operators. You need to use Perl's numeric operators when comparing scalar numeric values and Perl's string operators when comparing scalar strings.

 TRICK The if statement provides an alternate syntax for smaller, single expression conditional statements. Using this form of the if statement, you precede the statement with the code block, as demonstrated below.

```
print "Gee, you are old!" if ($myAge > $yourAge);
```

To use this format of the if statement, you are limited to executing a single expression and you must add a semicolon to the end of the if statement.

if...else

A variation of the if statement is the if...else statement. The syntax of the if...else statement is outlined here.

```
if (expression) {
  code block 1
} else {
  code block 2
}
```

Like the if statement, the if...else statement evaluates an expression to determine if it evaluates to a value of true and if it does, the first embedded code block is executed, after which the program flow jumps to the first code statement following the if...else loop. However, if the value of the tested expression evaluates as being false, the first code block is skipped and instead the statements that make up the second code block are executed.

To better explain the operation of the if...else statement, consider the following example.

```
if (the cost of an apple is under a dollar) {
  I'll add it to my cart
  I will buy it
} else {
  I'll put it back
  I'll buy something else
}
```

This English-like (*pseudo code*) example demonstrates how to apply the logic of an if...else statement to a typical everyday event. The first line in the example specifies the expression that is to be evaluated. If the value of the expression evaluates to true, the actions outlined in the first code block are performed. Otherwise, the actions specified in the second code block are performed.

TRICK *Pseudo code* is an English-like outline of the logic required to develop all or a portion of a script or computer program. By taking a little time to outline the overall design of a script using pseudo code, you force yourself to take time and plan out how you expect things to work. This provides you with the opportunity to review your thought process and potentially to identify, before writing any code, where you may run into problems. Pseudo code helps you to get your thoughts together and to develop an initial draft of your script.

You have already seen the if...else statement in action in Chapter 1, where you used the if...else statement when creating the Perl Humor Script as demonstrated here.

```
#Determine whether or not the player guessed the right answer
if ($reply ne 'silence') {
  print "\nSorry. Wrong answer. Think about it and try again later.\n\n";
} else {
  print "\nYes, that is right. Well done!\n\n";
}
```

Here, an if...else statement was used to evaluate a response that was collected from the user and stored in a scalar variable named $reply to determine whether the user wanted to hear the script's joke. Note that in this example, the user must type in the word silence in all lowercase characters in order for the first code block in the if...else statement to execute. Anything else will result in an evaluation of false and, as a result, the second code block would execute.

Let's take one more look at an example of an if...else statement; this time the expression that is tested compares numeric scalar variables.

```
if ($playerscore > $computerscore) {
  print "Congratulations! You have won.";
} else {
  print "Sorry, the computer has won.";
}
```

As you can see, this example uses the greater than numeric operator to compare two scalar variables and then determine which code block gets executed.

elsif

Another variation of the if statement is the if...elsif statement. Using this conditional statement, you can develop tests that can check for alternative conditions. The if...elsif statement has the following syntax.

```
if (expression1) {
  code block 1
} elsif (expression2) {
  code block 2
} else {
  code block 3
}
```

Each expression that is tested can evaluate completely different conditions and execute a different code block. The first condition that evaluates to true is executed and any remaining conditions are skipped. You can define as many elsif conditions as you wish as demonstrated next.

```
if ($playerscore > $computerscore) {
  print "Congratulations! You have won.";
} elsif ($playerscore == $computerscore) {
  print "Tie! There is no winner.";
} elsif ($playerscore < $computerscore) {
  print "Sorry, the computer has won.";
}
```

Be careful when comparing two numeric values to make sure that you use the == operator and not the = operator. The == operator is used when comparing numeric values and the = operator is used when making assignments. Otherwise, the results returned won't be what you expect. If you have warnings turned on, Perl will warn you if this situation occurs.

Here, three separate tests have been set up. The first test checks to see if the first scalar variable is greater than the second scalar variable. The second test checks to see if the values of two scalar variables are equal. The third test checks to see if the value of the second scalar variable is greater than that of the first.

Another pitfall to avoid is the accidental misuse of the == operators and the eq operator. The == operator is used to compare numeric values, whereas the eq operator is used to compare strg values. For example, consider the following statements.

```
$x = "Apples";
$y = "Oranges";
if ($x == $y) {
  print "Apples and oranges are the same.";
}
```

When executed, you might be surprised to learn that Perl will evaluate $x and $y as being equal. The reason for this is that the numeric == operator was used in place of the string eq operator when setting up this example. As a result, Perl tries to make the best out of this illogical situation by first converting the value of $x and $y to numeric values. In this case this means converting both scalar variables to a value of 0. As a result of this conversion, Perl reaches the conclusion that Apples are in fact the same as Oranges.

You can also add an optional else statement to an if…elsif code block that will execute in the event that none of the elsif statements evaluate to true. For example, take a look at the following example.

```
if ($playerscore > $computerscore) {
  print "Congratulations! You have won.";
} elsif ($playerscore == $computerscore) {
  print "Tie! There is no winner.";
} else {
  print "Sorry, the computer has won.";
}
```

Here, the else statement executes in the event that the expressions defined in the two elsif statements evaluate to false. An alternative to using if…elsif code blocks is to use a series of repeating if statements as demonstrated here.

```
if ($playerscore > $computerscore) {
  print "Congratulations! You have won.";
}
if ($playerscore == $computerscore) {
  print "Tie! There is no winner.";
}
if ($playerscore < $computerscore) {
  print "Sorry, the computer has won.";
}
```

As you can see, this solution requires more lines of code and also requires that Perl perform each test, which is less efficient than the if...elsif statement, which stops performing tests as soon as the first matching condition is found.

The unless Statement

Sometimes you may want to check for the falseness of a value. One way to do so is to negate the operator used in defining the tested expression in an if statement as demonstrated here.

```perl
$intCounter = 2;
if (not $intCounter > 3) {
  print "The counter is not greater than 3";
}
```

Alternatively, you could create an if...else code block and place the code you want executed for a false value in the code block belonging to the else statement as demonstrated here.

```perl
$intCounter = 2;
if ($intCounter > 3) {
  print "";
} else {
  print "The counter is not greater than 3";
}
```

Rather than testing for false by negating the test or testing for truth using an if...else statement, you can use Perl's unless statement to set up a test for a false value. The unless statement is basically the opposite of the if statement. Its syntax is outlined below.

```perl
unless (expression) {
  code block1
} else {
  code block2
}
```

To see how the unless statement works, take a look at the following example.

```perl
$intCounter = 2;
unless ($intCounter > 3) {
  print "The counter is not greater than 3";
}
```

In simple English, what this example does is check to see if the value of $intCounter > 3 is false and if it is, the statement in the embedded code block executes. Using the optional else statement, you can create unless code blocks that provide for an alternate course of action.

```
$intCounter = 4;
unless ($intCounter > 3) {
  print "The counter is not greater than 3";
} else {
  print "The counter is greater than or equal to 3";
}
```

CREATING MORE SOPHISTICATED CONDITIONAL LOGIC

In addition to working with each of the previously discussed variations of the if statements and the unless statement, Perl provides you with plenty of other options for implementing and controlling conditional logic in your Perl scripts. A number of these options are discussed in the sections that follow.

Nesting

Perl allows you to embed or *nest* conditional code blocks within one another. Doing so facilitates the development of more complicated conditional programming logic. The end result is that you can create conditional tests that start by evaluating one condition and then test the condition further using as many additional tests as required.

Take a look at the following example, where three if statements have been nested in order to create a piece of code that analyzes the value of the $playerscore scalar variable against a number of different values.

```
if ($playerscore > $computerscore) {
  print "Congratulations! You have won.\n";
  if ($playerscore > $highscore) {
    print "You have the high score!\n";
    if ($playerscore > 1000000) {
      print "You have earned the rank of Admiral!\n";
    }
  }
}
```

For starters, the first if code block tests to see if $playerscore is greater than the $computerscore. If this expression evaluates to true, the player is declared the winner of the game. Otherwise, nothing happens and all of the nested if statements are skipped. Assuming that the player won the game, the value of $playerscore is then tested to see if it is greater than $highscore. Assuming this is true, the value of $playerscore is evaluated to see if it exceeds 1,000,000.

 TRAP Perl will allow you to nest as many conditional code blocks as you want. However, nesting too deeply can result in program code that is difficult to read and follow along, making your Perl scripts more difficult to maintain.

Working with the ?...: Conditional Operator

Perl also allows you to define and execute conditional tests using the ?...: trinary conditional operator. This operator is especially handy in situations where the conditional test is simple and can be easily defined on a single line. The syntax for this form of conditional test is outlined below.

```
expression ? true_expression : false_expression;
```

Here, an expression is evaluated to see if it evaluates to true or false. If it proves true, the *true_expression* is then evaluated and its value is returned. Otherwise, *false_expression* is evaluated and its value is returned. The following statements provide an example of how you might use the ?...: trinary operator to perform a conditional test.

```
$playerscore = 10;
$computerscore = 5;

$result = $playerscore > $computerscore ? "player wins" : "computer wins";
print "$result";
```

In this example, the expression $result = $playerscore > $computerscore is evaluated to determine the true value of $result. If $result evaluates to true then the *true_expression* executes, in which case "player wins" is returned. If $result evaluates as being false, "computer wins" is returned. Note that while the previous example returned either of two scalar strings based on the results of the evaluation, Perl lets you use any expression as the true_expression and false_expression.

Creating Custom Conditional Structures

One type of conditional statement not found in Perl is one that allows you to compare one value or expression against a series of possible values. In most programming languages, this is accomplished through a Select Case, Case, or Switch statement. While Perl does not provide a similar statement, you can create a reasonable facsimile using a labeled block, the && logical operator, and do functions. The following example shows the syntax to follow to create your own custom Case-like conditional statement.

```
CASE: {
  expression && do {
    statements;
    last CASE;
  };
  expression && do {
    statements;
    last CASE;
  };
  expression && do {
    statements;
    last CASE;
  };
}
```

Here, CASE is the name assigned to the custom Case statement. Expression represents the expression to be tested. Statements is a placement holder representing statements placed within do code blocks that should be executed when one of the expressions evaluates to true. The statement last CASE; is used to exit the CASE code block as soon as one of the tested expressions evaluates to true.

To get a better look at how to put this custom CASE block to work, take a look at the following example.

```
$playerscore = 10;
$computerscore = 10;

CASE: {
  $playerscore < $computerscore && do {
    $winner = "Computer";
    last CASE;
  };
  $playerscore == $computerscore && do {
    $winner = "Tie";
    last CASE;
  };
  $playerscore > $computerscore && do {
    $winner = "Player";
    last CASE;
```

```
    };
}
```

```
print "The winner is $winner";
```

 HINT This example makes use of the do function and the last statement, both of which are covered later in this chapter. The do function is used here to set up code blocks that execute based on the value assigned to the $playerscore variable. The last statement is used to terminate the execution of code blocks.

Take note of the use of the && operator. It performs an operation known as *short-circuiting*, in which the operation on the right-hand side of the && operator is executed only if the operation on the left-hand side of the && operator evaluates to true.

In this example, three tests have been defined within the CASE block. Each expression that is evaluated performs a slightly different test. In this example, where $playerscore and $computerscore are both equal, the second expression will evaluate to true and its associated do code block will set $winner equal to Tie and exit the CASE code block.

SETTING UP LOOPS

By default, Perl scripts execute by processing code statements in the order they are written, starting at the beginning of the script and continuing on to the end of the script. This is sufficient for many scripts. However, in order to create Perl scripts that can handle large amounts of information, you need to learn how to create loops.

Loops provide additional control over the execution of code blocks by providing you with the ability to repeat the execution of statements defined within code blocks over and over again as necessary. A loop executes repeatedly until a specified condition is met or until a loop control statement executes, redirecting loop execution. As a result, it is possible to create small Perl scripts, which with just a few lines of code can process unlimited quantities of data. When combined with conditional statements, you have the ability to develop sophisticated scripts capable of performing just about anything.

Perl provides you with access to a number of different types of looping statements, including:

- while
- until
- do

- for
- foreach

By default, the while, until, and do loops execute until a specified condition is true or false. The for and foreach loops, on the other hand, are designed to execute a specific number of times. In most cases, you can substitute any one of the loops for another. However, each tends to be more appropriate for specific types of situations. Perl is an extremely flexible programming language. As such, it leaves it up to you to determine when and where you use each type of loop. Each of these different types of loops is examined in detail in the sections that follow.

while

The while loop is designed to execute a block of code statements as long as a tested condition remains true. Once that condition becomes false, the loop stops executing. The while loop has the following syntax.

```
while (expression) {
  code block
}
```

Perl begins executing a while loop by testing for the truth of its expression. If the value of the expression evaluates to true, the while loop's code block is executed. If the value of the expression is evaluated as being false, the while loop's code block is skipped and program execution continues on with the next code statement following the while loop. After each execution of a while loop's code block, the value of the expression is rechecked and as long as the expression evaluates to a value of true, the loop continues to execute. However, once the expression's value becomes false, the loop stops executing and script execution continues on with the next code statement following the while loop.

To see how the while loop really works, let's look at a few examples. First, consider the following example.

```
#!/usr/bin/perl

print "Let's count to 10\n\n";

$intCounter = 1;
while ($intCounter <= 10) {
  print "  $intCounter\n\n";
  $intCounter++;
```

```
}
```

```
$reply = <STDIN>;
```

Here, a `while` loop has been set up to execute 10 times. Upon each execution, the value of `$intCounter`, which was initially assigned a value of 1, is incremented by one. As soon as the value of `$intCounter` is set equal to 11, the loop stops executing. Figure 3.7 shows the output that is produced by this script when it is executed on a computer running Windows XP.

FIGURE 3.7

Counting to 10 using a `while` loop.

Next, take a look at this script:

```perl
#!/usr/bin/perl

while (lc ($reply) ne "quit") {
  print "\nType quit to terminate script execution\n\n>";
  chomp($reply = <STDIN>);
}
```

Here, a `while` loop has been set up to control interaction with the user. Specifically, the `while` loop has been set up to execute as long as the input keyed in by the user is not equal to quit. Note that the Perl `lc` function is used to automatically convert any user input to lower-case characters, thus allowing the user to enter the word `quit` using any combination of upper- and lowercase spelling.

Figure 3.8 shows the output generated by this script when the user presses the Enter key and then types in `exit`.

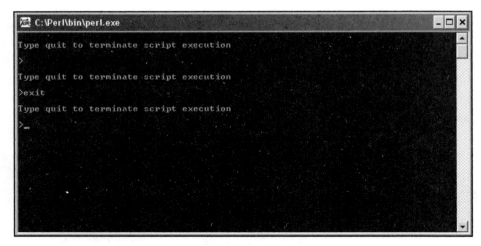

FIGURE 3.8

Using a while loop to control interaction with the user.

TRICK

The while statement provides an alternate syntax for smaller, single expression loop statements. Using this form of the while statement, you precede the while statement with another statement, as demonstrated below.

```
$intCounter = 1;
print $intCounter++ while ($intCounter <= 10);
```

When executed this script displays output of

12345678910

To use this form of the while statement, you are limited to executing a single expression and you must add a semicolon to the end of the while statement.

until

The until loop is pretty much the opposite of the while loop. Whereas the while loop executes as long as an expression is evaluated as being true, the until loop executes as long as an expression evaluates as being false. The until loop has the following syntax.

```
until (expression) {
    code block
}
```

Perl begins executing an until loop by testing for the truth of its expression. If the value of the expression evaluates as being false, the until loop's code block is executed. If the value of the expression is evaluated as being true, the until loop's code block is skipped and program execution skips on to the code statement immediately following the until loop. At the end of each execution of an until loop, the value of the tested expression is reevaluated and as long as the expression continues to remain false, the loop continues executing. Once the expression's value finally becomes true, the loop stops executing and program execution continues on with the code statement following the until loop.

To see the until loop in action, take a look at the following example.

```perl
#!/usr/bin/perl

print "Let's count to 10\n\n\n";

$intCounter = 1;
until ($intCounter > 10) {
  print "  $intCounter\n\n";
  $intCounter++;
}

$reply = <STDIN>;
```

This example is nearly identical to the example of the while loop that you looked at earlier in the chapter. The only real difference here is that the while statement has been replaced with an until statement and instead of running until $intCounter is less than or equal to 10, the loop now runs until $intCounter is greater than 10. The output that this script produces is identical to that shown in Figure 3.7. As already stated, you can usually use any of Perl's loops interchangeably, based on your personal preference.

 TRICK

Like the while statement, the until statement also provides an alternate syntax that lets you set up smaller, single expression loops. Using this form of the until statement, you precede the until statement with another statement, as demonstrated below.

```perl
$intCounter = 1;
print $intCounter++ until ($intCounter > 10);
```

When executed this script displays this output:

```
12345678910
```

To use this format of the until statement, you are limited to working with a single expression and you must add a semicolon to the end of the until statement.

do

Another option available to you for creating loops is the do loop function. The do function can be used to execute a block of statements before testing an assigned expression using a while or until statement, thus emanating the behavior of a loop. The syntax required to work with the do function when used with the while statement is outlined below.

```
do {
  code block
} while (expression);
```

Note that the last statement in the above example ends with a semicolon character. When executed, the do function automatically executes its code block and then tests the value of its assigned expression. If the value of the expression evaluates to true, the embedded code block executes again. Otherwise, the function stops executing and the statement following the function executes. To see an example of this in action, take a look at the following statements.

```
do {

  print "type exit to quit: ";
  chomp($reply = <STDIN>);

} while (lc $reply ne "exit");
```

Here, a code block is set up to automatically execute at least once. Next, the lc function is used to convert the value assigned to $reply. This value is then evaluated to determine if it is not equal to "exit". As long as it is not equal, the embedded code block executes again. As soon as the value evaluates to "exit", script execution continues on with the next statement following the function.

The second option for working with the do function replaces the while statement with the until statement and has the following syntax.

```
do {
  code block
} until (expression);
```

The only difference in the layout of this form of the do function is that the resulting loop runs until its expression evaluates to true instead of executing while the expression evaluates to true, as demonstrated in the following example.

```
do {

  print "type exit to quit: ";
  chomp($reply = <STDIN>);

} until (lc $reply eq "exit");
```

This example is almost exactly like the previous example, except that it executed until the lowercase value of $reply evaluates as true.

All in all, there is nothing that you can do using the do function that cannot be achieved using the while or until loops. General consensus among the Perl community favors the while and until loops. The do function and its ability to formulate loops is covered here for the sake of thoroughness and because you are likely to come across its use from time to time.

for

Unlike all of the previous types of loops that you have seen so far, the for loop does not execute based on the value of a tested expression. Instead, the for loop executes or *iterates* an arbitrary number of times. The syntax of the for loop is outlined here.

```
for (initialization; test; increment) {
  code block
}
```

Each section of the for loop is separated by a semicolon. The *initialization* parameter is used to specify an expression that is evaluated and incremented each time the loop executes. The *test* parameter is used to specify an expression that is evaluated each time the loop executes. The *increment* parameter is used to specify an expression that increments the value of a variable residing in the *initialization* expression.

When Perl encounters a for loop, it begins by evaluating the initialization expression. Next, Perl evaluates the test expression to determine its truth. As long as the test expression evaluates as being false, the loop will iterate. At the end of each iteration of the loop, Perl executes the increment expression and then reevaluates the value of the test expression to determine if the loop should execute again. For example, the following for loop begins by assigning a 1 to $intCounter, which is incremented by 1 each time the loop iterates. The loop will iterate as long as the value of $intCounter is less than or equal to 10.

```
for ($intCounter = 1; $intCounter <= 10; $intCounter++) {
  print "$intCounter ";
}
```

Note that each of the three expressions that make up the for loop are optional, meaning that you can omit one, two, or all three expressions when setting up a for loop. However, you still have to supply the semicolons. For example, the following code statements demonstrate a for loop where only the *test* expression has been supplied.

```
$intCounter = 1;
for ( ; $intCounter <= 10; ) {
  print "$intCounter ";
  $intCounter++;
}
```

Since the first parameter was omitted from the for loop, $intCounter had to be defined and initialized prior to the loop. This next example demonstrates a for loop where the second parameter has been omitted.

```
for ($intCounter = 0; ; $intCounter = $intCounter + 2) {
  print "$intCounter ";
    if ($intCounter == 10) {
    exit;
    }
}
```

In this example, the for loop has been set up to iterate 6 times. Upon the first iteration the value of $intCounter is 0. $intCounter is incremented by 2 each time the loop iterates and terminates when $intCounter equals 10.

TRICK   Note the use of the exit keyword in the previous example. exit is a built-in Perl function that instructs Perl to stop script execution. Optionally, you can pass the exit function an exit value. The exit value is used to provide the operating system with an indication of how successfully the Perl script ran. An exit value of 0 usually indicates that the script ran without any errors or problems.

foreach

Whereas the for loop is designed to iterate a predetermined number of times, Perl's foreach loop is designed to provide you with the ability to loop through all the members of a list or array as well as all of the keys in a hash.

TRICK   Lists, arrays, and hashes are collections of data that you can use to store and retrieve one or more elements of data as a unit. You'll learn how to work with lists, arrays, and hashes in Chapter 4.

The syntax of the `foreach` loop is outlined here.

```
foreach iterator  (arrayame) {
  code block
}
```

Iterator represents an element of the array. Note that *iterator* is not a variable that is temporarily assigned the value of the array element. It is a direct reference to the element itself, meaning that if you change its value in the embedded code block, its value is changed in the array. As an example of how to work with the `foreach` loop, consider the following example.

```
@playernames = qw(Alexander William Molly);

foreach $name (@playernames) {
  print "$name\n";
}
```

Here an array named `@playernames` is created and assigned three elements. The next three statements contain a `foreach` loop that iterates through each element in the array, displaying each name.

TRICK

Perl has a special `$_` variable that you can use as a shortcut when writing `foreach` loops. The `foreach` loop uses an iterator to represent the value of elements in lists, arrays, and hashes. If the iterator is omitted, Perl will automatically use the `$_` variable in its place, as demonstrated in the following example.

```
@playernames = qw(Alexander William Molly);

foreach (@playernames) {
  print "$_\n";
}
```

Adding Continue Blocks to Your Loops

One interesting feature that Perl allows you to add to the end of loops is a `continue` statement. The `continue` statement executes when the loop's code block finishes an iteration or whenever a `next` statement is executed within the loop. Once a `continue` statement finishes executing, the loop resumes its next iteration.

To better understand how to work with this optional loop feature, take a look at the following example.

```perl
while (lc ($reply) ne "quit") {
  print "\nType quit to terminate script execution\n\n>";
  chomp($reply = <STDIN>);
} continue {
  print "\nQuitting Script execution\n";
}
```

You can add continue blocks to your loops in order to group code statements that you'd like to execute at the end of each loop iteration but that you'd like not to execute whenever a redo or last statement is executed.

Loop Controls

Perl provides you with a number of statements that give you the ability to alter the logical processing flow within code blocks. These statement include

- Last
- Next
- Redo

Each of these statements is discussed further in the sections that follow.

The last Statement

There may be times when you want to terminate a loop's execution prematurely. To do so you can execute the last statement as demonstrated here.

```perl
$intCounter = 1;
while ($intCounter <= 20) {
  print "$intCounter ";
  if ($intCounter == 10) {
    last;
  }
  $intCounter++;
}
```

Here, the last statement is executed when the value of $intCounter becomes 10, stopping the execution of the while loop.

If you have nested one loop within another, using the last keyword by itself results in the termination of the loop containing the last statement. Any parent loops continue processing normally. As you will see a little later in this chapter, you can use the last statement with a label to terminate an outer loop.

The next Statement

The next statement provides you with the ability to skip the processing of any statements remaining in a code block after the next statement. When executed, the next statement arbitrarily ends the current execution of the loop and starts the loop over again, assuming that the loop is not finished.

The redo Statement

The redo statement terminates the current execution of the loop and starts the current iteration of the loop over again, without checking the value of the termination condition.

ADDING LABELS TO YOUR CODE BLOCKS AND LOOPS

Perl gives you added flexibility to control the logical flow of program code by allowing you to add labels to your code blocks, as well as to your while and for loops. A label is simply a unique identifier that you can use to mark certain locations in a Perl script that you can call from other parts of your scripts. Labels are commonly associated with looping statements where they can be used in conjunction with the last, next, and redo statements.

When used, labels are placed in front of a code block, as demonstrated here.

```
BLOCKNAME: {
  code block
}
```

By convention, label names are typed in all uppercase. Label names are governed by the same rules as variable names, with the exception that label names do not begin with a special character such as $ or @. Labels are commonly used to label loops that embed within other loops, as demonstrated below.

```
FIRSTLOOP: while (expression) {
  LASTLOOP: while (expression) {
    code block
  }
}
```

Note that a label must be followed immediately by a semicolon and can only occur at the beginning of the labeled statement. By labeling loops, you can specify which loop a loop control statement applies to, as demonstrated below.

```
FIRSTLOOP: while (expression) {
  LASTLOOP: while (expression) {
    if ($strikes == 3) {
      last FIRSTLOOP;
    }
  }
}
```

Here, the last statement tells Perl to terminate the execution of FIRSTLOOP if $strikes becomes equal to 3 in the embedded loop.

BACK TO THE PERL FORTUNE TELLER GAME

Okay, it is time to turn your attention back to the Perl Fortune Teller game. Through the development of this game, you will get the opportunity to work with the while loop and the if...elsif code block. You will also make use of the next statement to control loop execution. In addition, you will learn how to use the rand function to generate random numbers, thus providing the game with the ability to generate unpredictable responses.

TRICK

The rand function generates a random number between 0 and a value passed to the function as an argument. If the argument is omitted, rand returns a value between 0 and 1. For example, the following statement will assign a random number between 0 and 10 to a scalar variable named $secretnumber.

```
$randomnumber = rand 10;
```

The rand function returns a floating point number. If you want to generate a random number in the form of an integer, you will need to use the int function to round down the randomly generated number as demonstrated here.

```
$randomnumber = int(rand 10);
```

Designing the Game

The Perl Fortune Teller game is created in seven steps:

1. Creating a new script and adding opening comments.
2. Preparing the screen and the game.
3. Prompting the player for permission to continue.
4. Establishing the mood of the game.

5. Answering player questions.
6. Ending the game.
7. Keeping the screen clear.

Creating a New Perl Script

The first step in developing the Perl Fortune Teller game is to create a new Perl script and name it FortuneTeller.pl. Next, add the following statements to the script.

```perl
#!/usr/bin/perl
#
# The Perl Fortune Teller (FortuneTeller.pl)
```

By this point in the book, these statements should be pretty familiar to you. The first statement is the shebang, which is followed by comment statements that identify the game.

Preparing the Screen and the Game

Next, append the following statements to the end of the script.

```perl
clear_the_screen();

$reply     = "";
$question = "";
$randomnumber = 0;
```

The first statement executes the clear_the_screen() subroutine, which clears the screen in order to prepare it for the display of additional text. The remaining statements define variables that store information collected from the user as well as to store a randomly generated number.

Prompting the Player

Next, append the following statements to the end of the script.

```perl
print "Hello and welcome to the Perl Fortune Teller game.\n\n";
print "What you are about to see will thrill and amaze you!\n\n\n\n\n\n";
print "Press the Enter key to continue...";

$reply = <STDIN>;
```

The print statements are used to present the player with a welcome message. The last statement pauses script execution by telling Perl to wait until the user presses the Enter key.

Setting Up the Story's Background

Next, append the following statements to the end of the script.

```
clear_the_screen ();

print "The room goes black. You hear the creaking of an old\n";
print "door followed by the sound of someone coming towards you. Your\n";
print "heart begins to pound through your chest. For a few moments\n";
print "there is total silence. Suddenly, a bright light appears in the\n";
print "middle of the room, emanating from a crystal ball located on a\n";
print "small table.\n\n";


print "                       ****\n";
print "                    *       *\n";
print "                   *          *\n";
print "                  *            *\n";
print "                  *            *\n";
print "                  *           *\n";
print "                   *         *\n";
print "                    ****\n";
print "                    |  |\n";
print "                ----------------\n";
print "                |              |\n";
print "                |              |\n";
print "                |              |\n";
print "                |              |\n";
print "                ----------------\n\n";
print "Press the Enter key to continue...";

$reply = <STDIN>;
```

The first statement calls the clear_the_screen() subroutine. The remaining statements provide additional story information and display a text-based graphic of a crystal ball. The last statement pauses script execution, waiting for the player to press the Enter key.

Answering Player Questions

The Perl Fortune Teller game will allow the player to ask as many questions as she wishes, terminating only when the player types quit and presses the Enter key. To accommodate this requirement, you will need to set up a loop that will control the part of the script that displays player questions and generates computer responses.

So let's begin by adding the following statements to the end of the Perl script.

```perl
while (lc ($question) ne "quit") {

  clear_the_screen();

}
```

As you can see, a while statement has been defined to control execution of the loop. In addition, a call to the clear_the_screen subroutine has been added that will be used to clear the screen each time the loop iterates. The rest of the code statements presented in this section will be added to the while loop.

Begin by adding the following statements immediately following the clear_the_screen(); statement.

```perl
print "I see that someone has come to see me. Very well, ask me\n";
print "your question and I will tell you what it is that you wish\n";
print "to know.\n\n";
print "What is your question? ";
chomp($question = <STDIN>);
```

These statements instruct the player to type in a question, which is then assigned to a scalar string variable named $question. Next, add the following statements immediately after the previous statements.

```perl
clear_the_screen();

if (lc ($question) eq "quit") {
  next;
}
```

The first statement executes the clear_the_screen() subroutine. Next, an if block is set up to check and see if the player typed quit instead of entering a question. This is accomplished by first converting the value of $question to all lowercase characters and then comparing this new value to see if it equals quit. If it does, a next statement is executed, forcing a new iteration of the loop, and since the loop has been set up to terminate once the user enters quit, the loop stops executing. Otherwise, the next statement is not executed and the loop continues to run.

Next, add the following statements immediately below the previous statements.

```perl
if ($question eq "") {
  print "You did not ask a question.\n\n";
  print "Press the Enter key to continue...";
  $reply = <STDIN>;
  next;
}
```

As you can see, an if block has been set up to determine if the player pressed the Enter key without first keying in a question (e.g. to see if $question equals ""). If this is the case, the player is informed of the error and once the Enter key is pressed, the loop iterates and runs again, giving the player another chance to ask a question.

Next, add the following statement immediately below the previous statements.

```perl
$randomnumber = int(rand 6);
```

This statement is responsible for generating a random number. This is accomplished using the rand function. Rand is a Perl function that returns a randomly generated number between 0 and a specified value. By default, the rand function returns any valid number and not just whole numbers. To ensure that only integers are retrieved, the value retrieved by rand is then rounded down to a whole number using the int function. As a result, only integers in the range of 0 to 5 are retrieved.

Next, you need to add programming logic to the loop that analyzes the randomly generated number in order to determine which of 6 answers should be presented to the player. To do this, add the following statements immediately below the previous statement.

```perl
if ($randomnumber == 0) {
  print "The answer to your question is No.\n\n";
} elsif ($randomnumber == 1) {
  print "The answer to your question is Yes.\n\n";
} elsif ($randomnumber == 2) {
  print "The answer to your question is unclear. ";
  print "Try asking your question differently.\n\n";
} elsif ($randomnumber == 3) {
  print "The answer to your question is maybe.\n\n";
} elsif ($randomnumber == 4) {
  print "The answer to your question is that only time will tell.\n\n";
} elsif ($randomnumber == 5) {
```

```
  print "Ask a different question. I cannot answer this one.\n\n";
}
```

As you can see, an if…elsif block has been set up to process each of the possible values that might be returned as a random number. Based on the random number that is generated, the appropriate print statement is executed, thus answering the player's question.

To wrap up work on the code for the while loop, add the following statements immediately below the previous statements.

```
print "Press the Enter key to continue...";
$reply = <STDIN>;
```

These two statements force the script to pause in order to give the player the chance to read the Fortune Teller's answer.

Preparing to End the Game

To end the game, add the following script statements to the end of the script (e.g. as the first statement following the end of the while loop).

```
clear_the_screen();

print "Very well. I see that your business here is done. Please\n";
print "feel free to return any time to discover what else the future\n";
print "has in store for you.\n\n";
```

The first statement executes the clear_the_screen() subroutine. The remaining statements display text that invites the player to return and play again.

Clearing Screen Display

The last remaining task is to add the code statements that make up the clear_the_screen() subroutine. This is accomplished by appending the following statements to the end of the Perl script.

```
sub clear_the_screen {

  for ($i=0; $i < 25; ++$i){
    print "\n";
  }
}
```

The Final Result

If you haven't done so yet, save your Perl script as FortuneTeller.pl. By creating this script, you have reinforced your understanding of conditional and looping statements. For your convenience, the full version of the FortuneTeller.pl script is listed below. To help make things easier to follow along, comments have been added to document key script statements.

```perl
#!/usr/bin/perl
#
# The Perl Fortune Teller (FortuneTeller.pl)


clear_the_screen(); #Call subroutine that clears the screen

#Define a variable to hold user input
$reply    = "";
$question = "";
$randomnumber = 0;

#Display an introductory message and format display using carriage returns
print "Hello and welcome to the Perl Fortune Teller game.\n\n";
print "What you are about to see will thrill and amaze you!\n\n\n\n\n\n";
print "Press the Enter key to continue...";  #Prompt user before continuing
#Pause the script and wait for the player to press Enter
$reply = <STDIN>;


clear_the_screen();  #Call subroutine that clears the screen

print "The room goes black. You hear the creaking of an old\n";
print "door followed by the sound of someone coming towards you. Your\n";
print "heart begins to pound through your chest. For a few moments\n";
print "there is total silence. Suddenly, a bright light appears in the\n";
print "middle of the room emanating from a crystal ball located on a\n";
print "small table.\n\n";


print "                    ****\n";
print "                  *      *\n";
```

```perl
print "                       *        *\n";
print "                      *          *\n";
print "                     *            *\n";
print "                      *          *\n";
print "                       *        *\n";
print "                        ****\n";
print "                        |  |\n";
print "                ----------------\n";
print "                |               |\n";
print "                |               |\n";
print "                |               |\n";
print "                |               |\n";
print "                ----------------\n\n";
print "Press the Enter key to continue...";  #Prompt user before continuing


#Pause the script and wait for the player to press Enter
$reply = <STDIN>;


#Loop until the player types the word "quit"
while (lc ($question) ne "quit") {

  clear_the_screen();  #Call subroutine that clears the screen

  print "I see that someone has come to see me. Very well, ask me\n";
  print "your question and I will tell you what it is that you wish\n";
  print "to know.\n\n";
  print "What is your question? ";  #Capture the user's answer
  chomp($question = <STDIN>);


  clear_the_screen();  #Clear the screen


  #Terminate current iteration of the loop if the player typed "quit"
  if (lc ($question) eq "quit") {
    next;
```

```perl
}


#Terminate current iteration of the loop if the player did not type
#anything
if ($question eq "") {
  print "You did not ask a question.\n\n";
  print "Press the Enter key to continue...";  #Prompt user before continuing

  #Pause the script and wait for the player to press Enter
  $reply = <STDIN>;
  next;
}


#Generate a random number in the range of 0 to 5
$randomnumber = int(rand 6);

#Use the randomly generated number to select a response
if ($randomnumber == 0) {
  print "The answer to your question is No.\n\n";
} elsif ($randomnumber == 1) {
  print "The answer to your question is Yes.\n\n";
} elsif ($randomnumber == 2) {
  print "The answer to your question is unclear. ";
  print "Try asking your question differently.\n\n";
} elsif ($randomnumber == 3) {
  print "The answer to your question is maybe.\n\n";
} elsif ($randomnumber == 4) {
  print "The answer to your question is that only time will tell.\n\n";
} elsif ($randomnumber == 5) {
  print "Ask a different question. I cannot answer this one.\n\n";
}


print "Press the Enter key to continue...";  #Prompt user before continuing

#Pause the script and wait for the player to press Enter
```

```
   $reply = <STDIN>;

}  #End the loop


clear_the_screen();  #Call subroutine that clears the screen

print "Very well. I see that your business here is done. Please\n";
print "feel free to return any time to discover what else the future\n";
print "has in store for you.\n\n";


#This subroutine clears the screen by adding 25 blank lines
sub clear_the_screen {

  for ($i=0; $i < 25; ++$i){
    print "\n";
  }
}
```

Okay, it is time to run FortuneTeller.pl and see how it works. As long as you have not made any typos, the script should run as expected. If you receive any error messages, use the information provided to locate and track down each error and then try running the script again.

SUMMARY

In this chapter you learned how to define code blocks and to alter Perl's default top-down execution through the addition of conditional and looping programming logic. This included an overview of the if, if...else, if...elsif, unless, do, while, until, for, and foreach statements. You learned how to embed conditional statements in order to develop more complex tests. To exercise control over loops, you learned how to work with the last, next, and redo statements. You also learned how to combine these loop control statements with labels in order to jump around between embedded loops. On top of all this, you learned how to create the Perl Fortune Teller script, reinforcing your understanding of how to work with conditional logic and loops.

Before you move on to Chapter 4, take a few minutes to enhance the Perl Fortune Teller script by reviewing and implementing the following challenges.

CHALLENGES

1. The Perl Fortune Teller script's storyline is rather short. Expand upon the story to make it more descriptive.

2. Expand the if…elsif code block to support additional answers. Then modify the range of random numbers that the script generates in order to support the additional answers that you added.

WORKING WITH
COLLECTIONS OF DATA

U p to this point in the book, you have been writing Perl scripts that work with one piece of scalar data at a time. This is fine for many small scripts. However, at some point you will begin developing scripts that need to be able to process large amounts of data, and it will no longer be practical to define a unique variable for each data element. In this chapter, you will learn how to work with groups of scalar data. This will enable you to develop Perl scripts that can store any number of data elements. You will also learn how to retrieve, sort, and delete these data elements.

Specifically, you will learn how to

- Create and manipulate lists
- Use lists to assign data to arrays and hashes
- Create arrays and use them to store, retrieve, and sort array elements
- Create hashes and use them to store, retrieve, and sort hash contents
- Use loops to process the contents of arrays and hashes

PROJECT PREVIEW: THE STAR WARS QUIZ

This chapter's game project is the Star Wars Quiz. This game will reinforce your knowledge of how to work with arrays and how to use the `foreach` loop to process each element stored in an array. In addition, you will learn how to implement a text-based menu system from which help can be obtained and game play is initiated or terminated. The Star Wars Quiz begins by displaying a welcome message and a menu system, as demonstrated in Figure 4.1.

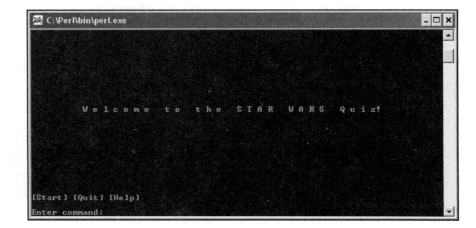

FIGURE 4.1

Executing the Star Wars Quiz script on a computer running Windows XP.

The user enters menu commands in order to control the script. Available menu commands include Start, Quit, and Help. In the event the user enters anything other than a valid menu command, the script responds by redisplaying the menu and waiting for a new menu command. Figure 4.2 demonstrates what happens when the user enters the Help command.

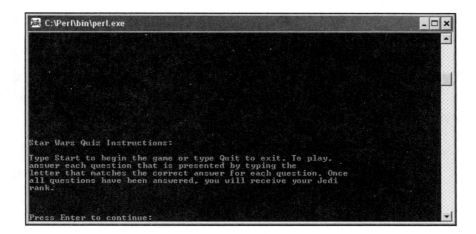

FIGURE 4.2

Viewing help information for the Star Wars Quiz.

Figure 4.3 shows the screen that is displayed if the user enters the Quit command.

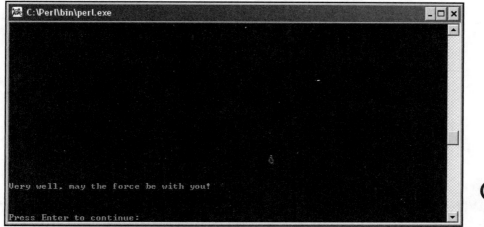

FIGURE 4.3

Quitting the Star Wars Quiz game.

To take the quiz, the user must enter the Start command. The script responds by displaying a series of questions. Each question is multiple choice, offering the user a selection of choices (A–D), as demonstrated in Figure 4.4.

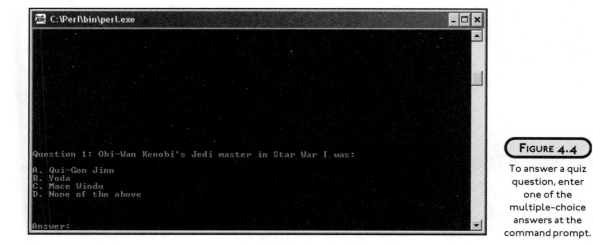

FIGURE 4.4

To answer a quiz question, enter one of the multiple-choice answers at the command prompt.

Once the last question has been answered, the game displays the player score and assigns a rank, as demonstrated in Figure 4.5.

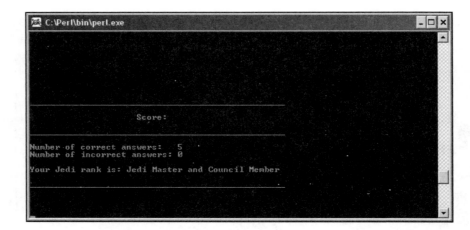

FIGURE 4.5

The game assigns the player a rank based on the number of correctly answered questions.

WORKING WITH COLLECTIONS OF RELATED DATA

Up to this point in the book, the focus has been on manipulating individual pieces of data in the form of scalar values and variables. Using scalar variables, you can store and retrieve individual items, such as a character, word, number, text string, or even a database record or a text document. This chapter changes focus a little bit by introducing you to different ways of representing, storing, and manipulating groups of related data.

Whenever you need to work with more than one piece of data at a time, such as when you need to manipulate a list of names or a collection of items such as an inventory of spare parts, you need to handle these items as list data. In Perl, *list data*, is represented in one of the following ways.

- Lists
- Arrays
- Hashes

ASSIGNING DATA TO A LIST

Of the three options available to you for storing and manipulating groups of data, lists are the most basic option and are often used as a starting point for creating arrays and hashes and populating them with data. A *list* is a collection of scalar data. Lists are created by enclosing comma-separated scalar data within a set of matching parentheses as demonstrated here.

```
("Alexander", "William", "Molly");
(1, 2, 3, 4, 5, 6, 7, 8, 9);
(A..Z);
qw($x, $y, $z);
```

Here four different lists have been created. The first list is a scalar string. Note that each list element is enclosed in matching double quotation marks. The second list is made up of a collection of numeric elements; therefore, quotation marks were not used. The third list uses the range operator to generate a list of uppercase characters from A to Z.

TRICK The *range* operator (..) provides you with the ability to generate a list of consecutive letters and numbers. For example, (1..10) is equivalent to (1 2 3 4 5 6 7 8 9 10). Likewise, (a..z) is equivalent to a list of lowercase characters from a to z and (A..Z) is equivalent to a list of uppercase characters from A to Z.

The fourth list generates a list that contains $x, $y, and $z and not the value that's assigned to these variables. The reason for this behavior is that the qw operator does not support variable interpolation. Beyond available computer memory, there is no limit to how large a list can be.

TRICK If you need to create a list that contains scalar data, you can omit the double quotation marks and the commas from any single word scalar entry when you define the list using the qw operator as demonstrated below.

```
qw(Alexander William Molly);
qw(Markland 40 Mike 40 Nick 40 Lee 41);
```

If you have any list elements that include blank spaces, you cannot use the qw operator when creating a list.

One capability of Perl not found in many other programming languages is the ability to populate a list of variables on the left-hand side of an expression from a list located on the right-hand side of the expression, as demonstrated below.

```
($x, $y) = qw(10 20);
```

Here, a list made up of two numeric scalar values is defined. The scalar values that make up the list are also assigned values corresponding to scalar variables located on the right-hand side of the equals assignment operator. In this example, $x is assigned a value of 10 and $y is assigned a value of 20. If the left-hand side of the assignment operator contains an array, the array will be assigned any remaining values on the right-hand side of the expression, as demonstrated here.

```
($x, @numbers, $y, $z) = qw(10 20 30 40 50);
```

Here, $x is assigned a value of 10 and the @numbers array is assigned the next four array elements (20, 30, 40, and 50). The $y and $z variables are each assigned a value of undefined. Arrays are discussed in detail in the next section.

HINT In Perl, an undefined value, commonly referred to as *undef*, is a value that has not been set. Perl will interpret an undefined value as being either 0 or an empty string, depending on the context in which it is used.

WORKING WITH ARRAYS

One way to use lists is to use them as the basis for populating an array with data. An array is a collection of scalar data that is stored in an indexed list. In Perl, array indexes start at 0 and are incremented by 1 each time a new element is added. Array indexes are made up only of whole numbers, although you can substitute a numeric scalar value in place of an actual number. Each item that is stored in an array is called an *array element*.

Arrays are ordered lists that have been assigned to an array variable. You can use arrays as substitutes for lists anywhere that lists can be used. Arrays have an initial element, a final element, and can have any number of elements in between. Individual array elements are accessed by referencing their index location within the array.

Arrays provide you with the ability to access array elements from any location within your Perl script. When creating an array, you must assign a unique array name. This name cannot conflict with other array names. Array names begin with the @ character, which is followed by a valid variable name.

TRICK Array names do not conflict with scalar variable names, meaning that $names and @names are not the same thing. However, in order to make your scripts as easy as possible to read and understand, it is best to avoid using similarly spelled variable and array names.

Declaring an Array

Perl does not require that you declare an array prior to using it. To create an array, all you have to do is reference it. Unlike many other programming languages, Perl does not require that you tell it in advance how large an array will be. Perl happily grows an array's size whenever a new array element is added.

One way to create an array is to assign a list to it as demonstrated below.

```
@names = ("Alexander", "William", "Molly");
```

or

```
@names = qw(Alexander William Molly);
```

In both of these examples, an array named @names is created and assigned a list made up of three scalar string values. An array can also be created by assigning it an empty list as shown below.

```
@names = ();
```

In this example, an array named @names is created but not assigned any data.

 TRAP Be careful when creating new empty arrays. If you accidentally create a new empty array that has the same array name as an existing array, the existing array will be replaced with the new array and any array elements in the old array will be lost.

Assigning the contents of one array to another array, as you see here, is another way of creating and populating arrays.

```
@usernames = @names;
```

In this example, any array elements stored in the @names array are copied into a temporary list and then reassigned to the @usernames array. In addition, if the @usernames array already exists, any of its old array elements are lost.

Perl is extremely flexible in the ways it allows you to work with and populate arrays. For example, if you want you can take two or more arrays and use them to create a new array as shown here.

```
@dolls = qw(Barbie, Ken);
@toys = qw(ball bat glove);

@kidsstuff = (@dolls, @toys);
```

In this example, a new array named @kidsstuff is created and assigned five array elements.

 TRICK Another way to create an array and assign data to it is with the split function. The split function takes two arguments. The first argument is a pattern that identifies the character or characters to use to break up the scalar value that makes up the second argument. For example, the following statement uses the split function to populate an array named @buddies with three elements.

```
@buddies = split(/ /, "Markland Nick Mike");
```

As you can see, in this example a blank space is passed to the split function as its first argument.

If you want, you can reverse this process by using the join function to take a list (or array) and merge it back into a scalar string as demonstrated below.

```perl
$x = join('', @buddies);
```

The join function takes two arguments: a string that identifies the character to be used to separate each element and a list or array name.

Populating and Modifying Arrays with Data

In addition to adding elements to an array when you first define it, Perl allows you to add or modify additional array elements any time you want. To do so you need to assign the new value to a specific location in the array. This is accomplished by specifying an index position within the array, which is accomplished using the following syntax.

```perl
$arrayname[indexposition]
```

TRICK Note that the syntax for referencing an individual element within an array may look a little strange. If you look closely at this reference, you will notice that it uses the $ character in place of the @ character when referring to the array. This may seem strange, but that is the way array references work in Perl. Think of it this way: In order to reference a scalar value, you must use the $ character. In this example, the value being added is a scalar. So you need to use the $ character in order to reference the scalar data, even though you are assigning it to an array. Yes, this can be confusing but you will get used to it.

For example, the following statements demonstrate how to add a new element to an already existing array.

```perl
@buddies = qw(Markland Nick Mike);
$buddies[3] = 'Lee';   #The array now contains Markland, Nick, Mike and Lee
```

In this example, a fourth element is added to the array by referencing the fourth index position as $buddies[3].

In addition to adding a new element as the last element in an array, you can also add array elements by reassigning the variable to itself as part of a list that also contains additional elements as demonstrated here.

```perl
@buddies = qw(Markland Nick Mike);
@buddies = (@buddies, "Alexander", "William");
```

Here, the @buddies array is increased in size by two elements.

To add a new element to the end of an array, you simply have to add it using an index number that is one greater than the last currently used index number in the array. Be careful when adding elements to the end of arrays not to add new elements too far beyond the last index position. Doing so will result in the assignment of undefined array elements in all index positions between the previous last index number and the new last index position as demonstrated below.

```
@buddies = qw(Markland Nick Mike);
$buddies[5] = "Molly";
```

Here, array element 5 is assigned a value of "Molly" and array elements 3 and 4 are created and assigned a value of undefined.

The push Function

Perl provides you with a number of other ways to add new elements to an array. For example, using the push function you can add an element or list to the end of any array as demonstrated here.

```
@buddies = qw(Markland Nick Mike);
push @buddies, "Alexander";   #Adds Alexander as the 4th element in @buddies
```

As you can see, the push function takes two arguments: the list to be modified and the element or list to be added.

The unshift Function

Another way to add a new element to an array is to use the unshift function, which adds an element or list to the beginning of the array, shifting any elements already stored in the array up by one index number. The unshift function takes two arguments: the name of the list to be modified and the list to add. An example of how to use the unshift function is provided here.

```
@buddies = qw(Markland Nick Mike);
$buddies = unshift @buddies, ("William", "Molly");
```

Here, the @buddies array is increased in size by two elements.

Retrieving Data from an Array

Perl provides you with a number of different ways of accessing the data stored in arrays. For example, you can display every element stored in an array.

```
@buddies = qw(Markland Nick Mike);
print "\n\nMy buddy list: @buddies\n\n";
```

Here, Perl interpolates the contents of the @buddies array and then displays them in the order they are stored in the array, with a blank space in between each element as shown in Figure 4.6.

```
Command Prompt                                            _ □ ×

C:\>BuddiesList.pl

My buddy list: Markland Nick Mike

C:\>
```

FIGURE 4.6

Displaying the
contents of an
array using the
print function.

TRAP If you attempt to access an array element that does not exist and you have warnings turned on, Perl will display a warning message. If not, a value of " " or 0 will be returned depending on the context in which the value is being used.

Perl provides a number of additional ways of accessing array elements, which include:

- Retrieving array elements one at a time
- Retrieving a series of array elements
- Retrieving every element in an array using a loop

Each of these options is examined more in the sections that follow.

Retrieving Individual Array Elements

You can retrieve individual elements from an array by setting up an assignment expression and placing a reference to a specific array index location on the right side of the equals operator.

```
@buddies = qw(Markland Nick Mike);
$myPizon = @buddies[2];  #Assigns Mike to $myPizon
```

TRICK Perl also allows you to access the contents of arrays using negative index numbers. For example, the last item in an array named @buddies can be referenced as $buddies[-1]. The next to the last element in an array would be referenced at $buddies[-2] and so on.

Retrieving a Slice from an Array

You can also retrieve a series of elements from an array, sometimes referred to as a slice, by enclosing a list of numbers representing the index locations of each element within a pair of matching square brackets.

```
@buddies = qw(Markland Nick Mike);
@localbuddies = @buddies[0, 2];  #Assigns Markland and Mike to @localbuddies
```

Looping Through Arrays

To loop through each element in an array and process it in some manner, you need to set up a loop. For example, the following statement demonstrates how to set up a while loop that displays each element in an array.

```
#!/usr/bin/perl

@buddies = qw(Markland Nick Mike);

$counter = 0;
$noOfElements = @buddies;
$count = 0;

print "\n\nBuddy List:\n\n";

while ($counter < $noOfElements) {

  $count = $counter + 1;
  print "$count. @buddies[$counter] \n";
  $counter++;

}
```

Here, an array named @buddies is defined and assigned three scalar values. Next, two scalar variables are defined. The first variable is assigned a value of 0 and will be used to control the execution of the while loop that follows. The second variable is assigned a numeric value representing the number of elements stored in the @buddies array. Next, a print statement is used to display a descriptive string and then a `while` loop is set up that iterates from 0 (the starting index number of any Perl array) to `$noOfElements`, which is a number representing the number of elements stored in the array. Each time the loop iterates, it displays an element from the array. Note that each text string that is displayed begins with a number. The number is derived by adding 1 to the value of `$counter`. Therefore, the first number displayed is 1, the second number is 2, and so on, as demonstrated in Figure 4.7.

```
C:\WINDOWS\system32\cmd.exe                                    _ □ ×

C:\>BuddiesList.pl

Buddy List:

1. Markland
2. Nick
3. Mike

C:\>_
```

FIGURE 4.7

Using a loop to iterate through and process each element stored in an array.

TRICK A quick way of ascertaining how many elements are currently stored in an array is to assign a scalar variable equal to the name of an array. In the previous example, the number of elements stored in the `@buddies` array was retrieved by assigning a scalar variable (`$noOfElements`) equal to the name of the array.

In Perl, there is always another way to get something done. For example, instead of retrieving the number of elements stored in an array, you could set up a `while` loop to process an array based on the number assigned to the last index position in an array.

```perl
@buddies = qw(Markland Nick Mike);

$counter = 0;
$count = 0;

print "\n\nBuddy List:\n\n";

while ($counter <= $#buddies) {
```

```
  $count = $counter + 1;
  print "$count. @buddies[counter] \n";
  $counter++;
}
```

Perl has a special variable named $#arrayname that can be used to retrieve the index number assigned to the last element stored in an array. The end of an array is one less than the index position of its last element. In this example, the while loop has been set up to loop as long as the value of $counter is less than or equal to $#buddies.

TRAP Be careful when working with the special $#arrayname variable. If you change the numeric value assigned to this variable, you modify the size of the array. By decreasing the value of $#arrayname, you shrink the size of the array, resulting in the loss of any truncated elements. On the other hand, if you increase the value of $#arrayname, new elements will be added to the end of the array and assigned a value of undefined.

While you can use any of the different types of loops supported by Perl to process the contents of arrays, you will usually want to stick with the foreach loop, which is specifically designed to process the contents of lists, arrays, and hashes. To see how easy it is to process the contents of an array using a foreach loop, look at the following example.

```
@buddies = qw(Markland Nick Mike);
foreach $friend (@buddies) {
  print "$friend is a friend of mine. \n";
}
```

Here a scalar variable named $friend is defined within the foreach loop and is used to represent a different array element upon each iteration of the loop. When executed, this example displays the following output.

```
Markland is a friend of mine.
Nick is a friend of mine.
Mike is a friend of mine.
```

Sorting Array Elements

Depending on the order in which data has been added to an array, array elements may or may not be stored in the order you want to work with them. Often, it helps to sort the contents of an array, which you can do using the sort function. As shown next, the sort function takes a list (or array) as an argument and returns a sorted list.

```
@buddies = qw(Markland Nick Mike);
@x = sort @buddies;
```

This example assigns a sorted list of elements from the @buddies array in a new array named @x. The elements stored in @x are arranged in ASCII order.

 TRICK Perl has a function named reverse, which you can use to reverse the order in which elements are stored in a list. You can use the reverse function to reverse the order in which elements are stored in an array by passing it the array name as demonstrated here.

```
@x = reverse @x;
```

The sort function also allows you to sort a list of numbers in numeric order. To accomplish this, you need to provide the sort function with a little extra information. Specifically, you need to insert the following expression after the sort function.

```
{$a <=> $b}
```

As an example of how to use the sort function to sort a numeric list, look at the following statements.

```
@num = sort {$a <=> $b} (9, 5, 7, 8, 2, 3, 3, 4, 9);
print "@num"; # Reorded as (2, 3, 3, 4, 5, 7, 8, 9, 9)
```

The {$a <=> $b} expression tells the sort function what to do when one value is greater than another. Specifically, it tells the sort function to sort from low to high. To reverse the sort order, change the order of $a and $b as demonstrated here.

```
{$b <=> $a}
```

Deleting Array Elements

There are a number of ways to delete elements stored in arrays. For example, you can use either Perl's delete or undef function to change the value assigned to an array element to undefined. These functions take one argument, the index position within the array whose value is to be changed, as demonstrated here.

```
@buddies = qw(Markland Nick Mike);
undef $buddies[1];    #Deletes Nick
delete $buddies[2];   #Deletes Mike
```

Of course, you will need to add programming logic to your script that knows how to deal with undefined values when processing the contents of the array, which is covered a little later in this chapter.

The shift Function

Another way of removing elements from an array is to use the shift function, which lets you delete the first element stored in an array and moves all of the remaining array elements down by one index position.

```
@buddies = qw(Markland Nick Mike);
shift @buddies;   #Removes Markland from @buddies
```

The pop Function

Instead of removing elements from the beginning of the array, you can remove them from the end of an array using the pop function. This function provides an easy means of deleting the last element stored in an array.

```
@buddies = qw(Markland Nick Mike);
$x = pop @buddies;   # @buddies now contains 2 elements
```

As you can see, the pop function takes a single argument, the name of the array from which the last array element should be removed.

Using Arrays to Populate Variables and Other Arrays

As is the case with lists, you can assign values to variables on the left-hand side of the assignment operator in an expression from an array located on the right-hand side, as demonstrated below.

```
@buddies = qw(Markland Nick Mike Lee);
($x, $y) = @buddies;
```

Here, $x is assigned a value of Markland and $y is assigned a value of Nick. The remaining values stored in the @buddies array go unassigned. If there are more scalar variables on the left-hand side than there are elements in an array, the scalar variables are assigned a value of undef.

```
@buddies = qw(Markland Nick Mike Lee);
($v, $w, $x, $y, $z) = @buddies;
```

Here, $z is set equal to undefined while the other four scalar variables are each assigned values corresponding to an element in the array.

Ensuring That Array Elements Exist

Perl provides another handy function that you can use to check for the existence of an array element before attempting to reference it. This function is the exists function. To use it, simply pass it the index position within an array.

```
if (exists $buddies[2]) {
  #Add statement here to process the array element
}
```

Dealing with Undefined Array Elements

Sometimes arrays end up with undefined elements. In most cases, you will want to avoid referencing these elements. This can happen, for example, if you accidentally increase the value of the special @#arrayname variable. This might also occur if you are collecting input from the user at the command prompt and the user presses the Enter key without typing anything and you don't have any logic in place to prevent the user from doing so.

One easy way of dealing with undefined array elements is to use Perl's undefined function to identify and skip the processing of any undefined array element, as demonstrated here.

```
if (defined $buddies[0]) {
  #Insert statements here to process the array element
}
```

As this example shows, all that you have to do to use this function is pass it the index position within an array.

CREATING HASHES

One of the problems with arrays is that it is difficult to keep track of where a given array element is stored. As a result, you typically have to set up a loop to process all the elements stored in an array in order to track down and find the one you want. As an alternative, you may instead want to store your data in a *hash*, also referred to as an *associative array*. Hashes store data in key-value pairs.

Like arrays, hashes can store any amount of data, limited only by the amount of available memory. Hash elements store data in values, which are directly associated with specific keys. Hashes can store any type of scalar data. To access an individual value in a hash, you need to know what its associated key is. Access to data stored in hashes is relatively fast and access time does not significantly increase as the hash grows in size.

Hash keys and values are made of scalar values, both of which can be of any length. Hash names begin with the % character followed by any valid variable name. Hash names are different from array and scalar variables' names. For example, as far as Perl is considered, each of the following is different.

- `$buddies`
- `@buddies`
- `%buddies`

Although it is not considered a good programming practice, Perl does not require that you declare a hash before you can use it. Instead, all that you have to do is to start assigning key-value pairs as demonstrated here.

```
$buddies{'pizon'} = 'Mike';
```

In this example, the hash is named `%buddies` and it contains one key named `pizon`, which has been associated with a value of `Mike`. Note that when referring to key-value pairs within a hash, you use curly brackets (`{}`) and not square (`[]`) as you do with arrays.

If you want, you can use a list to populate a hash when you first create it.

```
%buddies = ('pizon', 'Mike', 'coCaptain', 'Nick', 'bestMan', 'Markland')
```

In this example, the `%buddies` hash was created and assigned a key of `pizon` whose value is `Mike`, a key of `coCaptain` with a value of `Nick`, and a third key of `bestMan` with a value of `Markland`.

As you can see, when assigned in this manner, elements in a list are paired up to form key-value relationships. Be careful when assigning key-value pairs to hashes in this manner. If you assign an odd number of elements, the last element will be set up as a key and assigned a value of undefined.

While convenient, assigning a large number of key-value pairs as demonstrated in this manner can get confusing. Fortunately, Perl has a *comma-arrow* operator that you can use when instantiating a hash that helps to make the assignment of key-value pairs a lot clearer. The comma-arrow operator acts just like a comma yet looks like an arrow (=>). Using the comma-arrow operator, you can rewrite the previous example and make it easier to understand.

```
%buddies = ('pizon' => 'Mike',
  'coCaptain' => 'Nick',
  'bestMan' => 'Markland'
);
```

TRICK   The => operator automatically quotes the string on the left-hand side, allowing you to leave the quotation marks off each key as demonstrated here.

```
%buddies = (pizon => 'Mike',
   coCaptain => 'Nick',
   bestMan => 'Markland'
);
```

However, if a key includes a blank space, you must still enclose it within matching quotation marks.

 Perl requires that every key within a hash be unique. Adding a new key to a hash with the same name as an existing key results in a replacement operation. So be careful to ensure that you use unique keys for each new key-value pair that you add to a hash. Note that values, on the other hand, do not have to be unique.

Adding and Deleting Hash Elements

You can assign additional key-value pairs to a hash as shown below.

```
$buddies{'rebel'} = 'Dave';
```

Here, an additional key-value entry has been added to the %buddies hash. Note the use of the $ character in the example. Just as with arrays, you must use the $ character when referring to scalar data, even when you are assigning that data to a hash.

Another way to populate a hash is to copy the contents of an existing hash into a new hash.

```
%buddies = ('pizon', 'Mike', 'coCaptain', 'Nick', 'bestMan', 'Markland');
%associates = %buddies;
print %associates;
```

In addition, you can create and populate a new hash from two or more existing hashes.

```
%buddies = ('pizon', 'Mike', 'coCaptain', 'Nick', 'bestMan', 'Markland');
%associates = ('rebel', 'Dave');
%dudes = (%buddies, %associates);
```

As with arrays, you can use the delete function to delete individual hash key-value pairs as demonstrated here.

```
%buddies = ('pizon', 'Mike', 'coCaptain', 'Nick', 'bestMan', 'Markland');
delete $buddies{coCaptain};
```

To delete all the key-value pairs stored in a hash, all that you have to do is to assign an empty list to the hash.

```
%buddies = ('pizon', 'Mike', 'coCaptain', 'Nick', 'bestMan', 'Markland');
%buddies = ();
```

Processing Hash Contents

As with arrays, you can retrieve individual values from a hash. To retrieve an individual value from a hash, you need to refer to its key. In doing so you must use the $ character in place of the % character when referencing the hash name.

```
%buddies = ('pizon', 'Mike', 'coCaptain', 'Nick', 'bestMan', 'Markland');
$x = $buddies{'bestMan'};
```

Here, the value associated with the bestMan key is assigned to a scalar variable named $x.

TRICK If there is any doubt as to whether a particular key exists, you should first perform a check before attempting to retrieve its value. This can be done using the exists function, as demonstrated below.

```
%buddies = ('pizon', 'Mike', 'coCaptain', 'Nick', 'bestMan',
'Markland');
if (exists $buddies{bestMan}) {
    print "The best man at my wedding was $buddies{bestMan}";
}
```

Since hashes are not indexed like arrays, you cannot simply set up a loop that starts at the beginning of a hash and loops its way through. There is no beginning index to start at, nor is there a high-level ending index number that the loop can count to. Fortunately, Perl helps to solve this challenge by providing you with the keys function. This function is used to generate a list of all the keys stored in a hash. You can then set up a loop to iterate through the list of keys and access each key's corresponding value, as demonstrated in the following example.

```
%buddies = ('pizon', 'Mike', 'coCaptain', 'Nick', 'bestMan', 'Markland');
foreach $friend (keys %buddies) {
  print "My $friend is $buddies{$friend} \n";
}
```

In this example, a list of hash keys is generated by passing the keys function the name of the %buddies hash. This list is then iterated through. The scalar variable $friend represents the name of a different key each time the loop iterates. This variable is then used in the embedded print statement to display the name of the key and to reference its associated value ($buddies{$friend}).

TRICK In addition to the keys function, Perl also has a value function, which you can use to retrieve a list of all the values stored in an array.

Sorting Hash Values

Because you cannot control the order in which Perl stores and manages hash key-value pairs, the order in which key-value pairs are retrieved when using the keys function may not be optimal. Sometimes, it is preferable to first sort the list of keys that is returned before processing them. You can accomplish this using the sort function.

```perl
%buddies = ('pizon', 'Mike', 'coCaptain', 'Nick', 'bestMan', 'Markland');
foreach $friend (sort keys %buddies) {
  print "$friend \n";
}
```

Converting Between Arrays and Hashes

Because they are very similar, you can move data between arrays and hashes if you want. For example, the following statement initializes a hash named %buddies and then copies all of the key-value pairs stored in the hash into a similarly named array.

```perl
%buddies = ('pizon', 'Mike', 'coCaptain', 'Nick', 'bestMan', 'Markland');
@buddies = %buddies;
```

When executed, the @buddies array is assigned six array elements. Perl does not keep track of the order in which key-value pairs are added to hashes. As a result, there is no guarantee that the data copied from the hash to the array will reflect the order in which it was entered.

Conversion works just as easily the other way, as demonstrated in the following example.

```perl
@buddies = qw(pizon Mike coCaptain Nick bestMan Markland);
%buddies = @buddies;
```

UNDERSTANDING CONTEXT WITHIN PERL

At this point, it is probably a good idea that I pause for a moment and talk about a Perl concept known as context. *Context* is a term that means things in Perl behave differently depending on the situation in which they are used. Context is something that people have to deal with every day. For example, a physical gesture like a touch on the shoulder may mean one thing among friends and something very different when used to communicate with a stranger.

Another example where context is important is language. Take for example, the word *hit*. Depending on how it is used, hit has several different meanings, as demonstrated in the following list.

- He *hit* the baseball over the fence.
- He has a *hit* record.
- His play turned out to be a Broadway *hit*.

In the first example, the word hit is used as a verb. In the second sentence, it is used as an adjective, and in the last sentence, it is a noun. It is the same word but it has a different meaning in each context that it is used. Within Perl, things often work differently depending on context.

Functions and operators can behave quite differently based on context. In Perl, there are three major contexts: scalar, list, or Boolean. Of these three contexts, trying to determine whether you are working in a scalar or list context will cause you the most difficulty and confusion.

Scalar Context

You have already seen a number of different situations in which Perl automatically converts values between different contexts. For example, in a scalar context, Perl automatically converts values between numeric and string based on context.

```
$x = 7;
$y = "5.5";
print $x . $y;   # Displays 75.5
```

In this example, the print statement uses the string concatenation operator (.) to create an expression to be printed. Because the concatenation operator is used, Perl assumes a scalar string context and converts the numeric value stored in $x to a string value ("7") and then concatenates that value to "5.5", displaying 75.5.

Numeric Context

Perl will automatically convert a scalar string value to a numeric value based on context. For example, look at the following statements.

```
$x = "7";
$y = 5;
print $x + $y;   # Display 12
```

Here, Perl sees the + operator and assumes that it needs to work in a numeric scalar context. As such, it converts the value of "7" to 7 and then adds this value to 5. In this example, the result that was displayed was obvious. However, consider the following example.

```
$x = "seven";
$y = 5;
print $x + $y;  # Displays 5
```

Again, Perl will decide that a numeric context is appropriate. Only this time the conversion of $x is not as obvious and intuitive. Since it cannot reasonably guess what numeric value it should assign to $x when converting it from a string to a number, Perl assigns $x a value of 0. Since 0 plus 5 equals 5, the output displayed by this example is 5.

Boolean Context

Another context that you should be aware of is Boolean context. As you already know, Perl interprets any scalar value that is not 0, "", or undefined as being true. A value of 0, "", or undefined is evaluated as false.

Things work a bit differently when working with lists, arrays, and hashes in Boolean context. Lists, arrays, and hashes evaluate as false when they are empty and true when they have at least one element.

Scalar Versus List Context

Hopefully everything covered so far makes sense as far as the concept of context is concerned. Where things get a bit confusing is when you mix up scalar and list values. Unfortunately, there is no simple set of rules that you can follow in order to ensure that you always know how a particular function or operation behaves in a given context. Each function has its own rules. The only way to be 100 percent sure is to reference Perl's documentation for any function you want to work with in order to determine how it behaves in scalar and list context.

As an example of how things work differently based on context, look at the following statements.

```
$x = @buddies;
@x = @buddies;
```

In the first statement, a scalar variable has been defined on the left-hand side of the expression. This tells Perl to work in scalar context. As a result, Perl assigns the number of elements stored in the @buddies array to $x. However, the second statement sets up a list context, so Perl assigns a copy of the contents of @buddies into @x. Again, the point to understand here is that different contexts can yield different results.

Obviously, it is important to be able to determine when Perl will apply scalar context versus list content. The key to making this determination is to identify the context established on the left-hand side of an expression, as demonstrated in Table 4.1.

TABLE 4.1 DETERMINING SCALAR AND LIST CONTEXT		
Type of Expression	**Analysis**	**Context**
$x = $y	Scalar defined on the left	Scalar
$x = @x	Scalar defined on the left	Scalar
@x = @y	List (array) defined on the left	List
($x, $y, #z) = @x	List defined on the left	List
($x, @y) = @z	List defined on the left	List

As you can see in Table 4.1, when the left-hand side of an expression is scalar, the expression is evaluated in a scalar context, regardless of whether the right-hand side of the expression consists of scalars or lists. Likewise, when the left-hand side of an expression is a list (i.e. a list, array, or hash), the expression is evaluated in list context.

Context and Lists, Arrays, and Hashes

Lists, arrays, and hashes behave differently depending on the context in which they are used. Table 4.2 outlines the results that you can expect to be returned from lists, arrays, and hashes in both scalar and list context.

You have already seen different behavior for arrays when used in different contexts. For example, when used in scalar context, an array will return a number specifying the number of elements in the array.

```
@buddies = qw(Markland Nick Mike Lee);
$x = @buddies;
print $x;  # Prints 4
```

When used in list context, an array returns a list of its contents.

```
@buddies = qw(Markland Nick Mike Lee);
```

TABLE 4.2 DETERMINING SCALAR AND LIST CONTEXT		
Type	**Scalar Context**	**List Context**
List	Returns the last item in the list	Returns list contents
Array	Returns the length of the array	Returns array contents
Hash	Returns information about hash status	Returns hash contents

```
@x = @buddies;
print @x;  # Prints Markland Nick Mike Lee
```

Unfortunately, there is no set of rules that you can follow to determine how a given function will behave when used in a scalar or list context. To be sure, you must refer back to the Perl documentation. As an example, consider the print statement. By default, the print statement is designed to work in a list context, taking a list of arguments and printing them. Therefore, in the following example, the print statement prints out a list made up of all the elements in the @buddies array.

```
@buddies = qw(Markland Nick Mike Lee);
print @buddies;
```

If you wanted, you could force the print function to work in a scalar context using the scalar function. This function gives you the ability to tell Perl to evaluate any expression in scalar context.

```
@buddies = qw(Markland Nick Mike Lee);
print scalar(@buddies);
```

Since it is now operating in a scalar context, the print function displays a value representing the number of elements currently stored in @buddies.

BACK TO THE STAR WARS QUIZ

Now it is time to turn your attention back to the Star Wars Quiz game. The development of this game will give you another opportunity to work with arrays and to practice processing them using loops. You will also learn how to set up a while loop to create and control a script menu that includes options for accessing help information and for starting and terminating the quiz.

Designing the Game

The construction and development of the Star Wars Quiz game will be completed in nine steps.

1. Creating a new script and adding opening comments.
2. Initializing scalar variables.
3. Managing the main menu.
4. Asking the first quiz question.
5. Finishing the quiz.
6. Keeping count of player answers.
7. Determining player rank.

8. Displaying player score and rank.
9. Clearing the screen.

As you work your way through each step, pay attention to what that step is trying to accomplish. In particular, you may want to spend a little extra time on step 3 in order to make sure you understand how the game's menu system is set up. You may also want to spend a little extra time on step 6 where the user's answers are tabulated by using a `foreach` loop to iterate through the array that stores information regarding the correctness of each user answer.

Creating the Script File

The first step in creating the Star Wars Quiz is to create a new Perl script. Give the script file a name of SWQuiz.pl and add the following comment statements to it.

```perl
#!/usr/bin/perl
#
# The Star Wars Quiz (Star Wars Quiz.pl)
```

Declaring and Initializing Scalar Variables

Next, append the following statements to the end of the script. These statements define a number of scalar variables used by the script to store and process data collected as the script executes.

```perl
$reply = "";
$valid = "false";
$correct = 0;
$incorrect = 0;
$rank = "";
```

Managing the Quiz's Main Menu

One of the features of the Star Wars Quiz is that it is controlled by a text-based menu, which is displayed at the bottom of the screen just above the command prompt. This menu is controlled by a `while` loop, which is set up to execute as long as the value of `$valid` is not equal to true. `$valid` is set by default to false at the beginning of the script and remains that way until the user enters the `start` command.

To create the `while` loop, append the following code statement to the end of the script file.

```perl
while (! $isvalid) {

  clear_the_screen();
```

```perl
print "          ";
print "W e l c o m e   t o   t h e   S T A R   W A R S   Q u i z!";
print "\n\n\n\n\n\n\n\n\n\n\n\n";
print "[Start] [Quit] [Help]\n\n";
print "Enter command: ";

chomp($reply = <STDIN>);

if (lc ($reply) eq "start") {

  $isvalid = 1;

} elsif (lc ($reply) eq "quit") {

    clear_the_screen();

    print "Very well, may the force be with you!\n\n\n\n";
    print "Press Enter to continue: ";

    chomp($reply = <STDIN>);

    exit;

} elsif (lc ($reply) eq "help") {

    clear_the_screen();

    print "Star Wars Quiz Instructions:\n\n";
    print "Type Start to begin the game or type Quit to exit. To play,\n";
    print "answer each question that is presented by typing the\n";
    print "letter that matches the correct answer for each question. Once\n";
    print "all questions have been answered, you will receive your Jedi\n";
    print "rank.\n\n\n";
    print "Press Enter to continue: ";
```

```
        chomp($reply = <STDIN>);

    }


}
```

TRICK Instead of using multiple print statements to display the paragraphs that make up the game's story, you could instead group text using heredoc. Using heredoc, you can display multi-line strings using the following syntax.

```
print <<TAG

    . . .

TAG
```

Note that the text to be displayed is embedded inside the opening <<*TAG* and closing *TAG* markers. *TAG* is simply a placeholder for any marker you want to use. One of the conveniences of using heredoc is that it allows you to leave off quotation marks and semicolons while preserving the display of text exactly as you type it in. For example, using heredoc, you could display the text associated with the story's help screen as shown here.

```
print <<MSG;

Star Wars Quiz Instructions:\n
Type Start to begin the game or type Quit to exit. To play,
answer each question that is presented by typing the
letter that matches the correct answer for each question. Once
all questions have been answered, you will receive your Jedi
rank.\n\n\n
Press Enter to continue:

MSG
```

As you can see, the user also has the option of entering the help command in order to view instructions about how to control the script. In addition, the user can enter quit to terminate script execution, which occurs when the exit statement is executed. If the user enters anything other than start, help, or quit, the input is disregarded, the screen is cleared, and the menu is redisplayed.

Asking the First Quiz Question

Once the user finally decides to begin the quiz by entering the start command, the first of five questions is presented. This is accomplished by adding the following code statement to the end of the script file.

```perl
clear_the_screen();

print "Question 1: Obi-Wan Kenobi's Jedi master in Star Wars I was:\n\n";
print "A. Qui-Gon Jinn\n";
print "B. Yoda\n";
print "C. Mace Windu\n";
print "D. None of the above\n\n\n\n";
print "Answer: ";
chomp($reply = <STDIN>);

if (lc $reply eq "a") {
  $answers[0] = "correct";
} else {
  $answers[0] = "incorrect";
}
```

This section of the script begins by calling the clear_the_screen() subroutine, which is responsible for clearing the screen. Next a series of print statements are used to display the first question, which is collected and stored in $reply. The value of $reply is then converted to lowercase and checked to see if it is equal to the correct answer (a). Based on the result of this analysis, a value of correct or incorrect is then stored as the first element in the @answers array.

Asking the Remaining Quiz Questions

Since the Star Wars Quiz is made up of five questions, you need to add the code statements required to present and process the user's answers for the last four questions. The code statements required to do so, which should be added to the end of the script, are shown here.

```perl
clear_the_screen();


print "Question 2: The arch enemies for the Jedi are known as the:\n\n";
print "A. Sith\n";
print "B. Dark Lords\n";
print "C. Deviators\n";
```

```perl
print "D. None of the above\n\n\n\n";
print "Answer: ";
chomp($reply = <STDIN>);

if (lc $reply eq "a") {
  $answers[1] = "correct";
} else {
  $answers[1] = "incorrect";
}

clear_the_screen();


print "Question 3: Who did Yoda fight at the end of Star Wars II?\n\n";
print "A. Mace Windu\n";
print "B. Palpatine\n";
print "C. Count Dooku\n";
print "D. None of the above\n\n\n\n";
print "Answer: ";
chomp($reply = <STDIN>);

if (lc $reply eq "c") {
  $answers[2] = "correct";
} else {
  $answers[2] = "incorrect";
}

clear_the_screen();


print "Question 4: Who killed Mace Windu in Star Wars III?\n\n";
print "A. Palpatine\n";
print "B. The bounty hunter\n";
print "C. Count Dooku\n";
print "D. None of the above\n\n\n\n";
print "Answer: ";
chomp($reply = <STDIN>);
```

```
if (lc $reply eq "a") {
  $answers[3] = "correct";
} else {
  $answers[3] = "incorrect";
}

clear_the_screen();


print "Question 5: Who uttered the phrase \"Help me Obi-Wan Kenobi, you\n";
print "                are our only hope\" in Star Wars IV?\n\n";
print "A. Yoda\n";
print "B. Princess Leia\n";
print "C. Luke\n";
print "D. None of the above\n\n\n\n";
print "Answer: ";
chomp($reply = <STDIN>);
if (lc $reply eq "b") {
  $answers[4] = "correct";
} else {
  $answers[4] = "incorrect";
}

clear_the_screen();
```

As you can see, the code for each of these four questions is essentially the same as the code statements that were generated for the first question.

Keeping Count of Player Answers

Once all quiz questions have been presented and the user's answers collected, analyzed, and then recorded in the @answers array, it is time to count the number of questions that the user got right and wrong. This is accomplished by adding the following code statements to the end of the script file.

```
foreach $name (@answers) {

  if ($name eq "correct") {
    $correct++;
  } else {
```

```
    $incorrect++;
  }

}
```

As you can see, a `foreach` loop has been set up to iterate through each element stored in the array. An `if…else` code block is then set up that uses the autoincrement operator to increment the value of `$correct` by 1 for each correct answer and `$incorrect` for each incorrect answer.

Assigning Player Rank

Next, you need to add program logic that lets the script determine which rank to assign to the user based on the number of correctly answered quiz questions. You can accomplish this by adding the following code statements to the end of the script file.

```
%ranks = (0 => 'Beginner',
          1 => 'Padawan',
          2 => 'Jedi',
          3 => 'Jedi Night',
          4 => 'Jedi Master',
          5 => 'Jedi Master and Council Member'
);

$rank = $ranks{$correct};
```

As you can see, a hash has been created to associate rankings with different scores based on the number of correctly answered questions. The player's rank is then determined by using the `$correct` variable to look up the appropriate rank in the hash.

Displaying Player Score and Rank

Next, add the following code statement to the end of the script file.

```
$row = "_" x 50;
print "$row\n\n";
print "                        Score:\n\n";
print "$row\n\n";
print "Number of correct answers:   $correct\n";
print "Number of incorrect answers: $incorrect\n\n";
print "Your Jedi rank is: $rank\n\n";
```

```
print "$row\n\n\n\n";
```

```
chomp($reply = <STDIN>);
```

These statements are responsible for displaying the number of correctly and incorrectly answered questions and the player's assigned rank. Note that the x operator is used to generate top and bottom header lines that help to visually format the display of output. Also, note the last statement, which used the chomp function as a means of pausing the script to allow the user to view her score. As soon as the player presses the Enter key, the script ends and stops executing.

Clearing the Screen

The last few lines of code that you need to add to the script file is the code for the clear_the_screen() subroutine.

```
sub clear_the_screen {

  for ($i=0; $i < 25; ++$i){
    print "\n";
  }


}
```

The Final Result

At this point, the Star Wars Quiz is now complete. If you have not done so, save the script file and then execute it. As long as you did not make any typos when keying everything in, the script should run as advertised. If it does not, you will need to review any error messages that are displayed and use this information to track down where errors reside.

As a review, the complete version of the SWQuiz.pl script is provided below. As an added bonus, comments have been added throughout the script to document key functionality and to make the script easier to read and follow along.

```
#!/usr/bin/perl
#
# The Star Wars Quiz (Star Wars Quiz.pl)


#Declare and initialize script variables
$reply = "";         #Stores user supplied data
```

```perl
$isvalid = 0;        #used to control loop execution
$correct = 0;        #Used to keep count of correct answers
$incorrect = 0;      #Used to keep count of incorrect answers
$rank = "";          #Used to store player rank



#This loop manages the display of the game's main menu
while (! $isvalid) {  #Loop until the player types Start

  clear_the_screen(); #Call subroutine that clears the screen

  #Display the quiz's opening menu system
  print "           ";
  print "W e l c o m e   t o   t h e   S T A R   W A R S   Q u i z!";
  print "\n\n\n\n\n\n\n\n\n\n\n\n";
  print "[Start] [Quit] [Help]\n\n";
  print "Enter command: ";  #Prompt user for menu selection before continuing

  #Set variable equal to standard input and remove any trailing newline
  chomp($reply = <STDIN>);

  if (lc ($reply) eq "start") {  #See if the player typed Start

    $isvalid = 1;  #Set variable to enable loop termination

  } elsif (lc ($reply) eq "quit") {  #See if player typed Quit

      clear_the_screen(); #Call subroutine that clears the screen

      #Display closing message
      print "Very well, may the force be with you!\n\n\n\n";
      print "Press Enter to continue: ";

      chomp($reply = <STDIN>); #Force player to press Enter to continue

      exit;  #Terminate game execution
```

```perl
   } elsif (lc ($reply) eq "help") {   #See if the player typed Help

       clear_the_screen();  #Call subroutine that clears the screen

       #Display Help information
       print "Star Wars Quiz Instructions:\n\n";
       print "Type Start to begin the game or type Quit to exit. To play,\n";
       print "answer each question that is presented by typing the\n";
       print "letter that matches the correct answer for each question. Once\n";
       print "all questions have been answered, you will receive your Jedi\n";
       print "rank.\n\n\n\n";
       print "Press Enter to continue: ";

       chomp($reply = <STDIN>);   #Force player to press Enter to continue
   }

}


clear_the_screen();  #Call subroutine that clears the screen

#Question number 1
print "Question 1: Obi-Wan Kenobi's Jedi master in Star Wars I was:\n\n";
print "A. Qui-Gon Jinn\n";
print "B. Yoda\n";
print "C. Mace Windu\n";
print "D. None of the above\n\n\n\n";
print "Answer: ";
chomp($reply = <STDIN>);   #Force player to press Enter to continue

#Analyze the player's answer and determine if it is correct or incorrect
#and store the result of this analysis in the @answers array
if (lc $reply eq "a") {
  $answers[0] = "correct";
} else {
  $answers[0] = "incorrect";
}
```

```perl
clear_the_screen(); #Call subroutine that clears the screen


#Question Number 2
print "Question 2: The arch enemies for the Jedi are known as the:\n\n";
print "A. Sith\n";
print "B. Dark Lords\n";
print "C. Deviators\n";
print "D. None of the above\n\n\n\n";
print "Answer: ";
chomp($reply = <STDIN>);   #Force player to press Enter to continue

#Analyze the player's answer and determine if it is correct or incorrect
#and store the result of this analysis in the @answers array
if (lc $reply eq "a") {
   $answers[1] = "correct";
} else {
   $answers[1] = "incorrect";
}


clear_the_screen(); #Call subroutine that clears the screen


#Question Number 3
print "Question 3: Who did Yoda fight at the end of Star Wars II?\n\n";
print "A. Mace Windu\n";
print "B. Palpatine\n";
print "C. Count Dooku\n";
print "D. None of the above\n\n\n\n";
print "Answer: ";
chomp($reply = <STDIN>);   #Force player to press Enter to continue

#Analyze the player's answer and determine if it is correct or incorrect
#and store the result of this analysis in the @answers array
if (lc $reply eq "c") {
   $answers[2] = "correct";
} else {
   $answers[2] = "incorrect";
```

```perl
}


clear_the_screen(); #Call subroutine that clears the screen


#Question Number 4
print "Question 4: Who killed Mace Windu in Star Wars III?\n\n";
print "A. Palpatine\n";
print "B. The bounty hunter\n";
print "C. Count Dooku\n";
print "D. None of the above\n\n\n\n";
print "Answer: ";
chomp($reply = <STDIN>);  #Force player to press Enter to continue

#Analyze the player's answer and determine if it is correct or incorrect
#and store the result of this analysis in the @answers array
if (lc $reply eq "a") {
  $answers[3] = "correct";
} else {
  $answers[3] = "incorrect";
}


clear_the_screen(); #Call subroutine that clears the screen


#Question Number 5
print "Question 5: Who uttered the phrase \"Help me Obi-Wan Kenobi, you\n";
print "             are our only hope\" in Star Wars IV?\n\n";
print "A. Yoda\n";
print "B. Princess Leia\n";
print "C. Luke\n";
print "D. None of the above\n\n\n\n";
print "Answer: ";
chomp($reply = <STDIN>);  #Force player to press Enter to continue

#Analyze the player's answer and determine if it is correct or incorrect
#and add store the result of this analysis in the @answers array
if (lc $reply eq "b") {
```

```perl
    $answers[4] = "correct";
} else {
    $answers[4] = "incorrect";
}


clear_the_screen(); #Call subroutine that clears the screen


#Loop through the @answer array and count the number of answers the
#player got correct and incorrect
foreach $name (@answers) {

    #Analyze each element stored in the array
    if ($name eq "correct") {
        $correct++;  #Increment the number of correct answers by 1
    } else {
        $incorrect++;  #Increment the number of incorrect answers by 1
    }

}

#Set up a hash and use it when analyzing the player's
#score and assigning a Jedi rank
%ranks = (0 => 'Beginner',
          1 => 'Padawan',
          2 => 'Jedi',
          3 => 'Jedi Night',
          4 => 'Jedi Master',
          5 => 'Jedi Master and Council Member'
);


#Format the display of the player's score and rank
$row = "_" x 50;  #Set variable equal to 50 underscore characters
print "$row\n\n";
print "                    Score:\n\n";
print "$row\n\n";
print "Number of correct answers:   $correct\n";
```

```perl
print "Number of incorrect answers: $incorrect\n\n";
print "Your Jedi rank is: $rank\n\n";
print "$row\n\n\n\n";

chomp($reply = <STDIN>);  #Force player to press Enter to continue


#This subroutine clears the screen by adding 25 blank lines
sub clear_the_screen {

  for ($i=0; $i < 25; ++$i){  #Iterate 25 times
    print "\n";               #display a blank line
  }

}
```

Okay, that is it. It is time to run the Star Wars Quiz and see how it works. If you run into errors, read any error messages that are displayed and use this information to track down any typos that you may have made. Once you have eliminated any errors, you should find that the script works as described.

SUMMARY

In this chapter, you learned how to work with groups of scalar data using lists, arrays, and hashes. You learned how to add, retrieve, delete, and sort array and hash elements. You learned how to grow and shrink arrays and to eliminate undefined scalar data. You learned how to copy data between arrays and hashes and to retrieve a list of hash keys and then loop through and process each hash element. On top of all this you learned how lists, arrays, and hashes behave based on the context in which they are used. Finally, you learned how to create the Star Wars Quiz game.

Before you move on to the next chapter, take a few minutes to improve the Star Wars Quiz game by completing the following list of challenges.

CHALLENGES

1. As it is currently written, the Star Wars Quiz game does not prevent the user from entering invalid input. Add the programming logic required to check each answer to make sure the user only enters an answer between A–D.

2. The Star Wars Quiz game displays the number of correct and incorrect answers made by the user but does not tell the user which questions were missed. Modify the script to give the player the option of reviewing the correct answer to each missed question.

3. Rather than end the Star Wars Quiz game after displaying the user's score, add programming logic to allow the user to retake the quiz again until a perfect score has been reached.

CHAPTER 5

IMPROVING SCRIPT ORGANIZATION AND STRUCTURE

U p to this point in the book, you have been creating Perl scripts that, for the most part, execute sequentially from beginning to end. In this chapter, you will learn how to improve script organization by organizing groups of related statements into subroutines. This will help make your Perl scripts easier to read and understand. As an added benefit, you'll learn how to create subroutines that can limit access to variables defined in subroutines through the creation of private variables. In addition, you will learn how to create a new Perl script game, the Pick a Number game.

Specifically, you will learn how to

- Improve script organization using subroutines
- Pass arguments to subroutines for processing
- Return values from subroutines to calling statements
- Define private variables within subroutines

PROJECT PREVIEW: THE PICK A NUMBER GAME
This chapter's game project is the Pick a Number game. The game automatically selects a number in the range of 1 to 100, and prompts the player to guess the

number, allowing as many guesses as required. The game's overall execution is controlled by a text-based menu system, as demonstrated in Figure 5.1.

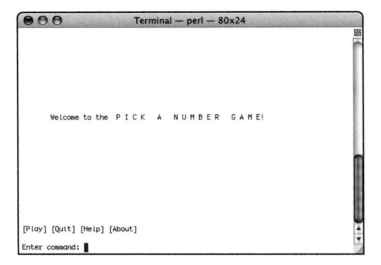

FIGURE 5.1

The Pick a Number game as seen running on Mac OS X.

The player can access the game's Help screen at any time, as demonstrated in Figure 5.2.

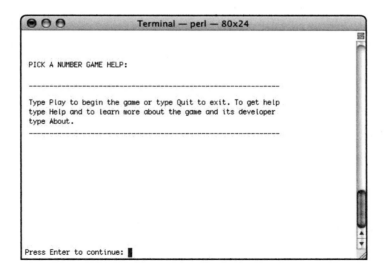

FIGURE 5.2

By entering the Help command, the player can view game instructions.

Information about the game and its developer is also available from the game's menu system, as demonstrated in Figure 5.3.

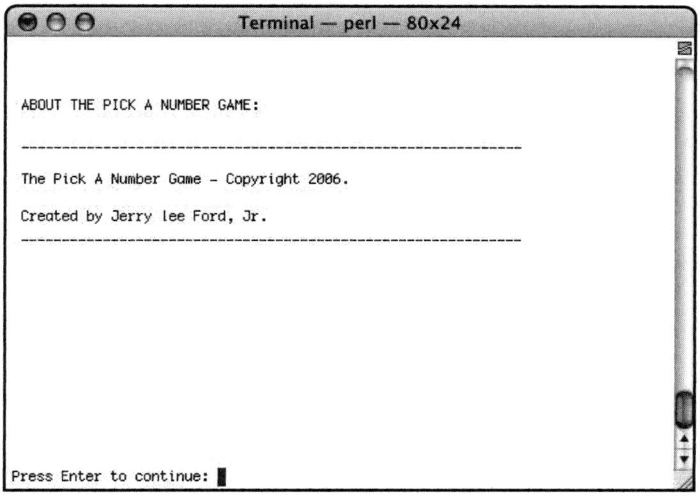

```
000              Terminal — perl — 80x24
ABOUT THE PICK A NUMBER GAME:

------------------------------------------------------------
The Pick A Number Game - Copyright 2006.

Created by Jerry lee Ford, Jr.
------------------------------------------------------------




Press Enter to continue: █
```

FIGURE 5.3

By entering the About command, the player can learn more about the game and its author.

The player is prompted to enter numbers in the range of 1 to 100, taking as many guesses as required, as demonstrated in Figure 5.4.

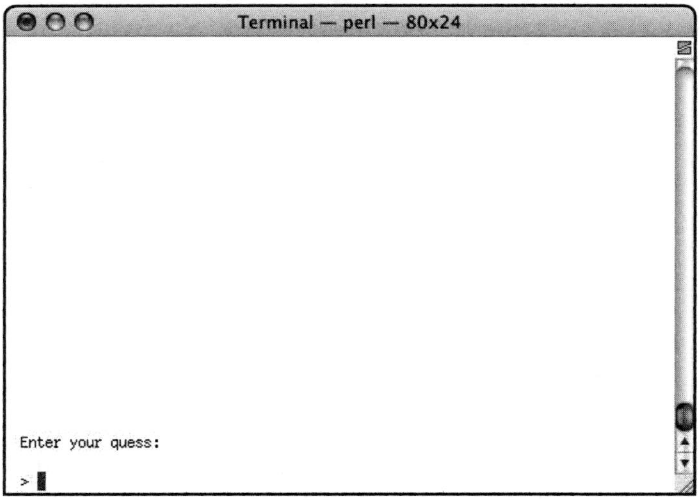

```
000              Terminal — perl — 80x24









Enter your guess:

> █
```

FIGURE 5.4

A valid guess is any number in the range of 1 to 100.

After each incorrect guess, the game provides the player with a hint that helps to guide the player's next guess, as shown in Figure 5.5.

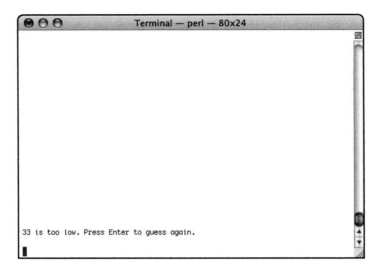

FIGURE 5.5

The game provides
clues that assist
the player with
honing in on the
correct answer.

Once the secret number has finally been guessed, the user is returned to the game's main menu, as demonstrated in Figure 5.6.

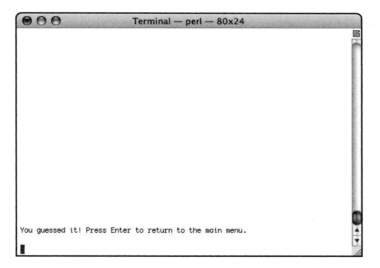

FIGURE 5.6

The player is
returned to the
game's main menu
as soon as the
secret number has
been guessed.

At the end of the game, the player is presented with game statistics, showing the number of games played, the total number of guesses made, and the average number of guesses per game, as demonstrated in Figure 5.7.

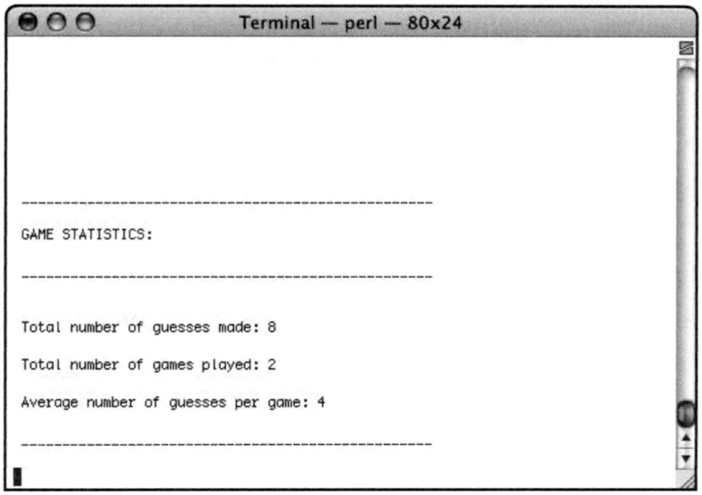

```
●  ○  ○              Terminal — perl — 80x24

-------------------------------------------------
GAME STATISTICS:

-------------------------------------------------

Total number of guesses made: 8

Total number of games played: 2

Average number of guesses per game: 4

-------------------------------------------------
```

FIGURE 5.7

Before ending, the game display statistics showing users how well they played.

ENHANCING SCRIPT ORGANIZATION

So far, all of the Perl game scripts that you have developed have been designed to logically run from beginning to end. By this I mean that the scripts have begun by defining variables used by the game, followed by the source code required to play the game. While this code contains conditional and looping code blocks, it has for the most part been sequential in nature. The one exception to this has been the inclusion of the `clear_the_screen` subroutine.

```perl
sub clear_the_screen {

  for ($i=0; $i < 25; ++$i){   #Iterate 25 times
    print "\n";                #Display a blank line
  }


}
```

A *function* is a group of related statements that are called and executed as a unit. Perl provides you with access to all sorts of built-in functions that speed up and simplify script development but provide access to pre-built collections of code. Perl's built-in functions typically accept input, process it, and return a result. Examples of built-in Perl functions include the `print`, `sort`, and `chomp` functions. Built-in functions are provided as part of the standard Perl library. In addition to Perl's built-in functions, you can also access predefined functions found in external modules written by other Perl programmers. You will learn how to access these types of functions later in Chapter 6, "Scope and Modules."

In addition to built-in and module functions, Perl allows you to create your own custom functions. Custom functions are commonly referred to as *subroutines* or *subs*. Your custom subroutines can be made to look and act just like built-in functions and can provide all the same capabilities, including the ability to accept and process arguments and to return a result.

The `clear_the_screen` subroutine, shown in the preceding code block, has been added to the end of every Perl game script you have created. Its purpose is to clear the screen each time it is called by using a for loop to iterate and display 25 blanks lines. Its execution is controlled by the placement of calling statements located throughout the scripts, allowing the script's logical flow to switch between sequential execution and subroutine execution as necessary, as demonstrated in Figure 5.8.

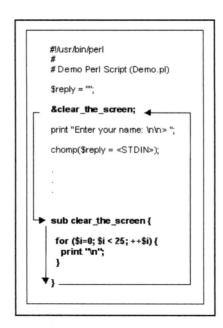

FIGURE 5.8

A call to a subroutine alters sequential program flow, transferring control to the subroutine, which executes and then returns controls back to the calling statement.

```
#!/usr/bin/perl
#
# Demo Perl Script (Demo.pl)

$reply = "";

&clear_the_screen;

print "Enter your name: \n\n> ";

chomp($reply = <STDIN>);
 .
 .
 .
sub clear_the_screen {

  for ($i=0; $i < 25; ++$i) {
    print "\n";
  }

}
```

In this chapter, you will learn how to construct subroutines like the `clear_the_screen` subroutine and to use these subroutines to create Perl scripts that are easier to read and maintain.

TRICK

Many programmers use the terms "function" and "subroutine" interchangeably. In this book, I use the term "function" when referring to built-in Perl functions and the term "subroutine" when referring to subroutines that you custom develop.

ORGANIZING PERL SCRIPTS USING SUBROUTINES

There are a number of good reasons for using subroutines to help organize scripts. For starters, any time you find that a script needs to execute the same set of statements over and over again in different locations within the script, it is usually a good idea to put these statements into a subroutine. This helps to reduce the overall size of your script by saving you from having to duplicate these statements over and over again at different points within your script. As a result, your Perl scripts are easier to read and to maintain.

Another good reason for organizing script statements into subroutines is to break a complex section of code down into smaller blocks, each of which accomplishes a specific task, thus simplifying the coding process. Subroutines also facilitate debugging because subroutines allow groups of statements to be tested independently from the rest of the script.

Defining Subroutines

In its simplest form, a subroutine accepts no arguments and does not return any results. All it does is execute the code statements embedded within its code block when called to execute. This form of the subroutine has the following syntax.

```
sub subroutinename {

    .
    .
    .

}
```

Subroutines start with the sub keyword followed by the name assigned to the subroutine and a pair of curly braces used to define the subroutine's embedded code block.

Subroutine names follow the same basic rules as scalar variable names. In fact, you can assign the same name to a subroutine that you assign to a scalar variable, array, or hash. However, doing so is poor programming practice and will make your Perl scripts harder to read and understand.

Do not give your custom subroutines the same name as an existing built-in Perl function. This is a bad programming practice. If you do, Perl will display a warning message if you have warnings (-w) turned on.

Also, do not create two different subroutines with the same name. If you do and you have warnings turned on, Perl will display an error message. Otherwise, Perl will run your script and disregard the first subroutine instance in favor of the second instance.

You can put a subroutine anywhere you want within a Perl script. However, for the sake of readability and maintenance, it is best to group them together in a common location, typically at the beginning or the end of the script.

Executing Subroutines

You can execute a subroutine by calling it from anywhere within a Perl script. Perl provides you with different ways of calling subroutines. For example, you can call any subroutine using the following syntax.

```
&subroutinename();
```

Here, the name of the subroutine is preceded by the & character and followed by a pair of parentheses. For example, using this syntax you could execute a subroutine named `clear_the_screen`.

```
&clear_the_screen();
```

This syntax provides you with the ability to call on a subroutine from any location within a Perl script. Alternatively, you can execute a subroutine using the following syntax.

```
subroutinename();
```

So, to call the `clear_the_screen` subroutine using this syntax you would type

```
clear_the_screen();
```

Both of these options for calling subroutines work the same way, and you may use whichever one suits your personal preference. For the sake of clarity and readability, it is probably best to pick one of these two options and to stick with it. Many Perl programmers use the & option in order to help identify calls to custom subroutines as opposed to calls to a built-in Perl function.

Another option for calling subroutines is to use the following syntax.

```
$variablename = &subroutinename();
```

or

```
$variablename = subroutinename();
```

This option is required when calling subroutines that return a value as discussed later in this chapter. Note that from this point on, this book will place all subroutines at the end of scripts and will call on them by preceding the subroutine name with the & character.

Subroutine calls can even be embedded within other subroutines.

```perl
sub play_game {
  $number = &get_random_number();
}
sub get_random_number {
  $randomnumber = int(rand 10) + 1;

}
```

Here, a subroutine named play_game contains a second embedded subroutine named get_random_number, which is called by the first statement in play_game. The value returned from get_random_number is stored in $number.

A Template for Organizing Your Scripts and Subroutines

It helps to develop Perl scripts (or any other type of script) using a consistent approach or pattern. One way of achieving this is to use a template that helps to organize your scripts into key sections. Going forward in this book, the following template will be used when developing new game scripts.

```perl
#!/usr/bin/perl
#
# Script Name (Xxxxxxx.pl)


#--------------------------------------------------------------------------------
# Initialization Section
#--------------------------------------------------------------------------------


#Define global variables, arrays and hashes here


#--------------------------------------------------------------------------------
# MAIN Processing Section
#--------------------------------------------------------------------------------


#Place controlling program statements and calls to custom subroutines here


#--------------------------------------------------------------------------------
# Subroutine Section
```

```
#- - - - - - - - - - - - - - - - - - - - - - - - - - - - - - - - - - - - - - - - - - - - - - - - - -

#Place your custom subroutines here
```

As you can see, this template organizes scripts into four major sections. At the top of the script file is the shebang followed by a comment statement that identifies the script's name. Next, the Initialization Section provides a place for declaring variables, arrays, and hashes used by the rest of the script. The MAIN Processing Section provides a place for putting the programming statements and subroutine calls that control the overall execution of the script. Lastly, the Subroutine Section provides a place for storing all the scripts' subroutines.

TRICK You might want to consider modifying the top portion of this template before using it to develop your own Perl scripts. For example, you might want to include a place to record the date the script is created and the date that it was last modified. You might also want to provide room for a description that documents the purpose of the script. It would not hurt to provide a place for keeping track of version information either.

THE FORTUNE TELLER GAME REVISITED

Now that you have learned how subroutines can be used to improve your Perl Scripts and have seen examples of how to create and call upon subroutines for execution, let's take a look at how you might use subroutines to improve on the Fortune Teller script. You created this script back in Chapter 3. Before continuing on, you might want to return to Chapter 3 and take a few minutes to reacquaint yourself with the original version of this script. Once you have done that, take a look at the reworked version shown here.

```
#!/usr/bin/perl
#
# The Perl Fortune Teller (FortuneTeller.pl)


#- - - - - - - - - - - - - - - - - - - - - - - - - - - - - - - - - - - - - - - - - - - - - - - - - -
# Initialization Section
#- - - - - - - - - - - - - - - - - - - - - - - - - - - - - - - - - - - - - - - - - - - - - - - - - -

#Define a variable to hold user input
$reply    = "";
$question = "";
$randomnumber = 0;
```

```
#-------------------------------------------------------------------------
# MAIN Processing Section
#-------------------------------------------------------------------------

&clear_the_screen();   #Call subroutine that clears the screen

&display_intro();   #Call subroutine that introduces the story

&display_crystal_ball();   #Call subroutine that displays the crystal ball

&clear_the_screen();    #Call subroutine that clears the screen

&provide_fortunes();    #Call subroutine that answers user questions

&clear_the_screen();    #Call subroutine that clears the screen

&display_closing_msg();  #Call subroutine that displays a closing message


#-------------------------------------------------------------------------
# Subroutine Section
#-------------------------------------------------------------------------

#This subroutine clears the screen by adding 25 blank lines
sub clear_the_screen {

  for ($i=0; $i < 25; ++$i){
    print "\n";
  }
}


sub display_intro {

  #Display an introductory message & format display using carriage returns

  print "Hello and welcome to the Perl Fortune Teller game.\n\n";
  print "What you are about to see will thrill and amaze you!\n\n\n\n\n\n";
```

```perl
    print "Press the Enter key to continue...";  #Prompt user to continue

    #Set variable equal to standard input and remove any trailing newline
    $reply = <STDIN>;

}


sub display_crystal_ball {

    print "The room goes black. You hear the creaking of an old\n";
    print "door followed by the sound of someone coming towards you. Your\n";
    print "heart begins to pound through your chest. For a few moments\n";
    print "there is total silence. Suddenly, a bright light appears in the\n";
    print "middle of the room emanating from a crystal ball located on a\n";
    print "small table.\n\n";

    print "                    ****\n";
    print "                 *       *\n";
    print "               *           *\n";
    print "              *             *\n";
    print "              *             *\n";
    print "               *           *\n";
    print "                 *       *\n";
    print "                    ****\n";
    print "                  |   |\n";
    print "          ----------------\n";
    print "          |              |\n";
    print "          |              |\n";
    print "          |              |\n";
    print "          |              |\n";
    print "          ----------------\n\n";
    print "Press the Enter key to continue...";  #Prompt user to continue

    #Set variable equal to standard input and remove any trailing newline
    $reply = <STDIN>;

}
```

```perl
sub provide_fortunes {

  #Loop until the player types the word "quit"
  while (lc ($question) ne "quit") {

    &collect_questions();  #Call subroutine that collects player questions

    &clear_the_screen();  #Call subroutine that clears the screen

    &test_for_quit(); #Call subroutine that determines when to quit

    &test_for_blank_space();  #Call subroutine that validates user input

    &generate_random_number();  #Call subroutine to retrieve random number

    &respond_to_questions();  #Call subroutine that answers user questions

    print "Press the Enter key to continue...";  #Prompt user to continue
    #Set variable equal to standard input and remove any trailing newline
    $reply = <STDIN>;

  }  #End the loop

}  #End sub


sub collect_questions {

  clear_the_screen();  #Call subroutine that clears the screen

  print "I see that someone has come to see me. Very well, ask me\n";
  print "your question and I will tell you what it is that you wish\n";
  print "to know.\n\n";

  $reply = <STDIN>;

  clear_the_screen();
```

```perl
    print "What is your question? ";  #Capture the user's answer
    chomp($question = <STDIN>);

}

sub test_for_quit {
  #Terminate current iteration of the loop if the player typed "quit"
  if (lc ($question) eq "quit") {
    next;
  }

}


sub test_for_blank_space {

  #Terminate current iteration of the loop if the player did not type
  #anything
  if ($question eq "") {
    print "You did not ask a question.\n\n";
    print "Press the Enter key to continue..."; #Prompt user to continue
    #Set variable equal to standard input and remove any trailing newline
    $reply = <STDIN>;
    next;
  }

}


sub generate_random_number {

  #Generate a random number in the range of 0 to 5
  $randomnumber = int(rand 6);

}


sub respond_to_questions {
```

```
#Use the randomly generated number to select a response
if ($randomnumber == 0) {
  print "The answer to your question is No.\n\n";
} elsif ($randomnumber == 1) {
  print "The answer to your question is Yes.\n\n";
} elsif ($randomnumber == 2) {
  print "The answer to your question is unclear. ";
  print "Try asking your question differently.\n\n";
} elsif ($randomnumber == 3) {
  print "The answer to your question is maybe.\n\n";
} elsif ($randomnumber == 4) {
  print "The answer to your question is that only time will tell.\n\n";
} elsif ($randomnumber == 5) {
  print "Ask a different question. I cannot answer this one.\n\n";
}

}


sub display_closing_msg {

  print "Very well. I see that your business here is done. Please\n";
  print "feel free to return any time to discover what else the future\n";
  print "has in store for you.\n\n";


}
```

As you can see, the Initialization Section contains declarations for each scalar variable defined in the script. The MAIN Processing Section consists of seven subroutine calls that control script execution by specifying which subroutines are executed and the order of their execution. Lastly, the code statements that made up the bulk of the previous version of this script have been grouped into ten subroutines, which are located in the Subroutines Section. Hopefully, as you look at this reworked version of the Fortune Teller script, you will agree that it is easier to read and understand than the original version.

PASSING ARGUMENTS TO SUBROUTINES

So far, all of the subroutines that you have seen execute when called using data already available when the subroutine call is made. For example, in the reworked Perl Fortune Teller script, the generate_random_number subroutine, shown below, generates a random number based in the range of 0 to 5 using data hard coded in the subroutine.

```
sub generate_random_number {

  #Generate a random number in the range of 0 to 5
  $randomnumber = int(rand 6);

}
```

Likewise, the test_for_blank_space subroutine, shown below, used the $question scalar variable to determine whether to display an error message. The $question scalar variable was declared and assigned a value earlier in the script.

```
sub test_for_blank_space {

  #Terminate current iteration of the loop if the player did not type
  #anything
  if ($question eq "") {
    print "You did not ask a question.\n\n";
    print "Press the Enter key to continue...";  #Prompt user to continue
    #Set variable equal to standard input and remove any trailing newline
    $reply = <STDIN>;
    next;
  }

}
```

While there is certainly value in being able to organize code statements into subroutines and to access data hard coded within subroutines or available globally as variables throughout the script, subroutines can be even more valuable when the script statements that call them pass them data for processing.

Passing Data to Subroutines for Processing

When you set up a subroutine to accept and process data, referred to as *arguments*, you make them independent of the script they reside in. In other words, you can copy and paste the subroutine into other scripts and, as long as you modify the other scripts to pass the right type and number of arguments to the subroutine, the subroutine should run without requiring any changes.

You pass arguments to subroutines in exactly the same manner that you have been passing arguments to functions throughout this book. For example, you could call a subroutine named display_names and pass it two arguments.

```
display_names("Alexander", "William ");
```

Alternatively, you could call the same subroutine as shown here.

```
&display_names("Alexander ", "William ");
```

 TRICK You can also call subroutines and pass them arguments without enclosing the arguments inside parentheses.

```
display_names "Alexander", "William";
```

However, in order to pass arguments to a subroutine in this way, the subroutine must have been previously declared. Otherwise an error will occur.

Accessing Subroutine Arguments

Any arguments passed to a subroutine are made available within the subroutine via the special @_ array variable.

```
&display_names("Alexander", "William", "Molly");

sub display_names {
  print "@_";

}
```

Here, a subroutine called display_names is called and passed three scalar variables. These variables are stored as elements in the @_ special array variable and are displayed by the subroutine's print statement. Individual arguments can be accessed by referencing their index position in the @_ array.

```
&display_names("Alexander", "William", "Molly");

sub display_names {
  print "$_[1]";  #Displays William

}
```

TRICK @_ directly references the arguments passed to the subroutine. If you change any of the arguments passed in @_, the change occurs both to the argument passed to the subroutine and to the original value that was passed. In other words, the change is not kept private to the subroutine. However, it is poor programming practice to modify the value of data passed to subroutines in this manner. Instead, if you need to change argument values, you should reassign subroutine arguments as explained in the next section.

Reassigning Subroutine Arguments

Referencing arguments within a subroutine via index position makes for some pretty cryptic code. Fortunately, Perl provides you with a way of assigning friendly names to arguments. To accomplish this, you can for example, assign scalar variables to each expected argument.

```perl
&display_stats(20, 10, 4);

sub display_stats {
  ($wins, $losses, $ties) = @_;
  print "Wins: $wins\n";
  print "Losses: $losses\n";
  print "Ties: $ties\n";
}
```

Here, three scalar variables are assigned arguments passed to the script. $wins is set equal to 20, $losses is set equal to 10, and $ties is set equal to 4.

TRICK Another way to reassign arguments to user-friendly variables within a sub-routine is to take advantage of the shift function. As you learned in Chapter 4, "Working with Collections of Data," this function removes the first element stored in an array and returns the deleted value. This allows you to use the shift function to assign friendly variable names to subroutine arguments as demonstrated here.

```perl
&display_stats(20, 10, 4);

sub display_stats {
  my $wins = shift;
  my $losses = shift;
  my $ties = shift;

  print "Wins: $wins\n";
  print "Losses: $losses\n";
```

```
        print "Ties: $ties\n";
    }
```

Passing Lists, Arrays, and Hashes as Arguments

Perl lets you pass more than just lists of scalar arguments to subroutines as argument inputs. Perl also allows you to pass arrays and hashes. Any time you pass an array or hash to a subroutine, Perl automatically converts its contents into an argument list which the subroutine has access to via the @_ special variable. For example, the following statements demonstrate how to call a subroutine named sort_names.

```
@children = qw(Alexander William Molly);

&sort_names(@children);

sub sort_names {
  @names = @_;
  print "Names: \n\n";
  foreach $i (@_) {
    print "$i \n";
  }
}
```

As you can see, the sort_names subroutine has been designed to accept any number of list arguments, which it then sorts and prints. You can just as easily pass a hash to a subroutine and Perl will convert it to a list made up of its associated keys and values. You can also pass any number of arrays and hashes to a subroutine as demonstrated here.

```
@children = qw(Alexander William Molly);
@buddies = qw(Mike Markland Nick);

&sort_names(@children, @buddies);

sub sort_names {
  @names = @_;
  print "Names: \n\n";
  foreach $i (sort @names) {
    print "$i \n";
  }
}
```

In this example, the contents of the two array arguments are converted into a single list and then processed by the subroutine.

TRICK There is one catch to passing multiple arrays and hashes to a subroutine. Once received by the subroutine, you lose the ability to easily tell which arguments belong to which array or hash. There are ways of working around this issue. For example, you could pass additional scalar string arguments in front of array or hash arguments identifying the number of elements in each and then use these arguments to reconstruct the contents of each array or hash. Another option is to use references. A *reference* is a pointer that, in the context of this discussion, provides access to external arrays and hashes. However, references are an advanced programming concept and covering them is beyond the scope of this book.

GETTING DATA BACK FROM SUBROUTINES

In addition to accepting and processing arguments, Perl subroutines can return a result back to any calling statement, in exactly the same manner that built-in Perl functions do. By default, the value returned by a subroutine is the value of the last evaluated expression. Consider the following example.

```
$result = &multiply_it(10, 5);

sub multiply_it {
  ($x, $y) = @_;
  $z = $x * $y;
}
```

In this example, the value assigned to $z (which is 50) is automatically returned to the calling statement and assigned to $result. While this method of returning a result works well a lot of the time, it can cause problems if a subroutine is designed in such a way that you cannot always guarantee what the last expression evaluated will be. For example, consider the following example.

```
$result = &multiply_it(10, 5);

sub multiply_it {
  ($x, $y) = @_;
  $z = ($x * $y);
  if ($z = 50) {
```

```
    $z = 100;   #order of 50 is automatically doubled
  }

}
```

Here, either of two different expressions may be returned to the calling statement depending on the value assigned to $z. Now, suppose that this was a much larger and more involved subroutine with many different logical flows and possible points of exit. As you can see, things can quickly get a little confusing. To help make them less confusing, you can instead explicitly identify possible return values within a subroutine using the return statement.

```
$result = &multiply_it(10, 5);

sub multiply_it {
  ($x, $y) = @_;

  $z = ($x * $y);

  if ($z <= 50) {
    return "Low";
  }

  if ($z > 50) {
    return "High";
  }

}
```

In this example, each possible location where a result might be returned has been clearly identified, making the subroutine easier to understand and maintain. As you would expect, Perl subroutines can also return arrays and hashes to calling statements if need be, as demonstrated here.

```
@children = qw(Alexander William Molly);
@buddies = qw(Mike Markland Nick);

@minilist = &get_short_list(@children, @buddies);

sub get_short_list {
  ($a, $b, $c, $d, $e, $f) = @_;
```

```
@names = ($a, $b, $e, $f);
return  @names;
```

}

In this example, two arrays containing a total of six elements are passed as arguments to the get_short_list subroutine. The subroutine creates an array named @names and assigns it elements consisting of the first two arguments and the last two arguments passed to it. The contents of the @names array are then returned to the calling statement, where they are stored in an array named @minilist.

CONTROLLING VARIABLE SCOPE

Another benefit provided by subroutines is the ability to limit the scope of variables. Scope is a term used to refer to the availability of a variable. By default, variables within Perl scripts are global in scope, meaning that they can be accessed from any location within the script. However, when defined within subroutines, variables can be kept private, limiting access to just within the subroutine. By defining *private variables*, you can develop subroutines that can execute in an independent manner, without reliance on the availability of global variables defined outside of the subroutine. This facilitates the development of portable subroutines that can be copied and pasted from script to script and then used without modification.

Creating Private Variables

In order to define a private variable within a subroutine, precede the variable declaration with the my operator using the following syntax.

my $variablename;

For example, the following statements define a subroutine that divides a value passed to it as an argument by 2.

```
sub divide_it {
  my ($x) = @_;

  $z = ($x / 2);
  print $z;

}
```

When used this way, the my operator only works with one variable at a time. Using list context, you can work with more than one variable at a time. For example, the following subroutine, named multiply_it, works with a list made up of two local scalar variables, $x and $y.

```
sub multiply_it {
  my ($x, $y) = @_;
  print $x * $y;
}
```

TRAP A subroutine's private variable is local to just the owning subroutine. If the subroutine calls other subroutines, those subroutines will not have access to the calling subroutine's private variables, nor will the calling subroutine be able to access private variables located inside the subroutines it calls.

Private subroutine variables cease to exist as soon as the subroutine finishes executing. Therefore, neither $x or $y are accessible outside of the subroutine. If another scalar variable with the same name exists outside of the subroutine, there will not be any conflicts—Perl will treat each variable independently. However, you should avoid duplicating variable names in this manner, since it can make scripts difficult to understand and maintain. The my operator also works with arrays and hashes.

TRICK You can also use the my operator to define private variables inside any code block, including, for example, if and while and for loop control blocks.

```
if ($x == $y) {
  my $z = 0;
    .
    .
    .
}
```

In this example, a private variable named $z is defined within an if statement control block and is therefore not accessible to any other area within the script. If the if statement code block were located within a subroutine, the $z variable would remain local to the if statement code block and would not even be accessible to other parts of the subroutine.

Getting Strict with Private Variables

As you have already witnessed, Perl is an extremely flexible scripting language that lets you accomplish the same task in many different ways. Perl is also very permissive in the way it lets you work with variables, allowing you to create them on the fly without declaring them in advance.

One way to add a little discipline to your scripting is to instruct Perl to be stricter in the way it enforces variable declaration. For example, you have already seen how the exclusion or inclusion of the warning switch (-w) determines whether Perl quietly allows your scripts to run or whether it spits out error messages. Turning on warnings tells Perl to generate error messages when you do something it does not like, such as declaring an unreferenced variable or using bare words.

One way to help yourself write better Perl code is to tell Perl to more strictly interpret the code statements that make up your scripts. You can do this by adding the use strict statement to your scripts. The use script statement tells Perl to generate an error message anytime it finds a scalar variable in your script that was not previously declared. For example, create a Perl script made up of the following statements.

```perl
#!/usr/bin/perl
use strict;
$x = 100;
```

When you run this script, Perl will stop the script's execution and display the following error message.

```
Global symbol "$x" requires explicit package name at C:\test.pl line 3.
Execution of C:\test.pl aborted due to compilation errors.
```

If, on the other hand, you edit the script and comment out or remove the use strict statement, Perl will allow the script to run without saying a word.

You can place the use strict statement anywhere you want within your scripts. However, it is common to include it at the beginning of your script, thus enabling script variable interpretation for the entire script. Alternatively, you can add it to the beginning of a function to limit its effect to an individual subroutine.

Creating Local Variables

Perl did not support private variables prior to Perl 5. Instead, Perl programmers had to make do with something called local variables. A *local* variable is very much like a private variable with one major exception: a local variable is accessible to the subroutine in which it is defined and to any subroutine embedded within the subroutine. To declare a local variable, you use the local operator, which has the following syntax.

```perl
local($localvariablename);
```

In the following example, a local variable named $name is defined within a subroutine.

```
sub display_it {
  local($name) = "William";
  print $name;
}
```

Local variables are covered here to make you aware of them, since you are likely to run across them from time to time in older Perl scripts. You should avoid using them in your own scripts and instead stick with private variables. If you need to share a value assigned to a private variable with an embedded subroutine, just pass the value as an argument to the embedded subroutine.

BACK TO THE PICK A NUMBER GAME

Now it is time to turn your attention back to the Pick a Number game. This script will rely heavily on subroutines as a means of organizing script logic and controlling script execution. In addition, while the script will use two global variables to track the total number of guesses made and the total number of games played, local subroutine variables will be used to localize the rest of the variables defined in the script. Data will then be passed between subroutines via arguments and, where appropriate, subroutine output will be explicitly returned to calling statements.

Designing the Game

The construction and development of the Pick a Number game will be completed in 9 steps:

1. Creating a new script.
2. Developing controlling logic.
3. Creating the clear_the_screen subroutine.
4. Creating the main_menu subroutine.
5. Creating the generate_number subroutine.
6. Creating the play_the_game subroutine.
7. Creating the display_stats subroutine.
8. Creating the display_help subroutine.
9. Creating the display_about subroutine.

Creating the Script File

The first step in creating the Pick a Number game is to create a new Perl script. Give the script file a name of PickANumber.pl and add the following code statements to it.

```perl
#!/usr/bin/perl
#
# The Pick A Number Game (PickANumber.pl)


$noOfGames = 0;
$noOfGuesses = 0;
```

The first three statements define the shebang and document the name of the script. The last two statements define and initialize two global scalar variables, which will be used to keep track of the total number of games played and the total number of guesses made while playing.

Controlling Game Play

The next step in creating the Pick a Number script is to set up the controlling logic that manages overall script execution. This is accomplished by setting up a while loop that executes for as long as the script runs, making subroutine calls based on the player's menu commands. The code statements that make up the while loop are shown here.

```perl
while (! $isvalid) {

  my $choice = "";
  my $secretnumber = 0;

  &clear_the_screen();

  $choice = &main_menu();

  if (lc ($choice) eq "play") {

      $noOfGames++;

      $secretnumber = &generate_number();

      $noOfGuesses = $noOfGuesses + &play_the_game($secretnumber);

  } elsif (lc ($choice) eq "quit") {

      if ($noOfGames != 0) {
```

```
        &display_stats();
    }

    $isvalid = 1;

} elsif (lc ($choice) eq "help") {

    &clear_the_screen();
    &display_help();

} elsif (lc ($choice) eq "about") {

    &clear_the_screen();
    &display_about();

  }


}
```

The first two statements in the while loop declare variables which are private to the while loop. The clear_the_screen subroutine is then called followed by the main_menu subroutine. The main_menu subroutine returns a scalar value representing the menu command entered by the player. An if...elsif control block then analyzes the value of $choice to determine which series of actions to take.

As you can see, the while loop has been set up to execute until the value of $value is set equal to true, which only happens when the player enters the quit command. When this happens, the script ends after calling the display_stats subroutine, which displays game statistics collected as the game is played. Note, however, that if the player enters the quit command without playing at least one game, the display_stats subroutine is not called. Regardless, $value is set equal to true, allowing the loop to terminate and end the game.

In addition to the play and quit commands, the if...elsif code block also looks for the help and about commands, clearing the screen and calling either the display_help or display_about subroutines as appropriate.

Clearing the Screen

As has been the case with each game script you have created so far, you need a means of clearing the screen at certain points during script execution. In this script, this is accomplished by adding the clear_the_screen() subroutine, shown here.

```
sub clear_the_screen {

  for ($i=0; $i < 25; ++$i){
    print "\n";
  }


}
```

Displaying the Main Menu

The code for the main_menu subroutine is outlined below. It consists of one local scalar variable and a number of print statements. It ends by explicitly returning the command entered by the player to the statement that called the subroutine.

```
sub main_menu {

  my $reply = "";

  print "        ";
  print "Welcome to the  P I C K   A   N U M B E R   G A M E!";
  print "\n\n\n\n\n\n\n\n\n\n\n\n";
  print "[Play] [Quit] [Help] [About]\n\n";
  print "Enter command: ";

  chomp($reply = <STDIN>);

  return $reply;

}
```

Generating a Random Number

The code for the generate_number subroutine is provided below. It consists of one local scalar variable and a return statement that returns a randomly generated number in the range of 1 to 100.

```
sub generate_number {

  my $randomnumber = 0;
```

```
return $randomnumber = int(rand 100) + 1;

}
```

TRICK

To make the Pick a Number script easier to test once you have finished keying it in, you might want to temporarily modify the code in the generate_number subroutine.

```
sub generate_number {

    my $randomnumber = 0;

    print "The randomly generated number is: $randomnumber \n\n";
    chomp($reply = <STDIN>);

    return $randomnumber = int(rand 100) + 1;

}
```

By adding the two statements shown above in bold, you will cause the script to pause and show you the game's randomly generated secret number each time a new game is played. This will help you to verify that things are working as they should. Once you have the script working correctly, you can come back and remove these extra statements.

Processing Player Guesses

The code for the play_the_game subroutine is provided here.

```
sub play_the_game {

  my $secretnumber = $_[0];
  my $isover = 0;
  my $userguess = 0;
  my $totalguesses = 0;
  my $reply = 0;

  until ($isover) {

    clear_the_screen();
    print " Enter your guess: \n\n > ";
```

```perl
chomp($userguess = <STDIN>);

$totalguesses++;

if ($userguess == $secretnumber) {

  clear_the_screen();
  print "You guessed it! Press Enter to return to the main menu.\n\n";
  chomp($reply = <STDIN>);
  $isover = 1;

} elsif ($userguess <= $secretnumber) {

  clear_the_screen();
  print "$ userguess is too low. Press Enter to guess again.\n\n";
  chomp($reply = <STDIN>);

} elsif ($userguess >= $secretnumber) {

  clear_the_screen();
  print "$userguess is too high. Press Enter to guess again.\n\n";
  chomp($reply = <STDIN>);

}

}

  return $totalguesses;
}
```

This subroutine begins by defining five local scalar variables, the first of which is used to set up a reference to the game's randomly selected number, passed to the subroutines as an argument.

The rest of the subroutine consists of an until loop that executes until the player guesses the game's random number. Each time a guess is made, the value of $totalguesses is incremented by one and the player's guess is analyzed using an if...elsif code block.

Each guess is analyzed to determine if it is correct, too low, or too high. When the player correctly guesses the game's number, the value of $over is set equal to true. Otherwise, the player is told that her guess is too low or too high and the loop iterates allowing the players to guess again.

Displaying Game Results

The code for the display_stats subroutine is outlined below.

```
sub display_stats {

  my $average = 0;
  my $reply = 0;

  clear_the_screen();

  $average = ($noOfGuesses / $noOfGames);

  $row = "_" x 50;
  print " $row\n\n";

  print " GAME STATISTICS:\n\n";

  print " $row\n\n\n";

  print " Total number of guesses made: $noOfGuesses\n\n";
  print " Total number of games played: $noOfGames\n\n";
  print " Average number of guesses per game: $average\n\n";

  print " $row\n\n";

  chomp($reply = <STDIN>);

}
```

This subroutine has two local scalar variables. It uses $average to store a value representing the average number of turns made by the player for each game that is played. This value is calculated by dividing $noOfGames by $noOfGuesses. A series of print statements is then used to display the value of each of these scalar variables.

Building a Help Screen

The code for the display_help subroutine is provided here.

```perl
sub display_help {

  my $reply = 0;
  my $row = "_" x 61;

  print " PICK A NUMBER GAME HELP:\n\n";
  print " $row\n\n";
  print " Type Play to begin the game or type Quit to exit. To get help\n";
  print " type Help and to learn more about the game and its developer\n";
  print " type About.\n";
  print " $row\n\n";
  print "\n\n\n\n\n\n\n\n\n\n\n";


  print "Press Enter to continue: ";
  chomp($reply = <STDIN>);

}
```

As you can see, this subroutine consists of two local scalar variables. $reply is used to store the player's input. $row is used to store a value generated using the x operator, which is used as a header to visually format the text displayed by the print statements that follow.

Providing Information About the Game

The code for the display_about subroutine is provided below. As you can see, except for the text in the print statements, it is identical to the display_help subroutine.

```perl
sub display_about {

  my $reply = 0;
  my $row = "_" x 61;

  print " ABOUT THE PICK A NUMBER GAME:\n\n";
  print " $row\n\n";
  print " The Pick A Number Game - Copyright 2006.\n\n";
  print " Created by Jerry Lee Ford, Jr.\n";
  print " $row\n\n";
  print "\n\n\n\n\n\n\n\n\n\n\n";
```

```perl
    print "Press Enter to continue: ";
    chomp($reply = <STDIN>);

}
```

The Final Result

At this point, you have everything you need to assemble the Pick a Number script. If you have not keyed it in yet, now is a good time to do so. For your convenience, a complete copy of the script is provided here. This version of the Pick a Number script includes the addition of comments that document key portions of the script and make the script easier to read and understand.

Note that if you have already created this script and elected to temporarily modify the code statements that make up the generate_number subroutine, you will want to go remove the temporary code statements that you added, as has been done in the completed version of the script shown here.

```perl
#!/usr/bin/perl
#
# The Pick A Number Game (PickANumber.pl)



#-------------------------------------------------------------------------
# Initialization Section
#-------------------------------------------------------------------------


#Declare and initialize script variables

$noOfGames = 0;    #Global variable used to track the number of games played
$noOfGuesses = 0; #Global variable used to track the total number of guesses



#-------------------------------------------------------------------------
# MAIN Processing Section
#-------------------------------------------------------------------------


#This loop is responsible for controlling the entire game
while (! $isvalid) {
```

```perl
my $choice = "";  #Local variable used to store the player's menu command
my $secretnumber = 0;  #Local variable that holds the game's random number

&clear_the_screen();  #Call subroutine that clears the screen

$choice = &main_menu();  #Call subroutine that displays the menu system

#Determine if player entered the play command
if (lc ($choice) eq "play") {

    $noOfGames++;  #Increment variable by one

    #Call subroutine that generates a random number and assign to a
    #local variable
    $secretnumber = &generate_number();

    #Call subroutine that controls the number guessing part of the game
    #and keep count of the total number of guesses made so far
    $noOfGuesses = $noOfGuesses + &play_the_game($secretnumber);

#Determine if the player entered the Quit command
} elsif (lc ($choice) eq "quit") {

    #Do not do anything if no games have been played
    if ($noOfGames != 0) {

      #As long as at least one game has been played, call the subroutine
      #that displays game statistics
      &display_stats();
    }

    $isvalid = 1;  #Set variable equal to true in order to exit script

#Determine if the player entered the Help command
} elsif (lc ($choice) eq "help") {

    &clear_the_screen();  #Call subroutine that clears the screen
    &display_help();  #Call subroutine that displays help text
```

```perl
    #Determine if the player entered the About command
    } elsif (lc ($choice) eq "about") {

        &clear_the_screen();  #Call subroutine that clears the screen
        &display_about();  #Call subroutine that displays game information

    }

}



#--------------------------------------------------------------------------
# Subroutine Section
#--------------------------------------------------------------------------

#This subroutine clears the screen by adding 25 blank lines
sub clear_the_screen {

  for ($i=0; $i < 25; ++$i){  #Loop 25 times
    print "\n";  #Print out a blank line
  }

}



#This subroutine displays a welcome message and game menu
sub main_menu {

  my $reply = "";  #Local variable used to hold the user's command

  #Display the game's opening menu system
  print "         ";
  print "Welcome to the  P I C K   A   N U M B E R   G A M E!";
  print "\n\n\n\n\n\n\n\n\n\n\n\n";
  print "[Play] [Quit] [Help] [About]\n\n";
  print "Enter command: ";  #Prompt user for selection before continuing

  #Set variable equal to standard input and remove any trailing newline
```

```perl
   chomp($reply = <STDIN>);

   return $reply;  #Return the command entered by the user


}


#This subroutine generates the game's random number between 1 and 100
sub generate_number {

   my $randomnumber = 0;  #Local variable used to store a random number

   #Return a random number between 1 and 100
   return $randomnumber = int(rand 100) + 1;

}


#This subroutine generates the game's random number
sub play_the_game {

   #Declare subroutine local variables
   my $secretnumber = $_[0]; #Stores the argument passed to the subroutine
   my $isover = 0;       #Used to control loop execution
   my $userguess = 0;        #Used to store the player's guess
   my $totalguesses = 0;     #Used to keep track the number of guesses made
   my $reply = 0;            #Used to store value entered by the player

   #This loop is responsible for collecting and analyzing player guesses
   until ($isover) {

      clear_the_screen();  #Call subroutine that clears the screen

      print " Enter your guess: \n\n > ";  #Instruction to the player to guess

      chomp($userguess = <STDIN>);  #Collect the player's guess

      $totalguesses++;  #Increment the variable by one
```

```perl
    #Determine if player guesses the game's secret number
    if ($userguess == $secretnumber) {

      clear_the_screen();  #Call subroutine that clears the screen
      print "You guessed it! Press Enter to return to the main menu.\n\n";
      chomp($reply = <STDIN>);  #Pause game until the player presses Enter
      $isover = 1;  #Set variable equal to true in order to leave loop

    #Determine if player's guess was too low
    } elsif ($userguess <= $secretnumber) {

      clear_the_screen();  #Call subroutine that clears the screen
      print "$ userguess is too low. Press Enter to guess again.\n\n";
      chomp($reply = <STDIN>);  #Pause game until the player presses Enter

    #Determine if player's guess was too high
    } elsif ($userguess >= $secretnumber) {

      clear_the_screen();  #Call subroutine that clears the screen
      print "$ userguess is too high. Press Enter to guess again.\n\n";
      chomp($reply = <STDIN>);  #Pause game until the player presses Enter

    }

  }

return $totalguesses;  #Return value representing the number of guesses made

}


#This subroutine displays help information about the game
sub display_stats {

  #Declare subroutine local variables
  my $average = 0;  #Used to calculate average number of guesses made
  my $reply = 0;    #Used to store value entered by the player
```

```perl
  clear_the_screen();  #Call subroutine that clears the screen

  #Calculate the average time of guesses required to win a game
  $average = ($noOfGuesses / $noOfGames);


  $row = "_" x 50;  #Format a header line of underscore characters
  print " $row\n\n";  #Display header line

  print " GAME STATISTICS:\n\n";

  print " $row\n\n\n";  #Display header line

  print " Total number of guesses made: $noOfGuesses\n\n";
  print " Total number of games played: $noOfGames\n\n";
  print " Average number of guesses per game: $average\n\n";

  print " $row\n\n";  #Display header line

  chomp($reply = <STDIN>);  #Pause game until the player presses Enter

}



#This subroutine displays help information about the game
sub display_help {

  #Declare subroutine local variables
  my $reply = 0;  #Used to store value entered by the player
  my $row = "_" x 61;  #Format a header line of underscore characters

  print " PICK A NUMBER GAME HELP:\n\n";
  print " $row\n\n";  #Display header line
  print " Type Play to begin the game or type Quit to exit. To get help\n";
  print " type Help and to learn more about the game and its developer\n";
  print " type About.\n";
  print " $row\n\n";  #Display header line
  print "\n\n\n\n\n\n\n\n\n\n";
```

```
    print "Press Enter to continue: ";
    chomp($reply = <STDIN>);   #Pause game until the player presses Enter


}


#This subroutine displays additional information about the game
sub display_about {

    #Declare subroutine local variables
    my $reply = 0;   #Used to store value entered by the player
    my $row = "_" x 61;   #Format a header line of underscore characters

    print " ABOUT THE PICK A NUMBER GAME:\n\n";
    print " $row\n\n";   #Display header line
    print " The Pick A Number Game - Copyright 2006.\n\n";
    print " Created by Jerry Lee Ford, Jr.\n";
    print " $row\n\n";   #Display header line
    print "\n\n\n\n\n\n\n\n\n\n\n";

    print "Press Enter to continue: ";
    chomp($reply = <STDIN>);   #Pause game until the player presses Enter


}
```

That's it. You have everything you need to create the Pick a Number script. If you have not done so, go ahead and save your script and then test it. As long as you have not made any typos, everything should work as expected. You might want to share this script with a few friends and ask them what they think and then look to incorporate any feedback they provide into changes that will make the game more fun.

SUMMARY

In this chapter, you learned how to organize your script statements into subroutines to make your scripts easier to read and maintain. In doing so, you learned how to create subroutines that act very much like Perl's built-in functions. For example, you learned how to create functions that accepted and processed any number of arguments as input and which could also return any amount of data as output to calling statements. You also learned how to define private variables within subroutines and to create portable subroutines that could be copied and pasted from script to script and then called on without requiring any modifications to the subroutines in order to get them to work. On top of all this, you got the opportunity to improve the organization of the Perl Fortune Teller script using subroutines and then learned how to create the Pick a Number game.

Now, before you move on to the next chapter, take a few minutes to improve the Pick a Number game by completing the following list of challenges.

CHALLENGES

1. As it is currently written, the Pick a Number script does not differentiate between different types of input. Add programming logic that tells the player when non-numeric input has been entered.

2. Currently, even though the Pick a Number script only expects guesses in the range of 1 – 100, it does not warn the player if guesses are made outside of this range. Modify the script to warn the player any time that an out of range guess is made.

3. The Pick a Number game only provides the player with hints of high and low. Add additional programming logic to notify players when they begin to make guesses that are close to the secret number. For example, you might tell players that they are getting warmer when their guesses are plus or minus five numbers from the secret number.

4. As it is currently written, the Help and About commands provide limited information. Enhance the script to provide the player with more useful information when the player executes the Help and About menu commands.

CHAPTER 6

SCOPE AND MODULES

So far, you have learned how to create global variables that are accessible to all portions of your scripts, as well as private and local variables, which restrict variable scope to inside functions and control blocks. In this chapter you will learn another way to create and restrict access to variables. This time you will learn how to create variables that are global only within the package that defines them. You will also learn how to create and access reusable units of code called modules. In doing so, you'll be able to create smaller scripts that are easier to develop and maintain. In addition, you'll learn how to find and use modules developed by other Perl programmers in order to save time and leverage work that is already done. On top of all this, you will learn how to create the Rock, Paper, Scissors game.

Specifically, you will learn how to

- Define packages and use them to manage variables
- Import and execute variables and subroutines stored in Perl library modules
- Build your own custom Perl modules
- Find Perl modules online that already solve the challenges you are trying to deal with
- Download, install, and use Perl modules developed by other Perl programmers

PROJECT PREVIEW: THE ROCK, PAPER, SCISSORS GAME

This chapter's game project is the Rock, Paper, Scissors game. This game is based on the classic game in which two opposing players, in this case the player and the computer, go head-to-head in an effort to out guess each other's moves. The development of this script will help to reinforce everything you have learned up to this point in the book, including the development and use of custom modules.

The Rock, Paper, Scissors game begins by displaying its main menu, as demonstrated in Figure 6.1.

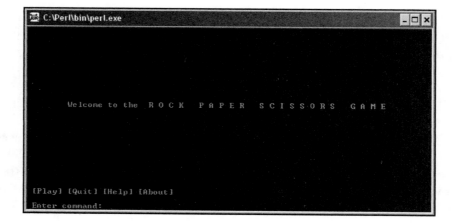

FIGURE 6.1

The Rock, Paper, Scissors game as seen on a computer running Windows XP.

The game provides the player with easy access to help information, as demonstrated in Figure 6.2.

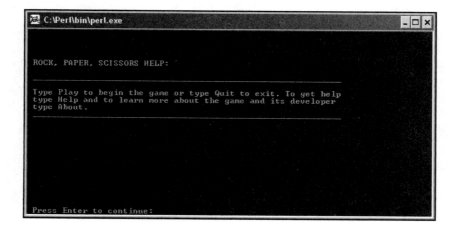

FIGURE 6.2

The game's help screen is available as an option on the main menu.

In addition, the game also provides access to an About screen, where the player can go to learn more about the game and its author, as shown in Figure 6.3.

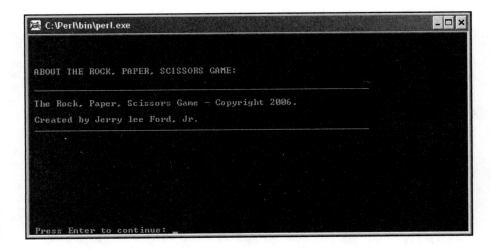

FIGURE 6.3

Viewing additional information about the game and its creator.

Once game play is initiated, the player is presented with instructions to enter a choice. Valid options, shown in Figure 6.4, are Rock, Paper, Scissors, and Back. To play, the player enters any of the first three options. To stop playing and return to the game's main menu, the player enters the Back command.

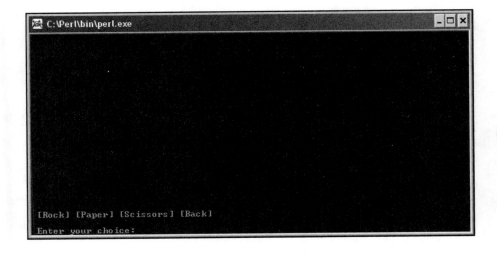

FIGURE 6.4

The player makes her selection by entering Rock, Paper, or Scissors at the game's Command Prompt.

The game automatically generates a random move on behalf of the computer and then displays the results, letting the player know whether she won, lost, or tied, as demonstrated in Figure 6.5.

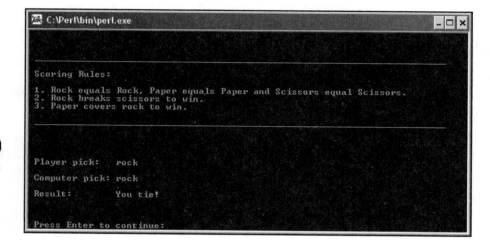

FIGURE 6.5

At the end of each turn, the user learns the computer's move and finds out who won.

Once the player decides to stop playing, the game displays statistics, showing the total number of games won, lost, and tied during the current playing session before exiting, as demonstrated in Figure 6.6.

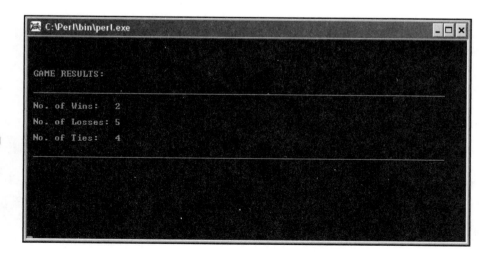

FIGURE 6.6

Before exiting, the Rock, Paper, Scissors game shows the player how many games have been won, lost, or tied.

EXERCISING ADDITIONAL CONTROL OVER VARIABLE SCOPE

So far, most of the examples that you have seen in this book have relied on global variables as the primary means of sharing access to different types of data, be it scalar, array, or hash. In Chapter 5, "Improving Script Organization and Structure," you learned how to refine your control over variables through the implementation of private and local variables placed inside subroutines and code blocks. Now it is time to introduce you to yet another means of controlling variable scope using packages.

Package definitions provide you with a tool for managing variables. Variables are global within the package. In addition, packages provide you with the ability to control access to their variables to other packages (e.g. other areas in the scripts that are outside of the package).

Each package has its own name. You probably have not realized it, but you have been working with packages from the very beginning of this book. By default, every Perl script is organized into at least one package. Perl's default package name for a new Perl script is *main*. To see what I mean, create the following script. Make sure that you enable warnings (-w), or this example will not work.

```
#!/usr/bin/perl -w
chomp($reply = <STDIN>);
```

Now, run the script and you should see output similar to that shown here.

```
Name "main::reply" used only once: possible typo at C:\Documents and
Settings\Owner\Desktop\Maindemo.pl line 3.
```

Take note that the error message that Perl displays begins by explaining that the error occurred because the $reply scalar variable was only used once in the main package. So, if you do not define a package definition within a script, Perl automatically defines one called main and places all the script's code within it. Based on this new information, you can see that a Perl script's global variables are really just global variables belonging to the main package and are therefore global within main.

Each package defines its own symbol table. A *symbol table* is a collection of variable names defined within a package. The symbol table keeps track of variable names and values and is also responsible for determining whether a variable can be accessed outside of the package. Symbol tables keep track of all variables defined inside a package, including scalar, array, and hash variables.

By defining additional packages within a Perl script, you can limit and/or control access to global variables between packages. To create a new package or to switch from one package to another, you need to use the package function, which has the following syntax.

```
package Namespace;
```

The rules for naming packages are the same as the rules for naming variables. However, by convention it is considered a good programming practice to begin package names with a capital letter. For example, to declare a new package named Override, you would add the following statement to your script.

```
package Override;
```

Perl treats any variable declarations that occur in the script after this statement as being part of the Override package, as long as none of the following conditions are met.

- **Another package is not declared or called.** If another package is declared, any new variable declarations are managed by that package's symbol table.
- **Variables are not declared using the my operator.** Any variable declared using my is excluded from the current package's symbol table and is truly global to the script itself.

Note that you can switch between packages at any time within a script using the package function by specifying the package name again. You can refer to any variable or subroutine declared within a package from outside that package by specifying the name of the package followed by two colons and the name of the variables or subroutines, as demonstrated here.

```
$Override::optional;
$Override::get_next_value();
```

In the first statement, a variable named $optional located in a module named Override is referenced. In the second statement, a subroutine named get_next_value located in the Override module is executed. You'll learn more about how to work with module variables and subroutines later in this chapter when you learn how to create your own custom modules.

TRAP Commonly accepted practices in the Perl community discourage the use of global variables. In fact, when Perl 6 finally arrives, you will find that much effort has gone into removing many built-in special global variables. While global variables can sometimes make life a lot easier, especially in small scripts, I strongly recommend that you limit your use of global variables and instead stick with private variables. When you need to share data between subroutines, you can pass it as arguments instead of using global variables.

WORKING WITH PERL MODULES

A big part of learning to be a Perl programmer is learning the basic syntax involved in using the language's basic programming statements. Another part of becoming a Perl programmer is learning how to master the art of putting this information to use through the development of Perl scripts. To be an effective programmer you also need to learn how to write scripts that are well structured, easy to understand, and, whenever possible, that take advantage of existing code.

The Perl Library

Perl stores built-in collections of pre-existing code in modules as part of the Perl library. The Perl library includes all of the modules, scripts, and other files shipped as part of the Perl distribution. Perl distributions vary based on platform. For example, in Perl distributions designed to run on Windows, you'll find a number of Win32 modules designed specifically for execution on Windows operating systems. Examples of these modules include:

- **Win32::Registry.** Facilitates the administration of the Windows registry.
- **Win32::Process.** Facilitates the creation and management of Windows processes.
- **Win32::Services.** Facilitates the administration of Windows services.

 TRICK Most, though not all, Perl modules are written in Perl. Therefore, you can read them to see how they are written. The Perl modules are provided as part of the standard Perl library and are typically stored somewhere in Perl's install directory. Some Perl modules are written in C, in which case you won't be able to read them.

Accessing Module Documentation

A great resource for locating documentation about Perl's core modules is perldoc.perl.org/index-modules-P.html, as shown in Figure 6.7. Here you will find an alphabetized listing of Perl's built-in code modules.

Perl modules generally include built-in documentation that you can view using the perldoc utility. For example, Figure 6.8 demonstrates how to use perldoc to view the documentation belonging to the Env module.

Importing Modules into Perl Scripts

To take advantage of Perl modules, you must import them into your Perl scripts, as demonstrated in the following example.

```
use Env;
print "Temp: $TEMP \n\n";
print "Path: $PATH"
```

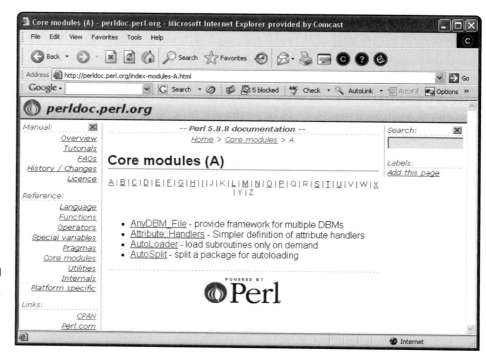

FIGURE 6.7

Reviewing the Perl module documentation available at perldoc.perl.org.

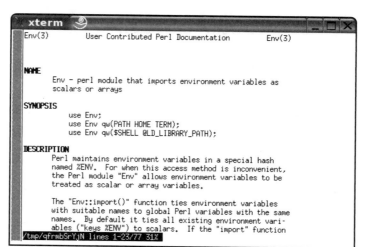

FIGURE 6.8

Viewing the documentation associated with Perl's Env module.

The use directive tells Perl to pause the interpretation of the current script and to search for the specified module. Once found, Perl opens and reads the module and loads all of its functions and variables. Once this has been completed, Perl resumes the interpretation of the original script. Once the entire script and any referenced modules have been interpreted, the script executes. This short two-line script imports the Env module. The Env module provides access to computer environment variables, allowing you to access them as scalar variables. In this example, the Env module's $TEMP and $PATH variables are referenced and the values are printed out as demonstrated below.

```
Temp: C:\Documents and Settings\Jerry\Local Settings\Temp
Path:
C:\Perl\bin\;C:\WINDOWS\system32;C:\WINDOWS;C:\WINDOWS\System32\Wbem;c:\Python22
```

TRICK In the preceding example, two Env module variables were referenced as $TEMP and $PATH. Alternatively, you could have explicitly referenced these variables as $main::TEMP and $main::PATH.

TRAP %ENV is a special hash variable that contains a key-value pairs listing of all the environment variables currently available. Don't confuse it with the Env module, which provides you with the ability to reference specific environment variable values as individual scalar values.

BUILDING CUSTOM MODULES

Modules are containers that you can use to create reusable collections of code. In Chapter 5, "Improving Script Organization and Structure," you learned how to create more efficient Perl scripts by grouping together related code statements into subroutines. One of the primary benefits of subroutines is that they facilitate code reuse. An example of one such subroutine is the clear_the_screen subroutine, which you have been adding to all your game scripts and then calling on whenever necessary to keep the screen clear.

TRICK The development of Perl modules is an extremely complicated task that can be a challenge to even the most advanced Perl programmer. A complete in-depth coverage of this topic is well beyond the scope of this book. In fact, entire books have been written about building Perl modules. While you will learn the basics of module development in this chapter, you will really only scratch the surface. To learn more, you might want to check out the following books: *Writing Perl Modules for CPAN* (ISBN: 159059018X) and *Learning Perl Objects, References and Modules* (ISBN: 0596004788).

The problem with creating reusable code inside of subroutines like the clear_the_screen subroutine is that you end up with copies of the subroutine in all your scripts. What happens if you one day decide that you want to modify the way the clear_the_screen subroutine is written? To make the change effective in all your scripts, you will have to edit every script where the subroutine has been defined and make the same change over and over again. Modules provide a solution to this maintenance dilemma by taking the concept of code reuse to a whole new level.

TRICK

Perl modules provide the foundation for the development of object-oriented programming (OOP) in Perl. In OOP, data, and objects, along with the program code that manipulates them are all stored together as a unit. A review of OOP is well beyond the scope of this book. While many Perl modules are object oriented in their design and require that you understand OOP to use them, many modules are not object oriented or have been designed to support both object-oriented and non-object-oriented scripting. Non-object-oriented modules are modules that contain collections of subroutines and variables which you can access after importing the module into your scripts. Modules are not intended to be full-fledged scripts that are capable of running on their own. In many cases they do not include any code statements that initiate any code execution and instead depend on the host script to perform this task. The information presented in this chapter covers module development from a non-object oriented point of view.

Modules provide a container for storing code that you want to share among multiple scripts. By storing shared variables and subroutines in a module, you make the code easily accessible, and, because it exists only in one place, it is easy to maintain an update. All you have to do, for example, is change the code for a given module subroutine and the change will affect any script that uses that module subroutine. Just be sure that you thoroughly test your changes to ensure that you did not make any errors. The end result is that you can save a great deal of time by creating and maintaining shared code within modules.

Defining a New Perl Module

It is customary to name a Perl module based on what it is designed to do. As you create your own custom modules, it is important that you avoid using names assigned to publicly available Perl modules that you may use in the future. One way to avoid this scenario is to include the underscore character as part of your module names since most publicly available Perl modules do not include underscores in their names. Perl module names must be the same as the name of the file that you store them in. In addition, Perl modules have a .pm file extension. Therefore, based on these rules, you might name a Perl module that is designed to return a random number something like `Random_no.pm`. Remember that by convention, you should begin your module names with a capital letter.

Perl modules use `package` definitions as a means of organizing their contents. Usually the `package` statement is the first statement in the module. For example, the following code statements represent a small Perl module named `Random_no`.

```
package Random_no;

use strict;
our $VERSION = 0.1;
my $randomnumber = 0;

sub get_random_no {
  $randomnumber = int(rand 100) + 1;
  return $randomnumber;
}

1;
```

`Random_no` is designed to return a randomly generated number in the range of 1–100. The file that contains the module must be named after the module that it contains, so this module should be stored in a file named `Random_no.pm`. Perl modules are required to return a value of `true` to calling scripts. Many Perl statements return a value of `true` after execution. However, one common way of ensuring that a module will always return a `true` value is to end the module by adding the following statement as the last line in the file. This ensures that the module will always return a value that Perl will interpret as being equal to `true`.

```
1;
```

Take note that the third line in the `Random_no` module declares a `package` variable that can be referenced by scripts that import the module. This is accomplished using the `our` function, which declares a scalar variable and makes it publicly available outside of the module. Had the `my` function been used in place of the `our` function, the `$VERSION` variable would not have been accessible outside of the module itself. The very next statement in the module defined a scalar variable named `$randomnumber` using the `my` operator. Therefore `$randomnumber` cannot be accessed outside of the module. Instead, access to the random number generated by the module's `get_random_no` subroutine is provided via the subroutine's `return` statement. Preventing direct access to module variables is considered a good programming practice because it provides tighter control over variables and forces you to make specific values explicitly available to external scripts.

TRICK

Note the availability of the scalar variable named $VERSION in the preceding example. This variable is used to provide version information about the script. If the script were later modified, it would be appropriate to modify the value assigned to $VERSION as demonstrated here.

```
our $version = 0.2;
```

The neat thing about embedding version information inside a module is that you can recode the use statement in external scripts, as demonstrated here.

```
use Random_no 0.2;
```

The net effect of this statement is that Perl will generate an error such as "Random_no version 0.2 required--this is only version 0.1" if the module's version number is not greater than or equal to the version number required by the script.

Saving Your Custom Modules

Once you have written the code for a custom Perl module, you need to save it. Any time it is asked to retrieve a module, Perl automatically searches a specific set of directories for the module (unless you specifically tell Perl to look somewhere else). The list of directories that Perl searches is maintained in a special array variable named @INC. You can view a list of these directories by writing a small Perl script such as the one shown here.

```
foreach $i (@INC) {
  print "$i \n";
}
```

For example, on a computer running Windows, this script might generate the following output.

```
C:/Perl/lib
C:/Perl/site/lib
.
```

As you can see, in this example Perl will search, by default, in three places when looking for modules. Typically, you will want to store your custom Perl modules in directories that contain the word site. site is a keyword intended to denote locally developed Perl modules. Take note of the last line in the above output. It consists of a single dot, which represents the current working directory. What this means is that Perl will check each directory in @INC, and if it cannot find the module it is looking for, it will check to see if the module resides in the current working directory. This is a great convenience when initially developing Perl modules because it allows you to store the module and the scripts that use them together. Once you have completed testing the module and have it working like you want, you can then move the module to an appropriate directory listed in @INC.

TRICK Another option for storing your custom modules is to create a directory on the computer and then to instruct Perl to search that directory. This can be accomplished as demonstrated here.

```perl
use lib qw(C:\MyModules);
```

Here, Perl has been instructed to search in C:\MyModules for the modules. If the module is not found there, Perl will still search in each of the directories listed in @INC.

Importing and Using Custom Perl Modules

As you have already seen, you import Perl modules by using the use function and specifying the name of the module, as demonstrated in the following example,

```perl
#!/usr/bin/perl

use Random_no;

$x = Random_no::get_random_no();

print "\n\nRandom number  = $x \n\n";
print "Module Version = $Random_no::VERSION \n\n";
```

In this example, the Random_no module is imported into the script and a scalar variable named $x is assigned a random value retrieved by calling on a subroutine named get_random_no located in the Random_no module. Also, the module's version number is retrieved and displayed.

TRICK In addition to the use function, you can also use the require function to import Perl modules into your scripts. Both functions work almost identically, the primary difference between the two being that use imports a module at compile time along with the rest of the script. The require function, on the other hand, waits to import a module until it is actually needed at runtime (e.g. after the script has already begun execution). Of the two functions, it is common practice to use the use function.

USING OTHER PEOPLE'S PERL MODULES

Perl programmers are not islands unto themselves. They exist as part of a greater Perl community on which they can draw for support. Perl programmers all around the world have invested countless hours developing Perl modules to help solve a host of common problems. Many have chosen to share their work and make their Perl modules publicly available. You will find copies of these modules at www.cpan.org. At the time that I was writing this book, over 9,800 modules, contributed by more than 5,000 authors were available on CPAN.

The modules that you will find at CPAN have module names that are fairly descriptive of what they are designed to do. If you find yourself facing a programming challenge that you think other people may have also had to deal with, there is a very good chance that somebody somewhere has created a Perl module to address it. Part of being a good Perl programmer is knowing when to write code and knowing when not to write code. There is no point to reinventing the wheel. Leveraging the work performed by other programmers can make you a more efficient Perl programmer and significantly speed up development time.

When you visit CPAN, you will find thousands of modules available that cover a wide range of categories, including:

- Database interface
- Web programming
- Commercial software interface
- Socket-based programming
- Encryption algorithms
- Compression algorithms
- Graphics
- Operating system interfaces
- Security

PPM

If you are writing Perl scripts that are going to run on Windows operating systems and are using ActiveState's Perl distribution, then the easiest way to locate and install new Perl modules is to use the Perl Package Module (PPM). PPM is a utility supplied with ActiveState Perl distribution that automates the process of locating, downloading, and installing Perl modules.

The ppm utility provides access to Windows Perl modules made available at CPAN. The number of modules available via ppm is limited to a subset made up of the most popular modules. If you cannot find a module that you are looking for, you may want to search CPAN, discussed in the next section.

PPM runs as a command-line utility. To start it, enter ppm and press Enter at the Windows Command Prompt, as demonstrated in Figure 6.9.

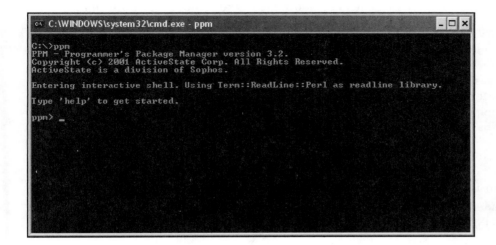

FIGURE 6.9

Using ActiveState's ppm utility, you can search for, download, and install Windows compatible Perl modules.

Once started, you can use ppm to search for Perl modules as demonstrated here.

```
ppm> search beep
Searching in Active Repositories
    1. Audio-Beep    [0.11] a module to use your computer beeper in fancy ways
    2. Audio-Beep    [0.11] Audio-Beep
```

In this example, a search is performed for a module that provides the capability to play a beep sound. As you can see, two different downloadable files are displayed. You can download and install the desired module as demonstrated here.

```
ppm> install Audio-Beep
====================
Install 'Audio-Beep' version 0.11 in ActivePerl 5.8.7.813.
====================
Downloaded 8165 bytes.
Extracting 8/8: blib/arch/auto/Audio/Beep/.exists
```

```
Installing C:\Perl\html\site\lib\Audio\Beep.html
Installing C:\Perl\html\site\lib\Audio\Beep\Win32\API.html
Installing C:\Perl\site\lib\Audio\Beep.pm
Installing C:\Perl\site\lib\Audio\Beep.pod
Installing C:\Perl\site\lib\Audio\Beep\Win32\API.pm
Successfully installed Audio-Beep version 0.11 in ActivePerl 5.8.7.813.
ppm>
```

Once installed, you can begin using the Perl module just like any of Perl's built-in modules.

TRICK Because Perl modules are developed by a host of different Perl programmers worldwide, you will find that the quality of documentation provided with each module varies substantially. You can view this documentation once the module has been installed using perldoc. You can also view the documentation associated with specific Perl modules at www.cpan.org/modules/. This documentation includes a description of the module, instructions for using it, as well as any instructions that you'll need to follow in order to install the module.

Some modules are dependent on other modules already being installed. The module's documentation should tell you if this is the case. For example, in order to use the Audio::Beep module downloaded in the previous example, you also need to download and install the Win-32-API module, which you can do using ppm. Once this is done you can import the Audio::Beep module and execute its beep function as demonstrated here.

```
#!/usr/bin/perl
use Audio::Beep;
beep;
```

CPAN

When you are working with Unix or Linux, the easiest way to install new Perl modules is to use a Perl utility named CPAN, which helps to automate the process of finding, downloading, and installing Perl modules. To begin using CPAN, enter the following command.

```
perl -MCPAN -e shell
```

TRICK Remember that under the covers, Mac OS X is really just a Unix operating system. Therefore, you can install Perl modules on Mac OS X Perl installations using the cpan utility just as you can do on Linux and Unix.

In order to install Perl modules, you usually need root authority on the computer on which you are working. The first time you use the CPAN utility, you will be prompted to answer a number of questions in order to configure CPAN and specify the websites that should be used when retrieving new Perl modules, as demonstrated in Figure 6.10. Read each question carefully and answer as best you can. In most situations, the default answers will be just fine.

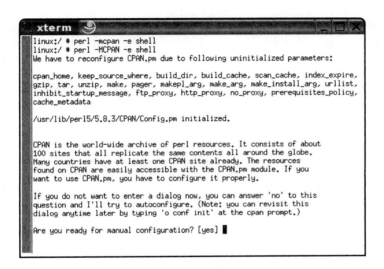

FIGURE 6.10

Using the CPAN utility you can search for, download, and install Perl modules.

Once you have finished answering the required configuration questions, you will be presented with the CPAN prompt shown here.

```
cpan>
```

At this point, you can begin searching for new Perl modules using the following syntax.

```
i /keyword/
```

Keyword represents a word that is part of the module names. Fortunately, Perl modules are generally given names that describe their purpose or function, which helps make the process of searching for new Perl modules fairly straightforward. For example, you might search for a Perl module that provides an HTML template for CGI scripting as shown below. (CGI stands for Common Gateway Interface and is a standard for developing interface web programs.)

```
cpan> i /HTML::Template/
```

Once you have found a module that you want to download and install, you can do so using the install command, as demonstrated below.

```
cpan> install HTML::Template
```

CPAN will then attempt to download and install the specified module. If the install is successful, you can begin using the new Perl module as described by its documentation.

 While you can install a great many Perl modules using the CPAN utility, there are a number of modules that won't install using CPAN. For these modules you will have to download and install them manually. Sometimes this just means retrieving the module from the downloaded archive file and moving it into one of the directories associated with @INC. Other times, you may have to compile the modules using a C compiler. Compiling C modules is well outside the scope of this book. To find specific instructions for a given module, refer to installation instructions provided as part of the module's online documentation at www.cpan.org/modules.

BACK TO THE ROCK, PAPER, SCISSORS GAME

Okay, let's turn our attention back to the development of the Rock, Paper, Scissors game. This game is based on the popular children's game of the same name. The game pits the player against the computer. The object of the game is for the player to attempt to out guess the computer by selecting superior choices each time a new round (or game) is played.

The rules for this game are quite simple. When prompted, the player enters a choice of Rock, Paper, or Scissors. The script then generates a random answer on behalf of the computer. The player's and computer's choices are then compared and a winner is determined using the criteria specified in Table 6.1.

TABLE 6.1   SCORING RULES FOR THE ROCK, PAPER, SCISSORS GAME

Player Choice	Computer Choice	Results	Explanation
Rock	Rock	Tie	-
Rock	Scissors	Player Wins	Rock breaks scissors
Rock	Paper	Player Loses	Paper covers rock
Paper	Paper	Tie	-
Paper	Rock	Player Wins	Paper covers rock
Paper	Scissors	Player Loses	Scissors cut paper
Scissors	Scissors	Tie	-
Scissors	Paper	Player Wins	Scissors cut paper
Scissors	Rock	Player Loses	Rock breaks scissors

Building the Clear_the_screen Module

The Rock, Paper, Scissors game will require the ability to clear the screen at various points of the game. In previous game scripts this has been accomplished by adding a copy of the clear_the_screen subroutine to each script. Since this chapter has focused on the development of modules, let's take a different approach and replace the clear_the_screen subroutine with a statement that imports a custom module that performs the screen clearing tasks. The code for this module file, which will be named Clear_the_screen.pm, is outlined here.

```
package Clear_the_screen;

#This subroutine clears the screen by adding 25 blank lines
sub clear {

  for ($i=0; $i < 25; ++$i){  #Loop 25 times
    print "\n";  #Print out a blank line
  }

}

1;
```

As you can see, this module consists of a package definition with a copy of the original clear_the_screen subroutine embedded inside. Once you have created and saved this module, you can move on to the next section and begin developing the rest of the Rock, Paper, Scissors game.

Designing the Game

The construction and development of the Rock, Paper, Scissors game will be completed in 13 steps:

1. Creating a new script.
2. Developing controlling logic.
3. Creating the main_menu subroutine.
4. Creating the play_the_game subroutine.
5. Creating the get_player_choice subroutine.
6. Creating the validate_player_choice subroutine.
7. Creating the generate_number subroutine.
8. Creating the determine_winner subroutine.
9. Creating the assign_computer_choice subroutine.

10. Creating the `display_result` subroutine.
11. Creating the `display_stats` subroutine.
12. Creating the `display_help` subroutine.
13. Creating the `display_about` subroutine.

Creating the Script File

The first step in developing the Rock, Paper, Scissors game is to create a new script file named RPS.pl and to add the following code statements to it.

```perl
#!/usr/bin/perl
#
# The Rock Paper Scissors Game (RPS.pl)

use Clear_the_screen;

$plays = 0;
$wins = 0;
$losses = 0;
$ties = 0;

$isvalid = 0;
```

As you can see, after the shebang and the rest of the opening comment statements, the `use` function is used to import the `Clear_the_screen` module you just created. Next, four global scalar variables are declared. The first three scalar variables will be used to keep track of game statistics and the fourth scalar variable will be used to control the execution of a `while` loop (created in the next section) that controls the overall execution of the game.

Controlling Game Play

The next step in creating the Rock, Paper, Scissors game is to set up a `while` loop that processes player commands and controls game execution based on those commands. The code statements that make up this loop are shown here.

```perl
while (! $isvalid) {

  my $choice = "";

  Clear_the_screen::clear();

  $choice = lc (&main_menu());
```

```perl
if ($choice eq "play") {

    &play_the_game();

} elsif ($choice eq "quit") {

    &display_stats();
    $isvalid = 1;

} elsif ($choice eq "help") {

    Clear_the_screen::clear();
    &display_help();

} elsif ($choice eq "about") {

    Clear_the_screen::clear();
    &display_about();

}

}
```

As you can see, the while loop has been set up to execute for as long as the value assigned to $valid is not equal to true. The first statement inside this loop declares a private scalar variable used to store commands entered by the player. Next, the clear subroutine located inside the Clear_the_screen module is executed. Then, a scalar variable named $choice is assigned a value returned by the main_menu subroutine (after being converted to lowercase).

The rest of the loop consists of an if…elsif code block that determines which script subroutines are executed based on the command entered by the player.

Building the Game's Main Menu

The code statements that make up the script's main_menu subroutine are shown here.

```perl
sub main_menu {

    my $reply = "";
```

```
print "          ";
print " Welcome to the  R O C K    P A P E R    S C I S S O R S    G A M E";
print " \n\n\n\n\n\n\n\n\n\n\n\n";
print " [Play] [Quit] [Help] [About]\n\n";
print " Enter command: ";

chomp($reply = <STDIN>);

return $reply;

}
```

The first statement in this subroutine declares a private variable named $reply, which is used to store the command entered by the player. Next, a series of print statements displays a menu made up of four options. The subroutine ends by returning the command entered by the player.

Controlling Game Play

The play_the_game subroutine, shown below, is responsible for controlling the play of individual games played between the player and the computer.

```
sub play_the_game {

  my $isover = 0;
  my $playerchoice = "";
  my $computerchoice = "";
  my $winner = "";
  my $evaluation = "";

  until ($isover) {

    Clear_the_screen::clear();

    $playerchoice = &get_player_choice();
    $evaluation = &validate_player_choice($playerchoice);

    if ($evaluation  eq "invalid") {
      next;
    }
```

```
if ($evaluation  eq "stop") {
  $isover = 1;
  next;
}

$computerchoice = &generate_number();

$computerchoice = &assign_computer_choice($computerchoice);

$winner = &determine_winner($playerchoice, $computerchoice);

Clear_the_screen::clear();

&display_result($playerchoice, $computerchoice, $winner);

  }

}
```

This subroutine begins by declaring five private variables. Next, an until loop is established that executes until the player enters the Back command. The first statement in the loop executes the clear subroutine located inside the Clear_the_screen module. The next statement executes the subroutine responsible for collecting the player's choice (of Rock, Paper, or Scissors). The command supplied by the player is then evaluated by this subroutine and checked to see if the player submitted an invalid command or if the player entered the Back command, signaling a decision to stop gameplay.

Next, the generate_number subroutine is called. This subroutine generates a number in the range of 1 to 3, representing the computer's choice. The assign_computer_choice subroutine is then called in order to associate the number representing the computer's choice with a valid game choice. Once both the player's and computer's choices have been made, the determine_winner subroutine is called and passed both choices. Finally, the clear_the_screen module's clear subroutine is called and then the display_result subroutine is executed in order to inform the player of the results of the game.

Collecting Player Choices

The code statements for the get_player_choice subroutine are shown here.

```perl
sub get_player_choice {

  my  $choice = "";

  Clear_the_screen::clear();

  print " [Rock] [Paper] [Scissors] [Back]\n\n";
  print " Enter your choice: ";

  chomp($choice = <STDIN>);

  return lc ($choice);

}
```

This subroutine is responsible for prompting the player to enter a selection of Rock, Paper, or Scissors. In addition, an option of Back is also presented, allowing the player to discontinue gameplay. The player's command is converted to lowercase and then returned to the calling statement located in the play_the_game subroutine.

Validating Player Choices

The validate_player_choice subroutine is responsible for determining whether the player entered a valid or invalid command or whether the player entered the Back command.

```perl
sub validate_player_choice {

  my $choice = $_[0];

  if ($choice eq "rock") {
    return "valid";
  } elsif ($choice eq "paper") {
     return "valid";
  } elsif ($choice eq "scissors") {
     return "valid";
  } elsif ($choice eq "back") {
    return "stop";
  } else {
```

```
    return "invalid";
  }

}
```

Generating Computer Game Choices

The code for the generate_number subroutine, shown below, should look familiar to you by now. It is responsible for generating a random number in the range of 1 to 3 in much the same way as you have seen random numbers generated in previous game scripts.

```
sub generate_number {

  my $randomnumber = 0;

  return $randomnumber = int(rand 3) + 1;

}
```

Determining Who Won the Game

The determine_winner subroutine is responsible for figuring out whether the player or computer won (or tied) in the last game played.

```
sub determine_winner {

  my ($player, $computer) = @_;

  CASE: {

  $player eq "rock" && do {
    if ($computer eq "rock") {
      $ties += 1;
      return "tie";
    } elsif ($computer eq "scissors") {
      $wins += 1;
      return "win";
    } elsif ($computer eq "paper") {
      $losses += 1;
      return "lose";
    }
```

```
      last CASE;
    };

    $player eq "paper" && do {
      if ($computer eq "rock") {
        $wins += 1;
        return "win";
      } elsif ($computer eq "scissors") {
        $losses += 1;
        return "lose";
      } elsif ($computer eq "paper") {
        $ties += 1;
        return "tie";
      }
      last CASE;
    };

    $player eq "scissors" && do {
      if ($computer eq "rock") {
        $losses += 1;
        return "lose";
      } elsif ($computer eq "scissors") {
        $ties += 1;
        return "tie";
      } elsif ($computer eq "paper") {
        $wins += 1;
        return "win";
      }
      last CASE;
    };

  }

}
```

As you can see, the code statements that make up this subroutine are organized into a custom-developed Case code block. A total of nine different scenarios are examined in order to determine the winner of the game.

Associating the Computer's Choice with a Valid Game Selection

The assign_computer_choice subroutine takes a randomly generated number passed to it as an argument and then associates it with one of three possible choices, thus assigning the computer's choice.

```perl
sub assign_computer_choice {

my $computerpick = $_[0];

  if ($computerpick == 1) {
    return "rock";
  } elsif ($computerpick == 2) {
    return "paper";
  } elsif ($computerpick == 3) {
    return "scissors";
  }


}
```

Displaying Game Results

The display_result subroutine is responsible for telling the player who won or lost (or tied) the game. It does so by displaying the scalar values passed to the subroutine as arguments.

```perl
sub display_result {

  my ($playermove, $computermove, $results) = @_;
  my $row = "_" x 75;

  Clear_the_screen::clear();

  print " $row\n\n";

  print " Scoring Rules:\n\n";
  print " 1. Rock equals Rock, Paper equals Paper and Scissors";
  print " equal Scissors.\n";
  print " 2. Rock breaks scissors to win.\n";
  print " 3. Paper covers rock to win.\n\n";

  print " $row\n\n\n\n\n";
```

```
print " Player pick:    $playermove\n\n";
print " Computer pick: $computermove\n\n";

print " Result:        You $results!\n\n\n\n";

print " Press Enter to continue: ";

chomp($reply = <STDIN>);

}
```

Displaying Game Statistics

The display_stats subroutine is called only at the end of the script, once the player has decided to stop the script's execution. This is accomplished by displaying the values of three global scalar variables that store values representing the number of games won, lost, and tied.

```
sub display_stats {

  my $row = "_" x 75;

  Clear_the_screen::clear();

  print " GAME RESULTS:\n\n";

  print " $row\n\n";

  print " No. of Wins:   $wins\n\n";
  print " No. of Losses: $losses\n\n";
  print " No. of Ties:   $ties\n\n";

  print " $row\n\n\n\n\n\n\n\n\n\n";

  chomp($reply = <STDIN>);

}
```

Developing the Help Screen

The code statements that make up the display_help subroutine consist of two private scalar variables and a series of print statements.

```perl
sub display_help {

  my $reply = 0;
  my $row = "_" x 61;

  print " ROCK, PAPER, SCISSORS HELP:\n\n";
  print " $row\n\n";
  print " Type Play to begin the game or type Quit to exit. To get help\n";
  print " type Help and to learn more about the game and its developer\n";
  print " type About.\n";
  print " $row\n\n";
  print "\n\n\n\n\n\n\n\n\n\n\n";


  print " Press Enter to continue: ";
  chomp($reply = <STDIN>);

}
```

Providing Information About the Game

The display_about subroutine is very similar to the display_help subroutine, differing only in the content of the text displayed by its print statements.

```perl
sub display_about {

  my $reply = 0;
  my $row = "_" x 61;

  print " ABOUT THE ROCK, PAPER, SCISSORS GAME:\n\n";
  print " $row\n\n";
  print " The Rock, Paper, Scissors Game - Copyright 2006.\n\n";
  print " Created by Jerry Lee Ford, Jr.\n";
  print " $row\n\n";
  print "\n\n\n\n\n\n\n\n\n\n\n";

  print " Press Enter to continue: ";
  chomp($reply = <STDIN>);

}
```

The Final Result

At this point, the Rock, Paper, Scissors game is complete. If you haven't done so already, save the game's script file. A complete copy of the RPS.pl script is listed below. It has been enhanced through the addition of an organizational script template and comments that document key functionality and make the script easier to read and understand.

```perl
#!/usr/bin/perl
#
# The Rock Paper Scissors Game (RPS.pl)


#-----------------------------------------------------------------------
# Initialization Section
#-----------------------------------------------------------------------

use Clear_the_screen;  #Import module responsible for clearing the screen

$plays = 0;    #Global variable used to track the number of games played
$wins = 0;     #Global variable used to track the number of games won
$losses = 0;   #Global variable used to track the number of games lost
$ties = 0;     #Global variable used to track the number of games tied

#Global variable used to control the loop in the Main Processing Section
$isvalid = 0;


#-----------------------------------------------------------------------
# MAIN Processing Section
#-----------------------------------------------------------------------

while (! $isvalid) { #Loop until the player enters the "quit" command

  my $choice = "";     #Local variable used to store the player menu command

  Clear_the_screen::clear(); #Module subroutine that clears the screen

  $choice = lc (&main_menu());  #Retrieve player's menu command
```

```perl
    if ($choice eq "play") {  #Determine if the player entered "Play"

        &play_the_game();  #Call subroutine that controls gameplay

    } elsif ($choice eq "quit") {  #Determine if the player entered "Quit"

        &display_stats();  #Call subroutine that displays game statistics
        $isvalid = 1;    #Time to prepare to exit the while loop

    } elsif ($choice eq "help") {  #Determine if the player entered "Help"

        Clear_the_screen::clear();  #Module subroutine that clears the screen
        &display_help();  #Call subroutine that displays help information

    } elsif ($choice eq "about") {   #Determine if the player entered "About"

        Clear_the_screen::clear();  #Module subroutine that clears the screen
        &display_about();  #Call subroutine that displays game information

    }

}


#-------------------------------------------------------------------------
# Subroutine Section
#-------------------------------------------------------------------------

#Display the game's main menu system
sub main_menu {

    #Declare subroutine local variables
    my $reply = "";  #Local variable that stores the player's menu command

    print "        ";
    print " Welcome to the  R O C K   P A P E R   S C I S S O R S   G A M E";
    print " \n\n\n\n\n\n\n\n\n\n\n\n";
    print " [Play] [Quit] [Help] [About]\n\n";
```

```perl
  print " Enter command: ";

  chomp($reply = <STDIN>);  #Collect the player's command

  return $reply;  #Return the command entered by the player

}


#This subroutine controls player and computer play
sub play_the_game {

  #Declare subroutine local variables
  my $isover = 0;  #Local variable that controls the subroutine's loop
  my $playerchoice = "";  #Local variable that holds the player's move
  my $computerchoice = "";  #Local variable that holds the computer's move
  my $winner = "";  #Local variable that stores a string indicating who won
  my $evaluation = "";  #Local variable that stores evaluation of player move

until ($isover) {  #Loop until the player decides to stop playing

    Clear_the_screen::clear();  #Module subroutine that clears the screen

    #Call subroutine that collects the player's selection
    $playerchoice = &get_player_choice();

#Call subroutine that validates the player's selection
    $evaluation = &validate_player_choice($playerchoice);

    #Restart the loop if the player made an invalid selection
    if ($evaluation  eq "invalid") {
      next;
    }

    #Terminate loop execution if the player elects to stop playing
    if ($evaluation  eq "stop") {
      $isover = 1;
```

```perl
      next;
   }

   #Call subroutine that generates the player's selection
   $computerchoice = &generate_number();

   #Associate computer selection with a valid move (rock, paper, scissors)
   $computerchoice = &assign_computer_choice($computerchoice);

   #Call subroutine that determines who has won the game
   $winner = &determine_winner($playerchoice, $computerchoice);

   Clear_the_screen::clear(); #Module subroutine that clears the screen

   #Call subroutine that displays the game results
   &display_result($playerchoice, $computerchoice, $winner);

  }

}


#This subroutine is responsible for collecting the player's move
sub get_player_choice {

  #Declare subroutine local variables
  my $choice = "";   #Local variable that stores the player's menu command

  Clear_the_screen::clear(); #Module subroutine that clears the screen

  print " [Rock] [Paper] [Scissors] [Back]\n\n";
  print " Enter your choice: ";

  chomp($choice = <STDIN>);

  #Return command entered by the player after converting it to lowercase
```

```perl
    return lc ($choice);

}



#This subroutine evaluates the player's move and returns its analysis
sub validate_player_choice {

  #Declare subroutine local variables
  my $choice = $_[0];     #Local variable passed the game selection
                          #made by the player

  if ($choice eq "rock") {   #A selection of rock is valid
    return "valid";
  } elsif ($choice eq "paper") {   #A selection of paper is valid
     return "valid";
  } elsif ($choice eq "scissors") {   #A selection of scissors is valid
     return "valid";
  } elsif ($choice eq "back") {   #A selection of back ends game play
    return "stop";
  } else {
    return "invalid";   #Any other selection is invalid
  }

}



#This subroutine is responsible for generating the computer's selection
sub generate_number {

  #Declare subroutine local variables
  my $randomnumber = 0;  #Local variable user to store a random number

  #Return a random number between 1 and 3
  return $randomnumber = int(rand 3) + 1;

}
```

```perl
#This subroutine is responsible for determining who won the game
sub determine_winner {

  #Declare subroutine local variables
  my ($player, $computer) = @_;   #Player and computer moves are
                                  #passed as arguments


  CASE: {

  $player eq "rock" && do {   #Determine winner if player picks rock
    if ($computer eq "rock") {
      $ties += 1;
      return "tie";
    } elsif ($computer eq "scissors") {
      $wins += 1;
      return "win";
    } elsif ($computer eq "paper") {
      $losses += 1;
      return "lose";
    }
    last CASE;   #End custom CASE block if a winner has been found
  };

  $player eq "paper" && do {   #Determine winner if player picks paper
    if ($computer eq "rock") {
      $wins += 1;
      return "win";
    } elsif ($computer eq "scissors") {
      $losses += 1;
      return "lose";
    } elsif ($computer eq "paper") {
      $ties += 1;
      return "tie";
    }
    last CASE;   #End custom CASE block if a winner has been found
  };

  $player eq "scissors" && do { #Determine winner if player picks scissors
```

```perl
    if ($computer eq "rock") {
      $losses += 1;
      return "lose";
    } elsif ($computer eq "scissors") {
      $ties += 1;
      return "tie";
    } elsif ($computer eq "paper") {
      $wins += 1;
      return "win";
    }
    last CASE;  #End custom CASE block if a winner has been found
  };

  }

}


#This subroutine associates the computer's selection with a game selection
sub assign_computer_choice {

  #Declare subroutine local variables
  my $computerpick = $_[0]; #Computer's selection is passed as an argument

  #If the computer's selection is 1, assign a selection of rock
  if ($computerpick == 1) {
    return "rock";
  #If the computer's selection is 2, assign a selection of paper
  } elsif ($computerpick == 2) {
    return "paper";
  #If the computer's selection is 3, assign a selection of scissors
  } elsif ($computerpick == 3) {
    return "scissors";
  }

}
```

```perl
#This subroutine displays the results of each individual game
sub display_result {

    #Declare subroutine local variables
    my ($playermove, $computermove, $results) = @_;
    my $row = "_" x 75;

    Clear_the_screen::clear(); #Module subroutine that clears the screen

    print " $row\n\n";

    print " Scoring Rules:\n\n";
    print " 1. Rock equals Rock, Paper equals Paper and Scissors";
    print " equal Scissors.\n";
    print " 2. Rock breaks scissors to win.\n";
    print " 3. Paper covers rock to win.\n\n";

    print " $row\n\n\n\n\n";

    print " Player pick:   $playermove\n\n";
    print " Computer pick: $computermove\n\n";

    print " Result:       You $results!\n\n\n\n";

    print " Press Enter to continue: ";

    chomp($reply = <STDIN>);  #Pause game until the player presses Enter

}


#This subroutine displays statistics for all games played
sub display_stats {

    #Declare subroutine local variables
    my $row = "_" x 75;

    Clear_the_screen::clear(); #Module subroutine that clears the screen
```

```perl
    print " GAME RESULTS:\n\n";

    print " $row\n\n";

    print " No. of Wins:    $wins\n\n";
    print " No. of Losses: $losses\n\n";
    print " No. of Ties:    $ties\n\n";

    print " $row\n\n\n\n\n\n\n\n\n\n";

    chomp($reply = <STDIN>);  #Pause game until the player presses Enter

}


#This subroutine displays help information about the game
sub display_help {

    #Declare subroutine local variables
    my $reply = 0;
    my $row = "_" x 61;

    print " ROCK, PAPER, SCISSORS HELP:\n\n";
    print " $row\n\n";
    print " Type Play to begin the game or type Quit to exit. To get help\n";
    print " type Help and to learn more about the game and its developer\n";
    print " type About.\n";
    print " $row\n\n";
    print "\n\n\n\n\n\n\n\n\n\n";


    print " Press Enter to continue: ";
    chomp($reply = <STDIN>);  #Pause game until the player presses Enter

}
```

```
#This subroutine displays additional information about the game
sub display_about {

    #Declare subroutine local variables
    my $reply = 0;
    my $row = "_" x 61;

    print " ABOUT THE ROCK, PAPER, SCISSORS GAME:\n\n";
    print " $row\n\n";
    print " The Rock, Paper, Scissors Game - Copyright 2006.\n\n";
    print " Created by Jerry Lee Ford, Jr.\n";
    print " $row\n\n";
    print "\n\n\n\n\n\n\n\n\n\n";

    print " Press Enter to continue: ";
    chomp($reply = <STDIN>);  #Pause game until the player presses Enter

}
```

At this point, assuming that you have not made any typos when keying it in, your copy of
RPS.pl should be ready to run. So, go ahead and see how it works. Not only do you have another
quality Perl game to add to your collection of scripts, but you also have a working example
of a custom-developed module which you can use in the development of new game scripts.

SUMMARY

In this chapter you learned how to define custom packages and to use them as a tool for
managing global variables. You learned how to import and access variables and subroutines
stored in the Perl library in order save yourself the trouble of reinventing the wheel as you
develop new Perl scripts. You also learned how to locate and download modules developed
by other Perl programmers. This included learning the basics of module installation. On top
of all this, you learned how to create your own custom modules and to use them to create
your own library of local modules. In doing so, you learned how to develop Perl scripts that
are easier to update and maintain. Finally, you finished the chapter by learning how to create
the Rock, Paper, Scissors game.

Before you move on to Chapter 7, "Regular Expressions," why not set aside a little extra time
to work on the following list of challenges in order to improve the Rock, Paper, Scissors game
and make it a little more fun.

CHALLENGES

1. Currently, the Rock, Paper, Scissors game displays game statistics even if the player quits without playing a single game. Prevent this action by adding logic that checks to make sure that at least one game has been played before displaying game statistics. Hint: Check out the Pick a Number script created in Chapter 5 for an example of one way to implement this feature.

2. Add an option to the game's main menu that allows the player to view game statistics at any time, rather than just at the end of the game.

3. As it is currently written, the Rock, Paper, Scissors game simply redisplays its menu system whenever the player enters an invalid command. To make the game more user-friendly, display a message that tells the player when an invalid command has been entered.

4. Spruce up the Help and About screens, adding additional information that the player will find useful.

Part
III

Advanced Topics

## CHAPTER 7

REGULAR EXPRESSIONS

U p to this point in the book, each of the game scripts that you have worked on has used data provided by the player which was more or less accepted as is. A limited amount of effort went in to validating the data provided by the player and ensuring that it was within expected parameters. In this chapter, you will learn how to improve your Perl scripts by using regular expressions to validate and analyze player input. The information that you'll learn can also be applied to many other programming aspects, such as validating text stored in any string or text file. Regardless of the source of the data, regular expressions are one of your primary tools for analyzing data. In addition to learning the theory behind regular expressions, you will also get the chance to put to practical use some of what you will learn through the development of the Lottery Picker game.

Specifically, you will learn how to:

- Build a variety of simple regular expression patterns
- Build regular expression patterns that match groups of characters or that match more than one instance of characters
- Work with metacharacters when building regular expression patterns
- Apply regular expression patterns as a controlling mechanism for conditional and loop control blocks

PROJECT PREVIEW: THE LOTTERY PICKER GAME

This chapter's game project is the Lottery Picker game. Its purpose is to automate the generation of lottery tickets. The game begins by prompting the player to specify how many lottery tickets she wishes to purchase. It then asks the player how many numbers are required to fill out a ticket. The game expects the player to enter numeric data, and it performs several input validation routines to ensure that only valid data is accepted.

Once both questions have been answered, the game generates the requested lottery tickets. The overall logical execution of the game is demonstrated in Figures 7.1 to 7.5. Figure 7.1 shows the game's opening screen, which welcomes the user and prompts her to begin gameplay.

FIGURE 7.1

The Lottery Picker game running on Linux.

Before proceeding, the game needs to know how many lottery tickets the player wants it to generate, as demonstrated in Figure 7.2.

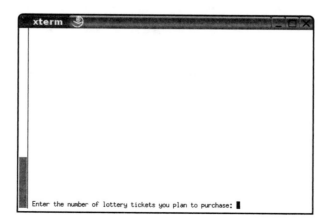

FIGURE 7.2

The Lottery Picker game will generate a list of up to 25 unique lottery tickets.

Next, the player is required to tell the game how many numbers it needs to generate in order to fill out a lottery ticket, as shown in Figure 7.3.

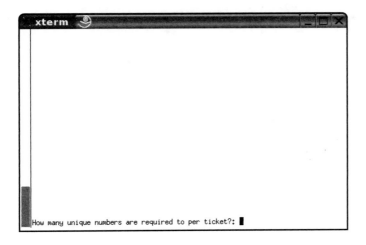

FIGURE 7.3

Because no two lottery games are the same, the Lottery Picker game requires that the player specify how many numbers make up a ticket.

Once both of the game's questions have been answered, it has all the information it needs. A list of lottery tickets is then displayed, as demonstrated in Figure 7.4.

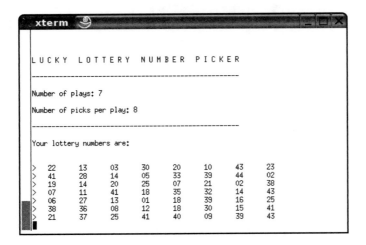

FIGURE 7.4

Once it has all the information it needs, the game generates unique lists of lottery numbers.

Finally, the game ends only after pausing to display a little information about itself and its author, as shown in Figure 7.5.

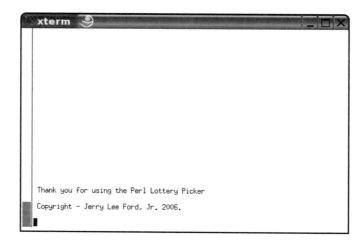

FIGURE 7.5

The game ends by displaying copyright information.

INTRODUCING REGULAR EXPRESSIONS

The scripts that you have developed up to this point in the book have all involved interacting with the user from the operating system Command Prompt in order to collect data needed for the scripts to execute. However, there are plenty of other sources of data, such as files and databases.

Regardless of where a script pulls its data from, there are going to be times where you will need to validate the data in order to make sure that it matches certain predefined criteria. In previous scripts you have performed different levels of data validation based on expected input. What I mean by this is that up to this point you have either presented the player with a specific set of valid responses such as Play, Quit, Help, and About or you have limited the range of responses to something like 1 to 100. By only accepting specific input, it is relatively easy to set up conditional code blocks to look for just those specific valid inputs and to reject all others. For example, in the Rock, Paper, Scissors game, you rejected as invalid any player selection (stored in all lowercase characters in a scalar variable named $choice) not equal to rock, paper, scissors, or back.

```perl
if ($choice eq "rock") {
  return "valid";
} elsif ($choice eq "paper") {
  return "valid";
} elsif ($choice eq "scissors") {
  return "valid";
} elsif ($choice eq "back") {
  return "stop";
```

```
} else {
  return "invalid";
}
```

Unfortunately, there will be times where you will not be able to count on working with restricted types of data. Instead, you may have to accept any of a host of different inputs. Still, this does not mean that you cannot perform some very sophisticated validation checking. For example, if you develop a script that requires the user to enter numeric input, you could check to ensure that the user did not supply alphabetic or special characters as part of the input. To accomplish this type of validation, you need a new tool in your programming toolbox: regular expressions. A *regular expression* is a pattern used to describe matching data.

> **Regular expressions are not unique to Perl. Regular expressions are used in numerous other programming languages, such as Java, Visual Basic .NET, Python, Visual Basic .C#, and Ruby. If you already have experience working with regular expressions in one of these or in any other programming language, you should not have a problem using them with Perl.**

Using regular expressions, also referred to as *regexps* or *REs*, you can search for extremely specific information using an absolute minimum of code. For example, you can define regular expression patterns that you can then use to:

- Perform validation of user input
- Search and replace pieces of strings
- Keep counts of instances of patterns
- Extract a substring from a larger string

TRICK

Regular expressions represents a topic that is too large to completely cover in just a single chapter of this book. A true, in-depth discussion of regular expressions merits its own book. In fact several good books have been dedicated to this topic alone. If you are interested in learning more, you might want to check out: *Mastering Regular Expressions, Second Edition* (ISBN: 0596002890), *Beginning Regular Expressions* (ISBN: 0764574892), and *Regular Expression Recipes: A Problem-Solution Approach* (ISBN: 159059441X).

Matching Simple Patterns

There are a few things you need to know about the manner in which regular expressions are evaluated. For starters, regular expression patterns are generally processed in a left to right order. A match occurs if the specified pattern is found anywhere in the source string. In addition, matches are, by default, case sensitive, and every character inside a pattern is taken literally, except for metacharacters, which have special meaning. However, metacharacters can be escaped (preceded with an \) in order to force them to be interpreted literally. You'll learn more about metacharacters and how to use them when building patterns shortly.

Creating Simple Patterns

The most basic regular expression pattern is one that matches against a specific pattern or one or more characters. This type of pattern is constructed using the m// match operator, which has the following syntax.

```
m/pattern/
```

For example, consider the following pattern.

```
m/ABC/
```

This pattern would match any string containing the capital letters A, B, and C, consecutively. If a match is found, a value of true is returned. Otherwise, a value of false is returned. To use this pattern to search for a match in a string, you would need to use it in a manner similar to the example shown here.

```
if ("Now I know my ABCs" =~ m/ABC/) {
  print "We have a match!";
}
```

Here the string "Now I know my ABCs" is searched to see if it contains ABC, which of course it does. Note the use of the =~ operator. This is a pattern-matching operator that looks for equality. Another pattern-matching operator that you should be familiar with is the !~ operator, which is used to perform "not equal" pattern-matching operations.

Shorter Pattern Footprints

In Perl, there is always another way to get something done. Perl's interaction with regular expressions is no exception. When you are creating simple pattern matches, as was done in the preceding example, the m part of m// is considered optional and is typically left off. Therefore, the previous example could be rewritten as shown here.

```
if ("Now I know my ABCs" =~ /ABC/) {
  print "We have a match!";
}
```

In addition, if you leave off the source string that is to be matched up against, the special $_ variable is used instead. When using the $_ variable, the =~ pattern-matching operator becomes optional. Therefore, the example shown here

```perl
if ("Now I know my ABCs" =~ m/ABC/) {
  print "We have a match!";
}
```

is functionally equivalent to this example, where both the m and the =~ have been eliminated.

```perl
$_ = "Now I know my ABCs";
if (/ABC/) {
  print "We have a match!";
}
```

As you can see, the second of these two examples requires fewer keystrokes. The tradeoff is that it is a little more difficult to figure out what is happening. You'll find that in the majority of the cases, Perl programmers will use the more cryptic style in place of the longer, more formal style. The good news is that it shouldn't take you long to get used to working with regular expressions, so after a while these kinds of patterns will become second nature.

TRICK

Remember that $_ is used by Perl as the default data source (variable) in a number of different situations. For example, if you do not specify a variable to store each element in an array when processing it with a foreach loop, $_ is used. Therefore, you could display each element in an array as demonstrated here.

```perl
foreach (@username) {
  print "$_";
  print "\n";
}
```

Note also that the print function also used $_ by default in the absence of any input. This means that you could rewrite the previous example as shown below and get the same results.

```perl
foreach (@username) {
  print;
  print "\n";
}
```

WORKING WITH METACHARACTERS

Most every character that you can place inside a pattern will match itself. However, one exception to this rule is metacharacters. A *metacharacter* is a character that changes the way pattern matches occur. For example, take a look at the following example.

```perl
if ("Please show Mrs. Ford to her seat." =~ m/Mr./) {
  print "Match!";
}
```

Here, the intention was to set up a pattern that matched up against the word Mr.. However, the . character is a metacharacter. It is used to create patterns that match any one character. Therefore, Mrs, Mr., Mrx will all match the /Mr./ pattern. In order to literally match the . character and prevent it from being treated as a metacharacter, you must escape it by preceding it with a \. So, you can fix the previous example so that only Mr. will match the pattern by escaping the . as shown below.

```perl
if ("Please show Mr. Ford to his seat." =~ m/Mr\./) {
  print "Match!";
}
```

TRICK You can also replace the opening and closing / characters in a pattern with another character. So instead of

```perl
m/Mr\./
```

you might write

```perl
m<Mr\.>
```

As you can see, even in this simple example, the combination of forward and backward slashes tends to make things confusing. By eliminating the / characters from the mix, the statement becomes easier to read.

The . character is just one of many metacharacters that you need to know about. Here's a list of the metacharacters you'll need to become familiar with.

```
^        (    )    \
|        $    [    {
?        .    +    *
```

Matching Patterns at the Beginning of a String

As has already been stated, regular expression patterns return a match if the pattern being searched for is found anywhere in the search string. However, there may be times in which you want to exercise control over where matches are allowed to occur. Using the ^ metacharacter, you can set up a pattern that only matches if its expression is found at the beginning of the search string. For example, a pattern of /^Please/ will result in a match only if it is found at the beginning of the search string, as demonstrated here.

```
if ("Please show Mrs. Ford to her seat." =~ /^Please/) {
  print "Match!";
}
```

On the other hand, a pattern of /^show/ will not result in a match since it does not occur at the beginning of the search string.

```
if ("Please show Mrs. Ford to her seat." =~ /^show/) {
  print "Match!";
}
```

Matching Patterns at the End of a String

You can just as easily reverse the above logic to instead restrict pattern matches to the end of the search string by using the $ metacharacter. For example, a pattern of /her seat\.$/ will result in a match only if the word her, followed by a blank space and then the word seat, with a closing period is found at the end of the search string, as demonstrated below.

```
if ("Please show Mrs. Ford to her seat." =~ /her seat\.$/) {
  print "Match!";
}
```

Note that in the pattern that the period (.) character, which is itself a metacharacter, was escaped in order to force the pattern to interpret it literally as a period.

TRICK You can combine the ^ and & metacharacters to produce more specific pattern matches. For example, /^winner$/ will only match a search string that contains only the word winner. Likewise, the /^$/ pattern will only match against empty strings (e.g. "").

TRICK In addition to ^ and $, you can also use the \b and \B metacharacter shortcuts to apply pattern matches on a word and non-word boundary. A word boundary is the position between a character or sequence of characters and a different character (as denoted by white space or some form of punctuation). For example, /at/ will match the sequential occurrence of the characters at if they occur anywhere in the search string. On the other hand, /\bat/ will only match the sequential occurrence of the characters if they are preceded by a blank space or a punctuation character, as demonstrated in the following strings.

```
He is at the store.
He is uncertain at which time he should arrive.
```

However, /\bat/ will not match anything in the following string.

```
It does not matter that Matt won the match.
```

Conversely, you can test for a non-word boundary as demonstrated below.

```
if ("It does not matter that Matt won the match." =~ /\Bat/) {
  print "Match!";
}
```

Matching One or Fewer Times

Sometimes when developing patterns, you may want to look for a character or group of characters that occur either once or not at all. Either results in a match. You can build such a pattern using the ? metacharacter. For example, the following pattern will match Mrs. In addition, if the s is not present, the pattern will also match the word Mr.

```
if ("Please show Mrs. Ford to her seat." =~ /Mrs?/) {
  print "Match!";
}
```

You can also use the ? metacharacter to look for a group of characters instead of just a single character by enclosing the characters inside matching parentheses.

```
if ($_ =~ /effort(less)?/) {
  print "Match!";
}
```

Here, an occurrence of effort or effortless in $_ will result in a match.

Matching Any Single Character

You can also set up patterns that match a specific character or group of characters using the . metacharacter. This character is used to represent any single character (except for the newline character). For example, the following statements demonstrate how to use the . metacharacter to match against the word Mrs..

```
if ("Please show Mrs. Ford to her seat." =~ /M.s/) {
  print "Match!";
}
```

The pattern set up in the previous example provides the ability to match against any number of words, provided they fit the pattern. For example, the pattern /M.s/ would also match Mss, Mts, and Mis. By stringing together a series of . metacharacters, you can set up a pattern that matches more than one character, as demonstrated here.

```
if ("Please show Mrs. Ford to her seat." =~ /Pl...e/) {
  print "Match!";
}
```

In this example, the pattern /Pl...e/ will match any portion of the target string that begins with the letters Pl, has three more characters, and ends with the letter e.

You can also create patterns that match specific characters found at the beginning or end of strings. For example, the following statements set up a pattern that looks for a colon (:) at the end of a string.

```
if ($_ =~ /:$/) {
  print "Match!";
}
```

You can combine the ^, $, and the . metacharacters to create a pattern that tests to see if a string is made up of a single character as demonstrated below.

```
/^.$/
```

Matching Zero or More Instances

The * metacharacter is similar to the . metacharacter, the difference being that the * metacharacter allows for matches of the preceding character zero or more times. For example, the pattern /c*r/ would match any of the following:

```
cccccr
cr
r
```

Note that the last example listed results in a match because the c character has been designated as optional.

Matching One or More Instances

To set up a pattern that matches one or more characters or groups of characters, you use the + metacharacter. This metacharacter is similar to the * metacharacter, except that it requires at least one instance of the preceding character or group of characters to be found. For example, the pattern /he+r/ will match her in the following example. It will also match heer but not hr or hear.

```
if ("Please show Mrs. Ford to her seat." =~ /he+r/) {
  print "Match!";
}
```

Matching a Range of Instances

Sometimes it may be useful to search for a given number of instances of a character. To do so, you can use the curly braces ({}) to quantify the number of instances that should be searched for, based on the following syntax.

```
/character{min,max}/
```

For example, to set up a pattern that looks for the lowercase letter a that occurs at least three times but no more than five times you would write the pattern as /a{3,5}/. To set up a pattern that looks for the lowercase letter a to occur no less than three times, you would leave off the max argument as shown here.

```
/a{3,}/
```

Similarly, you could develop a pattern that looks for the occurrence of the lowercase letter exactly five times.

```
/a{5}/
```

You can also look for groups of repeating characters by enclosing the set of characters inside parentheses.

```
/(123){4,5}/
```

Here, the pattern has been set up to search for four to five consecutive occurrences of the characters 123.

Matching Alternative Patterns

Another way to set up pattern matches is to look for either of a set of possible matches. To set up such a pattern, you need to use the | character to separate the list of possible matches.

```
if ("My company's stock rating is AAA." =~ /stock|bond/) {
  print "Match!";
}
```

Here, a pattern has been set up to look for either the string stock or the string bond. If either string is found, the match is successful. You can set up a pattern to match on as many different possible alternatives as you want, as demonstrated here.

```
if ($_ =~ /cars|bars|stars|jars/) {
  print "Match!";
}
```

In this example, if the $_ special variable contains cars, bars, stars, or jars, a match will occur. Setting up a pattern in this manner is fairly straightforward; however, it is not the most efficient way to do so. Instead, you could make the pattern more efficient by rewriting it as shown here.

```
/(ca|ba|sta|ja)rs/
```

As you can see, the unique portions of each potentially matching pattern have been grouped together inside matching parentheses while the shared portion of the string being searched for remains outside of the parentheses. This version of the pattern requires fewer keystrokes to write. In addition, it defines a more efficient search pattern from Perl's perspective. The downside of this version is that it is more cryptic. In the end, Perl leaves decisions as to how best to formulate regular expression patterns entirely up to your personal coding preference.

Matching Any of a Collection of Characters

Sometimes you will not necessarily need to develop patterns that match up against specific characters or groups of characters. Many times it may be sufficient to instead develop a pattern that looks for a data type or that searches for any character in a given range of characters. You can accomplish this using *character classes*. To set up a character class, you must enclose its characters inside a pair of match square brackets ([ ]).

Characters inside the character class are regarded as a single character. Character classes also provide you with the ability to write streamlined patterns by specifying ranges as demonstrated in Table 7.1.

The use of character classes is so common that a number of shortcuts have been developed to make them even easier to define. These shortcuts are specified as characters preceded by a backslash, as demonstrated in Table 7.2.

TABLE 7.1 SAMPLE CHARACTER CLASS PATTERNS	
Sample Pattern	**Description**
/[abc]/	Matches if any of these lowercase letters is found (a, b, c).
/[abcdefghijklmnopqrstuvwxyz]/	Matches any of the lowercase letters found in the alphabet.
/[a – z]/	Shorthand option for matching any of the lowercase letters found in the alphabet.
/[A – Z]/	Shorthand option for matching any of the uppercase letters found in the alphabet.
/[0123456789]/	Matches any number between 0 and 9.
/[0 – 9]/	Shorthand option for matching any number between 0 and 9.

TABLE 7.2 CHARACTER CLASS SHORTCUTS	
Shortcut	**Description**
\d	Same as /[0 – 9]/
\w	Same as /[0-9A-Za-z_]/
\s	Same as /[\t\f\r\n]/
\D	Any character other than /[0 – 9]/
\W	Any character other than /[0-9A-Za-z_]/
\S	Any character other than /[\t\f\r\n]/

For example, the following if code block checks to see if the $_ special variable contains any non-numeric characters.

```perl
if ($_ =~ /\D/) {
  print "Match!";
}
```

Similarly, the following statements check to see if input supplied by the user contains numeric input and displays an error message if it does not.

```perl
print "Enter a number between 1 and 10. \n>";
chomp($reply = <STDIN>);

if ($reply =~ /\d/) {
  print "Input accepted.";
} else {
```

```
    print "Invalid input, you must enter a number!";
}
```

OTHER REGULAR EXPRESSION TIPS AND TRICKS

There is a lot more to working with regular expressions than just creating simple patterns and metacharacter-based patterns. Searching strings for a match can be very helpful. However, depending on what your script is trying to do, you might want to change the contents of the string in the event a match occurs. In addition, you may want to make global changes based on multiple matches. In many cases, you may want to perform case-insensitive pattern searches. Finally, in addition to searching for patterns within strings, you may want to extend this capability to search for patterns in lists and arrays.

Using Patterns to Replace Data

In addition to locating and validating the contents of strings, you can also modify the contents of strings by specifying a search and replace pattern. To do so, you can use the s/// substitution operator, which has the following syntax.

```
s/search/replace/
```

To demonstrate how to search for and replace patterns located within a string, take a look at the following example.

```
$samplestring = "Once upon a time there was a small boy who climbed a ";
$samplestring = $samplestring . "small tree at the top of the hill.";

$samplestring =~ s/small/big/;
$samplestring =~ s/Once upon a time/Many years ago/;

print "$samplestring";
```

This example specified two search and replace patterns. When executed, this example replaces the first instance for any patterns that are matched. As a result, the following output is displayed.

```
Many years ago there was a big boy who climbed a small tree at the top of the hill.
```

TRICK In the preceding example, only the first instance of the pattern match is changed. This is why the word small was changed to big only for the first occurrence of the word. Using the global match modifier character (g), you could modify the example to replace every occurrence of small with big as shown below.

```
#$samplestring = "Once upon a time there was a small boy who climbed a
small tree at the top of the hill.";

$samplestring = "Once upon a time there was a small boy who climbed a ";
$samplestring = $samplestring . "small tree at the top of the hill.";


$samplestring =~ s/small/big/g;
$samplestring =~ s/Once upon a time/Many years ago/;

print "$samplestring";
```

Note that the global match modifier character (g) is placed at the end of the pattern. When executed, this example displays the following result.

```
Many years ago there was a big boy who climbed a big tree at the top of
the hill.
```

Performing Character Translation

In addition to replacing specific strings using the s/// substitution operator, you can also translate individual characters on a letter by letter basis using the tr/// operator, which has the following syntax.

tr/oldcharacters/newcharacters/

For example, you could replace all instances of the lowercase letter x with the uppercase letter X as shown here.

```
$_ =~ tr/x/X/;
```

Similarly, you could change every lowercase letter to all uppercase.

```
$_ =~ tr/a-z/A-Z/;
```

Handling Differences in Case

Thus far, each pattern you have seen is case-sensitive, meaning that a pattern of /big/ would not match a string of BIG. One way to work around this problem is to try and develop a pattern that anticipates each of the various formats that a string may be spelled in, as the following example demonstrates.

```
$story = "There is no pie as fine as apple pie.";

if ($story =~ /Apple|apple|APPLE/) {
  print "match";
}
```

The problem with this example is that while it has included the most likely spelling combinations of the word apple, the pattern cannot guarantee that it will match every possible spelling of the word. For example, as it is currently written, the pattern will not match ApplE, applE, ApplE, and so on. Fortunately, you can save yourself the hassle of trying to cover every base by disabling case-sensitivity using the optional i modifier as demonstrated here.

```
$story = "There is no pie as fine as apple pie.";

if ($story =~ /apple/i) {
  print "match";
}
```

In this new example, any spelling of apple will match the pattern, regardless of case usage.

TRAP

Perl regular expressions are greedy, meaning that they attempt to match the longest possible match. To best understand greed in this context, take a look at the following example.

```
if ("Mississippi " =~ m/i.*s/) {
  print "We have a match!";   #Matches on ississ
}
```

In this example, Perl will start the match at the first instance of the i character. It then looks at the character that follows, which is s, and then ends the match with the last s that is found. You can, however, modify the pattern by adding a ? character to make it less greedy, as demonstrated here.

```
if ("Mississippi " =~ m/i.*?s/) {
  print "We have a match!";   #Matches on is
}
```

Matching Data Stored in Lists

If the pattern you want to look for is stored inside a list, such as an array, you could always create a foreach loop to iterate through each element in the array and then perform the pattern comparison to see which elements match. Rather than go through all this effort, you can instead use the grep function to save both time and effort. The grep function has the following syntax.

```
grep(pattern, list)
```

The grep function automatically searches the specified list and sets $_ to each element, returning a new array whose elements are made up of elements that matched the specified pattern. Take the following statement for example.

```
@names = qw/Alexander William Molly Mary Lee/;
@m_names = grep(/^M/, @names);   #Contains Molly and Mary
```

The first statement creates an array made up of five names. The second statement uses the grep function to generate a new array named @m_names that is assigned two elements, Molly and Mary. Both of these elements matched the specified pattern, which was that the element name begins with a capital M.

 In the previous example, the $_ special value represents a reference to the actual value stored in the @names array. If you alter the value of $_, the change affects the value stored in the @names array, which may not be what you want.

BACK TO THE LOTTERY PICKER GAME

Now it is time to turn your attention back to the creation of the Lottery Picker game. This game automates the generation of lottery ticket numbers based on information provided by the player. To ensure that the player only provides valid input, the script incorporates the use of regular expressions when validating input in order to ensure that the player supplies only numeric data.

Designing the Game

The development of this game will follow the same basic pattern that you have followed when creating previous Perl script games. Its construction will be completed in 13 steps, starting with the creation of the script file and the development of the script's overall controlling logic. The rest of the Lottery Picker game will be organized and managed via individual subroutines, each of which is designed to perform a specific task. The overall plan for building this game is outlined here.

1. Creating a new script.
2. Developing controlling logic.
3. Creating the clear_the_screen subroutine.
4. Creating the display_welcome_screen subroutine.
5. Creating the determine_number_of_tickets subroutine.

6. Creating the `determine_number_range` subroutine.
7. Creating the `generate_lottery_tickets` subroutine.
8. Creating the `retrieve_random_no` subroutine.
9. Creating the `ensure_unique_numbers` subroutine.
10. Creating the `see_if_ticket_is_complete` subroutine.
11. Creating the `layout_ticket` subroutine.
12. Creating the `display_lottery_tickets` subroutine.
13. Creating the `about_lottery_picker` subroutine.

Creating the Script File

Let's begin the development of the Lottery Picker game by creating a new Perl script file named LotteryPicker.pl and adding the following code statements to it.

```perl
#!/usr/bin/perl
#
# The Perl Lottery Picker (LotteryPicker.pl)


my $tickets = 0;
my $picks = 0;
my $range = 44;
my $finalticket = "";
my $ticketlist = "";


my @lotterynumbers;
```

As you can see, these statements begin with the shebang followed by comments that identify the script. Next, four global variables used throughout the scripts are defined as an array, which the script will use as a tool for storing and evaluating the uniqueness of each lottery number that is generated. In other words, the array will be used to temporarily store lottery numbers for each new lottery ticket. Because duplicate lottery numbers are not allowed on the same lottery ticket, the script iterates through the array each time a new lottery number is generated to make sure that it has not already been created. If it has, the lottery number is discarded and another number is generated in its place.

Controlling Game Play

The next step in creating the Lottery Picker game is to add the statements that provide high-level control of the script. In the case of the Lottery Picker script, this means specifying the order in which major subroutines execute, as shown here.

```
&display_welcome_screen();
&determine_number_of_tickets();
&determine_number_range();
$finalticket = &generate_lottery_tickets();
&display_lottery_tickets($finalticket);
&about_lottery_picker();
```

The Lottery Picker script has a number of other supporting subroutines, which are called when necessary by the subroutines listed above.

Clearing the Screen

Let's begin by adding the code statements that make up the clear_the_screen subroutine, which is used extensively throughout various portions of the script.

```
sub clear_the_screen {

  for ($i=0; $i < 25; ++$i){
    print "\n";
  }

}
```

If you prefer, you might want to replace this subroutine and the statements that call it with the Clear_the_screen module developed in Chapter 7, "Scope and Modules."

Displaying the Welcome Screen

The display_welcome_screen subroutine, shown below, runs when the script first starts executing. Its job is to greet the player with an opening message. This screen remains displayed until the player presses the Enter key.

```
sub display_welcome_screen {

  my $reply = "";

  &clear_the_screen();

  print "        ";
  print "    Welcome to the  L O T T E R Y    P I C K E R    G A M E!";
  print "\n\n\n\n\n\n\n\n\n\n\n";
  print " Press Enter to continue: ";
```

```
    $reply = <STDIN>;

}
```

Collecting Ticket Information

The determine_number_of_tickets subroutine, shown here, is responsible for prompting the player to specify how many lottery tickets she plans on purchasing.

```
sub determine_number_of_tickets {

  my $valid = "false";
  my $pause = "";

  until ($valid eq "true") {

    &clear_the_screen();

    print "\n\n\n\n\n\n";
    print " Enter the number of lottery tickets you plan to purchase: ";

    chomp($tickets = <STDIN>);

    if ($tickets ne "") {
      $valid = "true";
    } else {
      print "\n\n Sorry. You did not enter anything.";
      $pause = <STDIN>;
      next;
    }

    if ($tickets =~ /[^0-9]/) {
      $valid = "false";
      print "\n\n Sorry. Your input must be numeric.";
      $pause = <STDIN>;
      next;
    } else {
      $valid = "true";
    }
```

```
if ($tickets > 25) {
  print "\n\n Sorry. A maximum of 25 tickets is allowed.";
  $valid = "false";
  $pause = <STDIN>;
  next;
}

  }

}
```

This subroutine begins by declaring two private variables. The rest of the subroutine is wrapped up inside an until loop, which executes until the player provides a valid response. The player's input is stored in a global scalar variable named $tickets. Rather than trust the player to supply valid input, the subroutine processes the player's response using three conditional code blocks.

The first code block tests to see whether the player simply hit the Enter key without first specifying the number of lottery tickers to be purchased. If this is the case, an error message is displayed and the next function is executed, prompting the player to enter a response by forcing the loop to run again.

The second code block uses a regular expression to check whether the player's input contains anything other than a number. If this is the case, an error message is displayed and the next function is executed, prompting the player to try again.

The third conditional block checks to see if the player supplied a value greater than 25, which is an arbitrary limit imposed by the game. If this is the case, an error message is displayed explaining why the input is invalid, and the loop executes again.

If the input provided by the player passes all three conditional tests, the until loop stops running, allowing the script to move on to the next subroutine.

Determining Ticket Number Range

The `determine_number_range` subroutine, shown here, is responsible for prompting the player to specify how many numbers are required to complete a lottery ticket.

```perl
sub determine_number_range {

  my $valid = "false";

  until ($valid eq "true") {

    &clear_the_screen();

    print "\n\n\n\n\n\n";
    print "How many unique numbers are required per ticket?: ";

    chomp($picks = <STDIN>);

    if ($picks ne "") {
      $valid = "true";
    } else {
      print "\n\n Sorry. You did not enter anything.";
      $pause = <STDIN>;
      next;
    }

    if ($picks =~ /[^0-9]/) {
      $valid = "false";
      print "\n\n Sorry. Your input must be numeric.";
      $pause = <STDIN>;
      next;
    } else {
      $valid = "true";
    }

    if ($picks > 10) {
      print "\n\n Sorry. A maximum of 10 numbers are allowed.";
      $valid = "false";
      $pause = <STDIN>;
```

```
      next;
   }


 }


}
```

As you can see, this subroutine is almost identical to the `determine_number_of_tickets` subroutine, performing the same three data validation checks on the player input.

Generating Lottery Tickets

The code for the `generate_lottery_tickets` subroutine, shown here, is responsible for creating the number of lottery tickets specified by the player.

```perl
sub generate_lottery_tickets {

  my $number = 0;
  my $done = "";
  my $count = 0;
  my $validpicks = 0;
  my $lotterynumbers = "";
  my $seeifvalid = 0;


  for ($i=0; $i < $tickets; ++$i) {

   $count = 0;
   @lotterynumbers = "";
   $done = "false";
   $validpicks = 0;
   $lotterynumbers = "";
   $finishedticket = "";

   until ($done eq "true") {

    $number = &retrieve_random_no();

    $count = $count + 1;

    $seeifvalid = &ensure_unique_numbers($number, $count);
```

```
        if ($seeifvalid == 1) {
         $validpicks = $validpicks + $seeifvalid;
         $lotterynumbers = $lotterynumbers . "  " . $number . "      ";
        }


        $done = &see_if_ticket_is_complete($validpicks);


       }


       $finishedticket = &layout_ticket($lotterynumbers);


      }


     return $finishedticket;


}
```

This subroutine begins by declaring a number of private variables used to keep track of lottery numbers and tickets as well as to store data returned by the various subroutines that are called.

The rest of the subroutine is enclosed inside a for loop. The loop executes once for each lottery ticket requested by the player. Because each iteration results in the creation of a new ticket, a number of variables must be reset at the beginning of the loop, to clear out any previously stored values.

Embedded inside the for loop is an until loop, which is responsible for generating the lottery numbers for each individual lottery ticket. It begins by calling the retrieve_random_no subroutine, which returns a randomly selected number. Next, the ensure_unique_numbers subroutine is called and passed variables representing the randomly selected number and a number representing a count of the number of randomly generated numbers created so far.

If the ensure_unique_numbers subroutine returns a value of 1, the number is unique, meaning that it has not already been selected. The number is then added to a scalar variable named $lotterynumbers. #lotterynumbers is a string containing a list of the lottery numbers for the current lottery ticket.

The see_if_ticket_is_complete subroutine is then called and passed the $validpick scalar variable. This variable represents the number of lottery ticket numbers selected so far. A value of true is returned if all the numbers required to complete the lottery ticket have all been generated. The layout_ticket subroutine is then called and passed the $lotterynumbers variable. The `generate_lottery_tickets` subroutine then ends, returning a scalar variable named $finishedticket, which is a string containing a list of each lottery ticket created so far.

Retrieving Random Numbers

The code for the `retrieve_random_no` subroutine is shown here.

```perl
sub retrieve_random_no {

  my $randomnumber = 0;

  $randomnumber = int(rand $range) + 1;
  $randomnumber = sprintf("%02d", $randomnumber);

  return $randomnumber;

}
```

This subroutine is responsible for generating a random number in the range of 1 to 44 ($range is a global variable set equal to 44 at the beginning of the script). It begins by declaring a private variable named $randomnumber, which is used to store the randomly generated number. For display purposes, the game displays all numbers as two digits, so the `sprintf` function is used to pad single digit numbers with leading zeros. The subroutine ends by returning its randomly generated, two-digit number to the `generate_lottery_tickets` subroutine.

Preventing Duplicate Numbers

The `ensure_unique_numbers` subroutine, shown below, is responsible for preventing duplicate numbers from being added to lottery tickets. It accomplishes this by adding lottery ticket numbers to an array named @randomnumber. New numbers are added to the array only if the array does not already have that number stored in it.

```perl
sub ensure_unique_numbers {


  my ($randomnumber, $indexno) = @_;

  CASE: {
    $randomnumber == $lotterynumbers[0]  && do { last CASE; };
    $randomnumber == $lotterynumbers[1]  && do { last CASE; };
    $randomnumber == $lotterynumbers[2]  && do { last CASE; };
```

```
    $randomnumber == $lotterynumbers[3]  && do { last CASE; };
    $randomnumber == $lotterynumbers[4]  && do { last CASE; };
    $randomnumber == $lotterynumbers[5]  && do { last CASE; };
    $randomnumber == $lotterynumbers[6]  && do { last CASE; };
    $randomnumber == $lotterynumbers[7]  && do { last CASE; };
    $randomnumber == $lotterynumbers[8]  && do { last CASE; };
    $randomnumber == $lotterynumbers[9]  && do { last CASE; };

    {
       $lotterynumbers[$indexno] = $randomnumber;
       return 1;
    }
  }


}
```

Note that before any numbers are added to the @lotterynumbers array, a custom CASE code block compares each number to every number already stored in the array, and if a match is found, the last function is used to exit the CASE block. However, if a matching number is not found in the array, the number is added to the array using an index number passed to the subroutine as an argument.

Determining when a Ticket Is Complete

The see_if_ticket_is_complete subroutine, shown here, is responsible for determining when all the numbers required to complete a lottery ticket have been selected. This subroutine accomplishes its job by comparing the value of $currentcount, whose value is passed to the subroutine as an argument, against a global scalar variable named $picks.

```
sub see_if_ticket_is_complete {

  my $currentcount = $_[0];

  if ($currentcount == $picks) {
    return "true";
  }


}
```

Laying Out Ticket Numbers

The layout_ticket subroutine, shown here, is responsible for formatting a new row in a string representing the lottery numbers generated by the script.

```perl
sub layout_ticket {

  my $rowofnumbers = $_[0];

  $rowofnumbers = "> " . $rowofnumbers;

  $ticketlist = $ticketlist . $rowofnumbers . "\n";

  return $ticketlist;

}
```

The string representing a full set of lottery numbers is pre-appended with the ">" character, which acts as a row marker that helps to visually improve the layout of each set of lottery numbers. This string is then appended to the end of another string named $ticketlist. This subroutine ends by returning the value of $ticketlist to the generate_lottery_tickets subroutine.

Displaying Lottery Tickets

Once all the lottery tickets requested by the player have been generated, they are displayed by the display_lottery_tickets subroutine shown here.

```perl
sub display_lottery_tickets {

  my $finallist = $_[0];

  my $reply = "";

  &clear_the_screen();

  print "L U C K Y   L O T T E R Y   N U M B E R   P I C K E R \n\n";
  print "---------------------------------------------------------- \n\n";
  print "Number of plays: $tickets \n\n";
  print "Number of picks per play: $picks \n\n";
  print "----------------------------------------------------------\n\n";
  print "Your lottery numbers are: \n\n\n";
```

```
print $finallist;

$reply = <STDIN>;
```

}

The subroutine displays the number of tickets that were generated (stored in $tickets) and the number of picks per ticket (stored in $picks). Finally, the value of $finallist is displayed. This global scalar variable contains a string representing each lottery ticket created by the game.

Displaying Additional Script Information

Before ending, the script calls on the about_lottery_picker subroutine, shown here. This subroutine displays a little information about the game and its author.

```
sub about_lottery_picker {

  my $reply = "";

  &clear_the_screen();

  print " Thank you for using the Perl Lottery Picker\n\n";
  print " Copyright - Jerry Lee Ford, Jr. 2006.\n\n";

  $reply = <STDIN>;

}
```

The Final Result

You have all the information you need to sit down and create your own copy of the Lottery Picker game. If you have not created the script yet, do so now. A complete copy of LotteryPicker.pl is provided below. This copy of the script has been enhanced through the addition of the book's Perl script template. In addition, comments have been embedded throughout the script to document key functionality and make it easier for you to follow along and understand what is going on at each point within the script.

```
#!/usr/bin/perl
#
# The Perl Lottery Picker (LotteryPicker.pl)
```

```perl
#-------------------------------------------------------------------------
# Initialization Section
#-------------------------------------------------------------------------

#Declare and initialize script variables

my $tickets = 0; #Specifies the number of tickets to be purchased
my $picks = 0;   #Specifies the number of lottery numbers per ticket
my $range = 44;  #Range from which to generate lottery numbers
my $finalticket = "";  #Stores the list of lottery tickets generated
                       #by the game
my $ticketlist = "";  #Stores a string representing the list of lottery
                      #tickets created by the game

my @lotterynumbers; #Stores randomly generated lottery numbers


#-------------------------------------------------------------------------
# MAIN Processing Section
#-------------------------------------------------------------------------

&display_welcome_screen();  #Display opening screen

&determine_number_of_tickets(); #Ask the player how many tickets to  create

&determine_number_range(); #Ask player how many numbers make up a ticket

$finalticket = &generate_lottery_tickets(); #Create list of lottery tickets

&display_lottery_tickets($finalticket);  #Display list of lottery tickets

&about_lottery_picker();  #Display game information before exiting


#-------------------------------------------------------------------------
# Subroutine Section
#-------------------------------------------------------------------------
```

```perl
#This subroutine clears the screen by adding 25 blank lines
sub clear_the_screen {

  for ($i=0; $i < 25; ++$i){  #Loop 25 times
    print "\n";  #Print out a blank line
  }


}



#This subroutine displays a message that welcomes the player to the game
sub display_welcome_screen {

  my $reply = "";  #Local variable used to store player input

  &clear_the_screen();  #Call subroutine that clears the screen

  #Display the game's opening menu system
  print "        ";
  print "    Welcome to the  L O T T E R Y   P I C K E R   G A M E!";
  print "\n\n\n\n\n\n\n\n\n\n\n\n";
  print " Press Enter to continue: ";  #Prompt user to press Enter
  $reply = <STDIN>; #Pause to allow the player to read the screen

}



#Prompt player for the number of ticket numbers to generate and validate
#player input
sub determine_number_of_tickets {

  my $valid = "false";  #Local variable used to control loop
  my $pause = "";  #Local variable used to store user input

  #Iterate until the player provides valid input
  until ($valid eq "true") {

    &clear_the_screen();  #Call subroutine that clears the screen
```

```perl
print "\n\n\n\n\n\n";
print " Enter the number of lottery tickets you plan to purchase: ";

chomp($tickets = <STDIN>);  #Collect player input

if ($tickets ne "") {  #Ensure the player enters numeric input
  $valid = "true";  #Input validation passed
} else {
  print "\n\n Sorry. You did not enter anything.";
  $pause = <STDIN>;  #Pause to display error message
  next;
}

if ($tickets =~ /[^0-9]/) {  #Do not allow non-numeric input
  $valid = "false";  #Input validation passed
  print "\n\n Sorry. Your input must be numeric.";
  $pause = <STDIN>;  #Pause to display error message
  next;
} else {
  $valid = "true";  #Input validation passed
}

if ($tickets > 25) { #Arbitrarily limit the plays to 25 tickets
  print "\n\n Sorry. A maximum of 25 tickets is allowed.";
  $valid = "false";  #Input validation passed
  $pause = <STDIN>;  #Pause to display error message
  next;
}

}

}


#Prompt player as to how many numbers make up a ticket
sub determine_number_range {
```

```perl
my $valid = "false";  #Local variable used to control loop

#Iterate until the player provides valid input
until ($valid eq "true") {

  &clear_the_screen();  #Call subroutine that clears the screen

  print "\n\n\n\n\n\n";
  print "How many unique numbers are required per ticket?: ";

  chomp($picks = <STDIN>);  #Collect player input

  if ($picks ne "") {  #Ensure the player enters numeric input
    $valid = "true";  #Input validation passed
  } else {
    print "\n\n Sorry. You did not enter anything.";
    $pause = <STDIN>;  #Pause to display error message
    next;
  }

  if ($picks =~ /[^0-9]/) {  #Do not allow non-numeric input
    $valid = "false";  #Input validation passed
    print "\n\n Sorry. Your input must be numeric.";
    $pause = <STDIN>;  #Pause to display error message
    next;
  } else {
    $valid = "true";  #Input validation passed
  }

  if ($picks > 10) { #Arbitrarily limit the range to 10 numbers
    print "\n\n Sorry. A maximum of 10 numbers are allowed.";
    $valid = "false";  #Input validation passed
    $pause = <STDIN>;  #Pause to display error message
    next;
  }

}
```

```perl
}


#This subroutine manages the generation of lottery tickets
sub generate_lottery_tickets {

  my $number = 0; #Local variable used to store lottery numbers
  my $done = ""; #Local variable used to control inner loop
  my $count = 0; #Local variable used to keep track of the number
                 #unique lottery number created so far
  my $validpicks = 0; #Local variable used to keep track of the number
                      #of valid lottery ticket numbers picked so far
  my $lotterynumbers = ""; #Local variable used to store the numbers
                           #that make up an individual lottery ticket
  my $seeifvalid = 0; #Local variable that stores a value that determines
                      #whether a lottery number is valid
  for ($i=0; $i < $tickets; ++$i) { #For each set lottery ticket

   $count = 0; #Reset variable to zero each time a new ticket
               #is started
   @lotterynumbers = ""; #Reinitialize the array each time a new ticket is
                         #started
   $done = "false"; #Reset local variable to prepare for next ticket
   $validpicks = 0; #Local variable used to keep track of the total number
                    #of valid lottery numbers generated so far
   $lotterynumbers = ""; #Local variable used to build a lottery ticket
   $finishedticket = ""; #Local variable used to store a completed lottery
                         #ticket

  until ($done eq "true") { #Create a new lottery ticket

   #Call subroutine that generates ticket numbers
   $number = &retrieve_random_no();

   $count = $count + 1; #Increment value by one

   #Call subroutine that ensures unique lottery numbers are generated
   $seeifvalid = &ensure_unique_numbers($number, $count);
```

```perl
    if ($seeifvalid == 1) { #A non-duplicate number has been generated
      $validpicks = $validpicks + $seeifvalid;  #Increment value by one
      #Add new number to the list of numbers representing the current ticket
      $lotterynumbers = $lotterynumbers . " " . $number . "   ";
    }

    #call subroutine that determines when a ticket is ready
    $done = &see_if_ticket_is_complete($validpicks);

  }

    #Call subroutine that formats the display of the ticket
    $finishedticket = &layout_ticket($lotterynumbers);

  }

  return $finishedticket;

}


#This subroutine generates the game's random lottery numbers
sub retrieve_random_no {

  my $randomnumber = 0;  #Local variable used to store a random number

  $randomnumber = int(rand $range) + 1; #Generate random number
  $randomnumber = sprintf("%02d", $randomnumber);  #Apply padding

  return $randomnumber;  #Return the randomly generated number

}


#This subroutine ensures that duplicate numbers are eliminated
sub ensure_unique_numbers {
```

```perl
#Local variables set equal to a randomly generated number and
#the current array index
my ($randomnumber, $indexno) = @_;

#Custom CASE block used to store lottery ticket numbers
#Duplicate lottery numbers are not added to the array
CASE: {
  $randomnumber == $lotterynumbers[0]  && do { last CASE; };
  $randomnumber == $lotterynumbers[1]  && do { last CASE; };
  $randomnumber == $lotterynumbers[2]  && do { last CASE; };
  $randomnumber == $lotterynumbers[3]  && do { last CASE; };
  $randomnumber == $lotterynumbers[4]  && do { last CASE; };
  $randomnumber == $lotterynumbers[5]  && do { last CASE; };
  $randomnumber == $lotterynumbers[6]  && do { last CASE; };
  $randomnumber == $lotterynumbers[7]  && do { last CASE; };
  $randomnumber == $lotterynumbers[8]  && do { last CASE; };
  $randomnumber == $lotterynumbers[9]  && do { last CASE; };

  {
    #Store lottery number in the game's array
    $lotterynumbers[$indexno] = $randomnumber;
    return 1;
  }
}

}


#This subroutine determines when a lottery ticket is complete
sub see_if_ticket_is_complete {

  my $currentcount = $_[0]; #Local variable representing the number of
                            #valid lottery numbers generated so far for
                            #the current ticket

  if ($currentcount == $picks) {  #A full set of lottery numbers has been
    return "true";                #generated
  }
```

```
}


#This subroutine lays out a string representing one lottery ticket
sub layout_ticket {

    my $rowofnumbers = $_[0]; #A list of lottery numbers passed as arguments

    $rowofnumbers = "> " . $rowofnumbers;  #Add a start of line indicator

    #Add the row representing the new ticket to the string being used to
    #display a list of lottery tickets
    $ticketlist = $ticketlist . $rowofnumbers . "\n";

    return $ticketlist; #Return the string being used to store the list of
                        #lottery tickets generated by the game

}


#This subroutine displays the lottery tickets generated by the script
sub display_lottery_tickets {

    my $finallist = $_[0];  #Local variables containing the list of lottery
                            #tickets generated by the script
    my $reply = "";

    &clear_the_screen();  #Call subroutine that clears the screen

    print "L U C K Y   L O T T E R Y   N U M B E R   P I C K E R \n\n";
    print "------------------------------------------------------- \n\n";
    print "Number of plays: $tickets \n\n";
    print "Number of picks per play: $picks \n\n";
    print "-------------------------------------------------------\n\n";
    print "Your lottery numbers are: \n\n\n";
    print $finallist;
```

```
  $reply = <STDIN>; #Pause to allow the player to read the screen

}


#This subroutine displays information about the game and its creator
sub about_lottery_picker {

  my $reply = "";

  &clear_the_screen();  #Call subroutine that clears the screen

  #Display information about the game and its author
  print " Thank you for using the Perl Lottery Picker\n\n";
  print " Copyright - Jerry Lee Ford, Jr. 2006.\n\n";

  $reply = <STDIN>;  #Pause to allow the player to read the screen

}
```

That's it. Your copy of the Lottery Picker game should be ready to go. So, crank it up and make sure that it is working exactly as you expected before you use it to select numbers and purchase the next winning lottery ticket.

Summary

In this chapter you learned how to build an assortment of different types of regular expressions. This included learning how to build regular expressions that matched individual characters, simple patterns, groups of characters, and repeating sets of characters. You learned the basic rules behind building regular expressions and how to incorporate metacharacters in order to build more efficient and more complex regular expressions. You also learned how to incorporate regular expressions into conditional and loop control blocks and to use regular expressions to extract data.

Before you move on to Chapter 8, "Debugging," why don't you spend a little extra time working on the following list of challenges to see if you can improve the Perl Lottery Picker game and make it a little more useful.

CHALLENGES

1. Give the Perl Lottery Picker game an opening menu and provide it with an effective Help screen.

2. As it is currently written, the range of numbers that the Perl Lottery Picker game pulls from is hard coded in the script. Modify the script to give the user the option of accepting this value or changing it.

3. Currently, the Perl Lottery Picker game prevents the player from attempting to enter a blank space or non-numeric input when answering questions. However, the game does not prevent the player from entering outrageous input such as a negative number or a number that exceeds the range of valid lottery numbers. Modify the script to prevent illogical inputs.

4. Right now, the Perl Lottery Picker game only allows the player to generate one set of lottery numbers and then terminates the game. Modify this behavior by adding a controlling loop that allows the player to generate as many lists of lottery numbers as she wants and to exit only when the player decides to do so.

5. The Perl Lottery Picker script includes a `clear_the_screen` subroutine. You might consider importing the `Clear_the_screen` module developed in Chapter 6, "Scope and Modules," in place of this subroutine.

DEBUGGING

U p to this point in the book, your primary tools for dealing with script errors have been to type carefully when keying in script statements and to use the information presented by Perl's error messages when mistakes were made. As you have no doubt learned, with a little time and patience and the information presented in error messages, many errors can quickly be tracked down. However, as your Perl scripts grow in size and complexity, errors will become more and more difficult to track down using this technique. Fortunately, Perl comes equipped with a built-in debugger that you can use to eliminate pesky bugs from your scripts. This chapter will teach you how to work with Perl's debugger and provide you with a number of other programming tips and techniques for dealing with script errors.

Specifically, you will learn how to

- Use error messages to track down and fix errors
- Trace a script's logical execution using `print` statements
- Start and stop the Perl debugger
- Use the Perl debugger to control the execution of script and subroutine statements
- Use the Perl debugger to monitor and modify variable values

- Use the Perl debugger to set breakpoints that halt script execution at specific locations within the script
- Use the Perl debugger as an interactive test environment

PROJECT PREVIEW: THE TIC TAC TOE GAME

This book's final game project is the Tic Tac Toe game. This game is a computerized version of the classic children's game where two players compete in an effort to line up three Xs or Os in a row on the Tic Tac Toe game board. The development of this game will help tie together everything you have learned in this book. This includes the use of private and global variables, conditional logic, loops, subroutines, and regular expressions.

As shown in Figure 8.1, the Tic Tac Toe game begins by displaying a welcome message and a menu of commands that control game play.

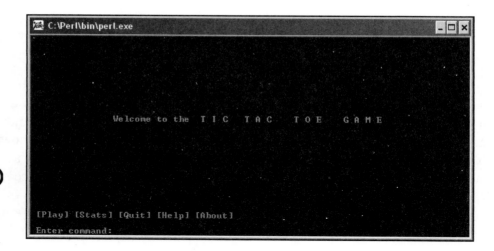

FIGURE 8.1

The Tic Tac Toe game as seen running on Windows XP.

To play a game of Tic Tac Toe, the player enters the Play command. In response, the game displays a blank game board and prompts the first player (Player X) to make a move as demonstrated in Figure 8.2.

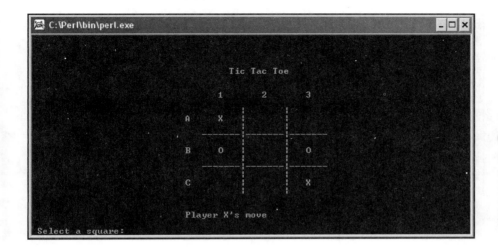

Each player's move is evaluated to ensure that a valid game board square was specified and that the specified square has not already been selected. Otherwise, an error message is displayed, as demonstrated in Figure 8.3.

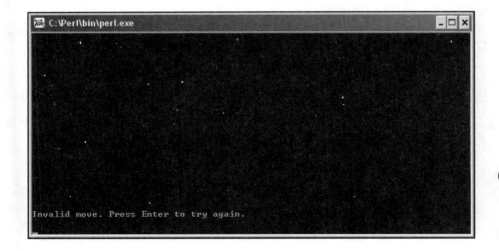

As game play continues, the game keeps track of each player's turn. Game play ends when one of the players gets 3 squares in a row or when every square on the game board has been selected. A message is displayed at the end of each game identifying who won or if the game ended in a tie, as demonstrated in Figure 8.4.

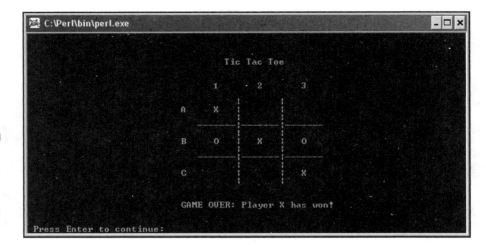

FIGURE 8.4

Games end when one of the players has managed to get three squares in a row or when all squares have been selected.

By entering the Stats command at the game's main menu, players can view statistics showing the number of games won by each player as well as the number of games that have ended in a tie as demonstrated in Figure 8.5.

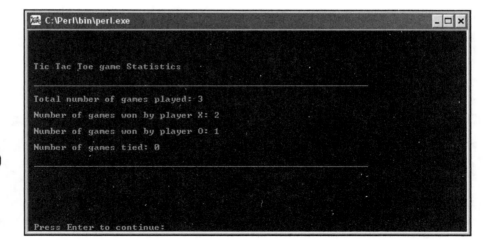

FIGURE 8.5

Players can view game statistics at any time by entering the stats command.

By entering the Help command at the game's main menu, players can read instructions on how the game is played, as shown in Figure 8.6.

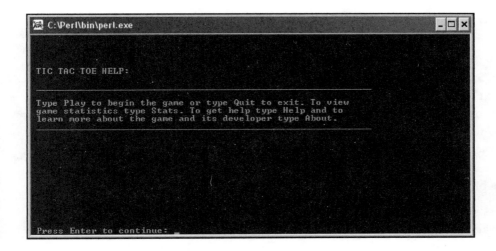

FIGURE 8.6

Instructions for playing the game are also available.

Additional information about the game and its author is also available by keying in the About command, as demonstrated in Figure 8.7.

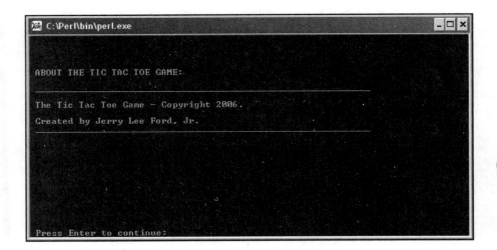

FIGURE 8.7

Copyright and author information are also available as a menu command.

UNDERSTANDING PERL SCRIPT ERRORS

As you worked your way through the various game scripts presented in this book, you likely ran into a number of errors. Perhaps you mistyped a keyword or left off an occasional semicolon. Not to worry, even the most experienced and talented programmers run into errors. For programmers, errors, which are often referred to as bugs, are simply a fact of life. To help keep you on the straight and narrow, this chapter is designed to equip you with the information you need to track down and fix scripting errors.

Syntax Errors

Errors can occur at many different places within your Perl scripts for many different reasons. One type of error that you will run into a lot is syntax errors. *Syntax errors* are errors that occur when you fail to follow the rules for formatting your Perl code statements. Syntax errors occur, for example, when you mistype a keyword, leave off the ending semicolon after a statement, or when you forget to add matching closing curly braces to the ends of loops, conditional code blocks, or subroutines.

When it discovers syntax errors, the Perl interpreter automatically halts execution and displays error messages describing each error. By using the information presented in error messages, you can usually track down and fix syntax errors with little trouble.

TRICK When making a number of changes to a Perl script, it is easy to introduce syntax errors. To discover problems as quickly as possible, pause along the way to test your script each time you make a change. Even a minor change has the potential to lead to unexpected results. Alternatively, perform a quick compile check of your script to see if Perl detects any errors partway through making your changes. You can accomplish this using the -c switch as demonstrated below.

```
perl -c test.pl
```

Here, a Perl script named test.pl is compiled without being executed. The -c switch compiles the script without turning warnings on. If you want, you can add the -w switch to include Perl warnings as demonstrated here.

```
perl -wc test.pl
```

Runtime Errors

Another type of script error that you will run into is runtime errors. These types of errors occur after Perl has finished interpreting your script and begins executing it. *Runtime* errors occur when your scripts attempt to perform some type of illegal action. Runtime errors can be a bit tricky to track down and fix. For example, you might have a runtime error embedded deep inside a seldom-used subroutine that you failed to catch when testing the script during development. Suppose, for example, that you wrote a small Perl script that was designed to display the results of 100 divided by a number supplied by the user.

```
$x = 100;
print "Enter a number that you wish to divide into 100: ";
chomp($y = <STDIN>);
print $x / $y;
```

Syntactically, there is nothing wrong with this example. However, there is a flaw that can easily lead to the generation of a runtime error. It is illegal to divide any number by zero. Therefore, if the user enters zero and presses Enter, the following runtime error will be generated.

```
Illegal division by zero at test.pl line 9, <STDIN> line 1.
```

To prevent this type of error from occurring, you must carefully test out every part of your script. In the case of this example, what is needed is a little input validation, perhaps using a regular expression. Unfortunately, you will not always be able to anticipate every possible type of runtime error. For example, if you develop a Perl script that is designed to copy files from one network drive to another, a number of runtime errors could occur over which you have no control. Examples of these types of problems include the network going down, one of the network drives crashing, or a network drive filling up. As a programmer, your job is to anticipate, as best as possible, the places where runtime errors are likely to occur and to try and prevent them from impacting your script as much as possible.

Logical Errors

A third category of error that you need to be on the lookout for is *logical errors*. These types of errors happen when you make a mistake in your Perl scripts that does not lead to syntax or runtime errors, but it does not lead to the expected result either. For example, a logical error can be something as simple as accidentally adding two numbers instead of multiplying them or specifying the wrong variable when building an expression.

You'll know when you run into a logical error because your script will not behave correctly. It may produce incorrect output or execute the wrong subroutines. Because logical errors do not result in the generation of error messages, they can be particularly difficult to track down and fix. Fortunately, there are a number of debugging techniques and tools available that you can use to locate and fix logical errors, including Perl's built-in debugger.

EXAMINING PERL ERROR MESSAGES

Many times Perl gives you all the information that you need to know in order to locate and correct an error just by analyzing the error message it displays. For starters, Perl tells you the line number where it believes the error may reside and provides a brief description of the error. For example, the following statements show a syntax error generated on a computer running Windows where a semicolon was left off the end of a statement.

```
C:\Documents and Settings\Owner\Desktop>test.pl
syntax error at C:\Documents and Settings\Owner\Desktop\Test.pl line 5,
near "chomp"
Execution of C:\Documents and Settings\Owner\Desktop\Test.pl aborted due
to compilation errors.
```

Sometimes the error message will tell you exactly what the error is. More often than not, however, error messages tend to be a little vague. In the previous example, you are told that a syntax error has occurred. Using this information and the line number provided in the error message, locate the specified line number within your script. If the specified line does not appear to have a syntax error, examine the code statements immediately preceding and following the specified line number to see if you can find the syntax error in either of these two places. The following list provides you with a number of items to look for when tracking down syntax errors.

- Double-check the spelling of language keywords
- Look for unmatched parentheses, curly braces, and square brackets
- Look for missing punctuation such as the semicolon character or required commas
- If you cannot find an error in the statement where the error was reported, check out lines immediately preceding and following the statement

Many times, a mistake may result in more than one error message. Often, the first error message will provide you with the best clue as to what the problem is and where it lies. Fix this error and the other error messages may well go away.

TRICK
The best way of dealing with errors is to prevent them from occurring in the first place. To accomplish this lofty task, begin all new script development by setting up the contents of the Initialization Section. Then, before adding any additional statements, run the script even though it does not do anything yet. Running it now will let you track down and eliminate any syntax errors, while they are still easy to find. Then continue writing the script, developing it a subroutine at a time, pausing to test each subroutine before moving on. By building new scripts in this modular fashion, you greatly simplify the debugging process, because if an error does occur, it will most likely be located in the most recently developed subroutine.

TRACING LOGICAL FLOW WITH THE PRINT FUNCTION

Sometime errors are not so easy to track down and find. This is particularly true in situations where Perl is unable to point you back to the actual location in your script where the error initiated and instead displays an error message much later when the error impacts another portion of the script. One technique for tracking down errors is to use the print statement to trace the overall logical flow of your Perl scripts. To do this, you could place print statements at the beginning and ending of the script's Initialization and Main Processing Sections. You might also insert print statements in each of the script's subroutines in order to be able to tell when they are executed. For example, the following subroutine has been modified using this technique.

```
sub generate_number {

  print STDERR "The main_menu subroutine is now executing\n";

  my $randomnumber = 0;
  $randomnumber = int(rand 100) + 1;

  print STDERR "Exiting main_menu subroutine, returning: $randomnumber";

  return $randomnumber

}
```

TRICK

By default Perl provides you with easy access to three separate sources of reading from input and writing to output, as listed here.

- **STDIN.** Standard input.
- **STDOUT.** Standard output.
- **STDERR.** Standard error.

You have seen how to use STDIN in numerous occasions to collect user input. STDOUT identifies the default location for all output. Perl automatically uses STDOUT for any print statement, allowing you to leave STDOUT off of your print statement. Using STDERR you can write error messages to a different location than STDOUT. However, both default to the terminal. It has been applied to the previous example to help make the extra print statements stand out from other print statements that belong in the Perl script.

By inserting `print` statements in subroutines, as shown above, you can monitor the logical execution of your script. In addition, by displaying the value or variables within `print` statements, you can keep an eye on the variables to make sure that they are being assigned values in the manner you expect. Once you have finished debugging your script, you can delete these extra `print` statements. Alternatively, you can simply comment them out so that they remain in place should you need to come back and debug the script again in the future.

USING THE PERL DEBUGGER TO TRACK DOWN PESKY BUGS

Embedding `print` statements to trace script execution in small scripts is often the quickest and easiest way to track down a problem. However, for larger and more complicated scripts, you need a more powerful tool than just `print` statements. Fortunately, the Perl interpreter includes a built-in command line debugger. It allows you to step through your Perl scripts, so that you can monitor the logical execution flow of script statements, pausing when necessary to inspect variable values. The debugger also allows you to modify variable values, stop script execution, and to restart the script over again. While you are given detailed control over the manner in which your script executes, the script itself executes as it normally does.

Learning all of the ins and outs involved in debugging Perl programs is an extensive topic. This chapter provides you with a solid foundation that covers all the basics. However, if you wish to learn more, there are a number of books dedicated solely to debugging Perl scripts, including *Pro Perl Debugging* (ISBN: 1590594541) and the *Perl Debugger Pocket Reference* (ISBN: 0596005032).

Starting the Debugger

Not all script errors are obvious. Some are hidden deep within your script and are not readily obvious because while they result in unexpected output, they do not prevent the script from executing. For these situations, you may need something more than the basic debugging techniques discussed up to this point in the chapter. Specifically, you need a tool that lets you exercise tight control over your scripts, controlling when each statement executes, and which allows you to check on the status of script variables. This tool is the Perl debugger.

Thankfully, Perl's debugger is built-in, meaning that it is integrated into Perl itself and always available to you. However, before you can use the Perl debugger to debug a Perl script, the script must compile cleanly. This means that you must first track down and correct any syntax errors that would otherwise keep your script from executing, which you can do using the debugging tricks you have already covered in this chapter.

To use the debugger, you must start it using the following syntax.

```
perl -d scriptname.pl
```

The -d parameter tells Perl to start in debug mode and scriptname.pl is the name of the Perl script to be debugged. When started, the debugger displays a number of pieces of information about itself, as demonstrated in Figure 8.8.

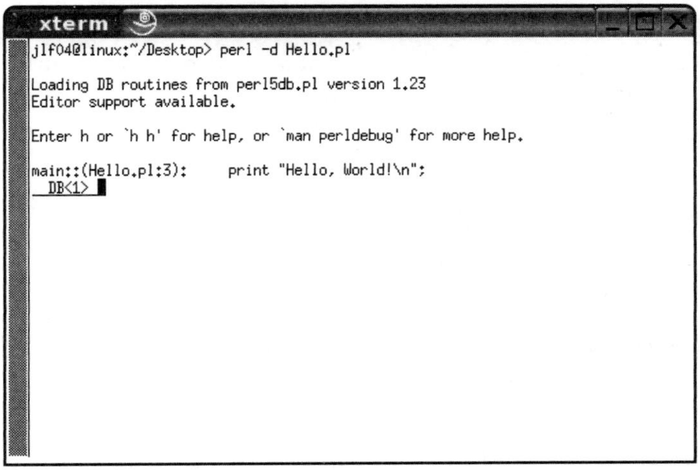

```
xterm
jlf04@linux:~/Desktop> perl -d Hello.pl

Loading DB routines from perl5db.pl version 1.23
Editor support available.

Enter h or `h h' for help, or `man perldebug' for more help.

main::(Hello.pl:3):     print "Hello, World!\n";
  DB<1>
```

FIGURE 8.8

Using Perl's built-in debugger to debug a Perl script running on Linux.

When first started, the Perl debugger loads debugging routines and displays version information similar to that shown here.

```
Loading DB routines from perl5db.pl version 1.28
Editor support available.
```

Next, the debugger displays a line telling you how to access its online help.

```
Enter h or 'h h' for help, or 'perldoc perldebug' for more help.
```

Finally, the debugger displays the first executable line in the script.

```
main::(hello.pl:3):     print "Hello, World!\n";
```

It is important to understand that the statement displayed by the debugger has not been executed yet. Instead, the debugger displays the next statement to be executed, which is of course the script's first executable statement when the script initially starts executing. Take note of the information that is displayed just to the left of the actual script statement. As you can see, the current package name is displayed as well as the name of the script and the line number of the statement. The last thing the debugger does is display its Command Prompt as shown here.

```
DB<1>
```

To continue working with the debugger and to track down where problems lie in the script, you must enter debugging commands at the Command Prompt. Note that the Command Prompt shown above displays the letters DB followed by <1>. The debugger keeps track of every command that is entered. In this example, it is waiting on the first command.

TRICK If you think that you are going to be spending a lot of time debugging a particular script, you can modify its shebang statement as shown below in order to automatically start the Perl debugger every time the script is run.

```
#!/usr/bin/perl -wd
```

Executing Additional Code Statements

To execute the next statement within the script, you can use either the n or the s command. The difference between the two commands is as follows:

- **n.** Executes the next code statement and then pauses. If the next statement is a call to a subroutine, the entire subroutine executes without stepping through its statements one at a time.

- **s.** Executes the next code statement and then pauses. If the next statement is a call to a subroutine, the first statement in the subroutine is executed and then the script pauses awaiting the next user command.

To get a feel of the differences between these two commands, let's use the Perl debugger to process the following script.

```
#!/usr/bin/perl -w
#
# JokeMachine.pl

clear_the_screen();

$reply = "";

while ( $reply ne 'yes') {
  print 'Would you like to hear a joke? (yes/no): ';
  chomp($reply = <STDIN>)
  if( $reply ne 'yes') {
    print "\nHum... Perhaps you misunderstood.\n\n";
  }
}
```

```perl
clear_the_screen();

print "\nWhat disappears the moment you say its name?";
chomp($reply = <STDIN>);

if( $reply ne 'silence') {
  print "\nSorry. Wrong answer. Think about it and try again later.\n\n";
} else {
  print "\nYes, that is right. Well done!\n\n";
}

sub clear_the_screen {
  for ($i=0; $i < 25; ++$i){
    print "\n";
  }
}
```

When initially started, the debugger displays the following output, pausing at the first statement within the script.

```
C:\>perl -d JokeMachine.pl

Loading DB routines from perl5db.pl version 1.28
Editor support available.

Enter h or 'h h' for help, or 'perldoc perldebug' for more help.

main::(JokeMachine.pl:5):        clear_the_screen();
  clears the screen
  DB<1>
```

The first statement in the script is a call to a subroutine named clear_the_screen. If you type the n command and press Enter, the debugger executes this subroutine without pausing to display its statements and then pauses at the first statement that follows the subroutine calls as shown here.

```
main::(JokeMachine.pl:7):        $reply = "";
player reply
  DB<1>
```

Alternatively, you could have used the s command to step through the clear_the_screen subroutine.

```
DB<1> s
main::clear_the_screen(JokeMachine.pl:31):
31:         }
  DB<1>
```

To execute either the n or s command again, you can do so by pressing the Enter key as demonstrated below, where the previously entered s command is automatically repeated four times by simply pressing the Enter key over and over again.

```
  DB<1>
main::clear_the_screen(JokeMachine.pl:29):
29:        for ($i=0; $i < 25; ++$i){
  DB<1>

main::clear_the_screen(JokeMachine.pl:30):
30:            print "\n";
  DB<1>

main::clear_the_screen(JokeMachine.pl:30):
30:            print "\n";
  DB<1>

main::clear_the_screen(JokeMachine.pl:30):
30:            print "\n";
  DB<1>
```

Note that the clear_the_screen subroutine iterates 25 times, which explains why you see the print "\n"; statement repeat over and over again.

Resuming or Restarting Execution

The Perl debugger provides other commands for controlling script execution, allowing you to execute more than one statement at a time or even to start the debugging process over again. Any time you want to stop stepping through script execution, you can execute the c command. Once this command has been issued, the script continues its execution, pausing only if it comes across a breakpoint or some other halting statement, such as a command that pauses to collect user input.

If you are stepping through the inside of a subroutine and want to skip the step by step execution of the rest of the statements in that subroutine, use the r command. The r command executes the rest of the subroutine and returns control back to the statement that called the subroutine.

At any point during debugging, you can stop and restart the debugging of the script again using the R command. The R command automatically resets any variables set during the previous execution of the script back to their default values. However, any breakpoints that you have already set remain in tact. (Bookmarks are discussed a little later in this chapter.)

Tracing Logic Flow

Another helpful debugger feature is the ability to enable tracing, which is done using the t command. When tracing is enabled, the debugger displays both script statements and any script output as it runs. Executing the t command again disables tracing. Tracing is helpful in situations where you want to allow the script to run normally without stepping through it line by line but still want to view what is occurring. Tracing is often used in conjunction with breakpoints, discussed a little later in the chapter, to allow small portions of the scripts to run at a time. To see the trace command in action, run the following script using Perl's debugger.

```perl
#!/usr/bin/perl

my $randomnumber = 0;
$randomnumber = getnumber();
print "The randomly generated number is $randomnumber";

sub getnumber {
  my $number = 0;
  $number = int(rand 100) + 1;
  return $number;
}
```

As you can see, when this script is executed, it pauses just before the execution of the first statement. trace is then enabled and the c command executes to allow the script to continue running.

```
C:\>perl -d test.pl

Loading DB routines from perl5db.pl version 1.28
Editor support available.
```

```
Enter h or 'h h' for help, or 'perldoc perldebug' for more help.

main::(test.pl:3):       my $randomnumber = 0;
  DB<1> t
Trace = on
  DB<1> c
main::(test.pl:5):       $randomnumber = getnumber();
main::getnumber(test.pl:11):    my $number = 0;
main::getnumber(test.pl:13):    $number = int(rand 100) + 1;
main::getnumber(test.pl:15):    return $number;
main::(test.pl:7):       print "The randomly generated number is
$randomnumber";
The randomly generated number is Debugged program terminated.
Use q to quit or R to restart,
  use O inhibit_exit to avoid stopping after program termination,
  h q, h R or h O to get additional info.
  DB<1>
```

As the debugger executes the script, both script statements and output are displayed.

Quitting the Debugger

Once you are done using the debugger to analyze the execution of your Perl script, you can quit it by entering the q command. Entering this command returns you to the operating system Command Prompt, where you can run the script normally.

Locating Your Position within the Script

Sometimes it is difficult to determine just exactly where you are within your script when stepping through it. To help you get your bearings, you can use the l command to list the next ten lines (after the current line). Hopefully this will help you figure out your exact position. The l command is also useful in situations where you want to look ahead to see what statements are about to execute.

Displaying and Modifying Variable Values

Each time your script pauses in the debugger, you have the opportunity to display variable values or even to change variable values if you need to. Both of these tasks are accomplished using the x command. For example, you could use the x command to display the value of a variable scalar named $x as shown below.

```
main::(test.pl:3):      $x = 100;
DB<1> n
main::(test.pl:5):      print $x;
  DB<1> x $x
0  100
  DB<2>
```

You can also use the x command to display the contents of an array using the following syntax.

x *@arrayname*

Likewise, you could display the contents of any hash using the following syntax.

x *%hashname*

You can also change the value of any variable (scalar, array, or hash) when the script is paused in the debugger.

```
main::(test.pl:3):      $x = 5;
  DB<1> n
main::(test.pl:5):      print "$x \n";
  DB<1> $x = 100

  DB<2> n
100
main::(test.pl:7):      chomp($reply = <STDIN>);
  DB<2>
```

In this example a script has been executed that sets a variable named $x equal to 5. However, the x command is then used at the debugger Command Prompt to change the value of $x to 100. The next statement in the script, which is a print statement, is then executed. It prints out the value of $x, which as you can see is now 100.

 TRICK   You can also use the x command to execute small pieces of Perl code. For example, x $x[2] would retrieve the third element stored in the array @x.

Displaying Help Information
You can view debugger help information at any time by entering the h command as demonstrated in Figure 8.9.

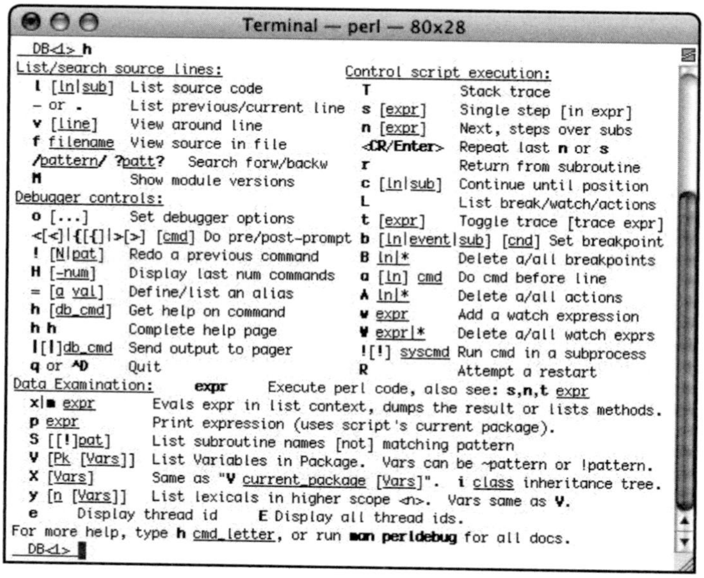

FIGURE 8.9

Using the h command to display information about available debugger commands as seen on MAC OS X.

The h command displays a list of debugger commands. There are a number of variations of this command that you may find useful. For example, h *command* displays information about a particular debugger command.

```
DB<1> h r
r         Return from current subroutine.
rerun             Rerun session to current position.
rerun n           Rerun session to numbered command.
rerun -n          Rerun session to number'th-to-last command.
  DB<2>
```

Executing Any Perl Statement

Perl's built-in debugger is an extremely powerful and flexible tool. In addition to using it to view values stored in variables, you can also use it to execute any valid Perl command. As an example of how to do this, consider the following.

```
C:\Documents and Settings\Owner\Desktop>perl -d test.pl

Loading DB routines from perl5db.pl version 1.28
Editor support available.

Enter h or `h h' for help, or 'perldoc perldebug' for more help.
```

```
main::(test.pl:3):        @names = ("Alexander", "William", "Molly");
DB<1> n
main::(test.pl:6):        chomp($reply = <STDIN>);
  DB<1> foreach $i (@names) { print "$i \n"; }
Alexander
William
Molly


  DB<2>
```

In this example, the debugger executes a small script. The debugger stops running at a statement just before the execution of a statement that sets up an array. The n command is then used to run that statement. To verify that things worked as expected, a small foreach code block is then manually entered at the debugger Command Prompt. In response the debugger displays the contents of the array. At this point additional commands can be entered, for example, to add additional elements to the array or to continue the execution of the script.

Setting and Working with Breakpoints

Stepping through small scripts a line at a time is a relatively easy and useful exercise. However, stepping through scripts a line at a time can be a daunting task for large scripts. A better way to tackle larger scripts is to set up breakpoints at different places within your script where you would like to pause and check things out. A breakpoint is simply a marker set by the debugger that tells it when to pause script execution.

The Perl debugger lets you set as many breakpoints as you want. Breakpoints can be specified for any executable Perl statement or subroutine. Breakpoints cannot be set for:

- A brace "}"
- A blank line
- A comment line
- Punctuation (for example: ");")

To set a breakpoint, you use the b command. If you enter the b command by itself, the breakpoint is assigned to the current line. If you specify a specific line number, the breakpoint is set at that line. Lastly, if you specify the name of a subroutine, the breakpoint is set at the first statement within the subroutine.

In order to set breakpoints you need to know either the line number of the statement or the name of the subroutine where you want to set the breakpoint. Using the l command, you can view a list of statements that follow the current statement as demonstrated here.

```
DB<1> l
3==>     my $randomnumber = 0;
4
5:       $randomnumber = getnumber();
6
7:       print "The randomly generated number is $randomnumber";
8
9        sub getnumber {
10
11:          my $number = 0;
12
```

To the left of each statement is that statement's line number. You can issue the l command repeatedly to view additional code statements.

Once you have located a line where you want to add a breakpoint, you can do so using the b command.

```
DB<1> b 5
```

You can also establish a breakpoint for a subroutine.

```
DB<2> b getnumber
```

TRICK It is easy to lose track of your breakpoints when you set a lot of them. Using the L command you can display a list of every breakpoint set within the script as demonstrated here.

```
  DB<3> L
test.pl:
 5:      $randomnumber = getnumber();
   break if (1)
 11:        my $number = 0;
   break if (1)
  DB<3>
```

Once your have set up breakpoints you can resume script executing using the c command. Your script will continue to execute normally until it reaches either a breakpoint or the end of the script.

Using the Perl Debugger as an Interactive Test Environment

If you want, you can use the Perl debugger as an interactive test environment by starting it using the following command.

```
perl -d -e1
```

You can then enter any valid Perl statement to see how Perl processes it. For example, look at Figure 8.10, which shows an example of how to interactively declare two scalar variables, add them together, and then display the result.

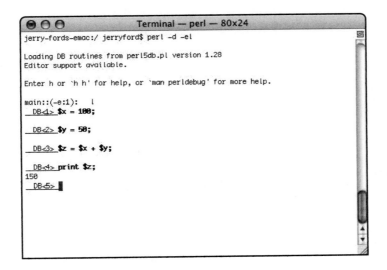

FIGURE 8.10

You can also use the built-in Perl debugger to experiment with different Perl commands to test their execution.

Although it is a rather simplistic example, Figure 8.10 clearly demonstrates how to interactively experiment with and test different Perl statements to see if Perl processes them as you expect. Once tested, you can add your tested statements into actual Perl scripts with the confidence of knowing that the statements will execute as expected.

Using a Graphical Perl IDE/Debugger

If you find working with Perl's built-in debugger a bit challenging or simply prefer working in a GUI-based development and debugging environment, then you may be better off installing a graphical Perl IDE/Debugger. For example, ActiveState has developed the Komodo integrated development environment. This application includes a powerful Perl script debugger. Komodo is an extremely flexible development application that supports a number of different programming languages including Perl, Python, Ruby, and PHP. It runs on Linux,

Mac OS X, Windows, and Solaris UNIX. It comes in both Professional and Personal editions and can be downloaded for a free trial at www.activestate.com/Products/Komodo.

Komodo's IDE provides many powerful scripting features that you will find useful, including:

- Automatic statement color coding
- Automatic statement indentation
- Support for simultaneously editing multiple scripts
- An AutoComplete feature that assists in completing code statements

In addition to these features, Komodo provides powerful Perl script debugging capabilities. Its debugging features include support for :

- Breakpoints
- Stepping
- Watching variables
- Call stack

For a sneak peak at Komodo's debugging capabilities, look at Figure 8.11.

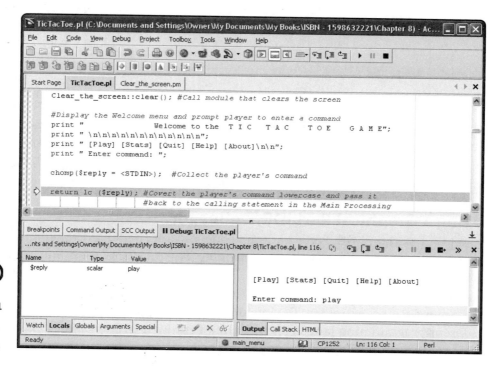

FIGURE 8.11

The ActiveState Komodo graphical IDE includes a powerful time-saving debugging.

ActiveState also offers another graphic debugging application as part of its Perl Dev Kit software package. ActiveState's Perl Dev Kit is a collection of applications designed to help streamline the process of developing and deploying Perl scripts. ActiveState advertises the debugger supplied with the Perl Dev Kit as a lightweight GUI debugger for Perl. Once installed, it automatically sets itself up in place of Perl's built-in debugger, although you can easily switch back if you want. It works with Windows, Solaris, AIX, HP-UNIX, and Linux and can be downloaded for a free trial at www.activestate.com/Products/Perl_Dev_Kit.

TIPS FOR WRITING CLEANER CODE

The best way to deal with errors is to prevent them from occurring in the first place. To achieve this objective you should carefully plan out your Perl scripts before you begin writing them and thoroughly test them during development. In addition to following these principles, there are a number of additional steps that you can take in your effort to reduce the number of errors in your scripts, as outlined in the sections that follow.

Document What Your Script Is Doing

One of the most important things to do when developing your Perl scripts is to embed documentation directly into the scripts using comment statements. This type of documentation is essential because in addition to making your scripts easier to maintain and support in the long run, it also helps you to focus on the task at hand and in doing so also helps you to catch little mistakes that might lead to errors.

When each game script was developed in this book, comments were left out in order to streamline the presentation and discussion. However, even though each game script developed in this book is initially described in a step by step fashion, each chapter ends by presenting a complete copy of the chapter's game script packed full of comments.

In addition to providing plenty of documentation, make sure that you indent your code statements to make them easier to read and make liberal use of blank space in order to make your scripts as easy to understand as possible.

Enable Warnings

Each of the game scripts that you have developed in this book begin with an opening shebang statement as shown below.

```
#!/usr/bin/perl
```

Game scripts of the type presented in this book do not impose any strict requirements on the programmer. However, if you make the transition to software development at a professional level, you may find that you are required to hold yourself to a higher standard, which you can do by turning on warnings as part of your shebang statement as demonstrated here.

```
#!/usr/bin/perl -w
```

As has already been discussed in this book, enabling warnings tells Perl to display warnings for anything it sees as a potential problem, allowing you to address issues that you might otherwise miss.

Add Use Strict

If necessary, you can instruct Perl to warn you of any undeclared variables in order to further tighten down the execution of your scripts. To accomplish this, you add the use strict statement to the beginning of your Perl scripts. An example of the effect of using the use strict statement is shown here.

```
$x1 = 10;
$y1 = 20;
$z1 = 0;

$z1 = $x1 + $y2;

print $z1;
```

If you look closely, you see that this script contains a logical error. Instead of adding together the value of $x1 and $y1, the script adds $x1 to $y2. Perl, being an extremely flexible scripting language, happily allows $y2, an undeclared variable to spring to life at its mere reference. The end result is that $z1 is set equal to 10, which is not at all what was intended.

To detect this type of error during script development, you can add use strict; to the beginning of the example and then run the example again. In doing so, the following errors will be reported.

```
C:\ >test.pl
Global symbol "$x1" requires explicit package name at C:\test.pl line 5.
Global symbol "$y1" requires explicit package name at C:\test.pl line 6.
Global symbol "$z1" requires explicit package name at C:\test.pl line 7.
Global symbol "$z1" requires explicit package name at C:\test.pl line 9.
Global symbol "$x1" requires explicit package name at C:\test.pl line 9.
Global symbol "$y2" requires explicit package name at C:\test.pl line 9.
Global symbol "$z1" requires explicit package name at C:\test.pl line 11.
```

```
Execution of C:\test.pl aborted due to compilation errors.

C:\ >
```

Once aware of this situation, you could modify the script by adding my before each of the first three statements as shown here.

```
use strict;

my $x1 = 10;
my $y1 = 20;
my $z1 = 0;

$z1 = $x1 + $y2;

print $z1;
```

Now, when you run the example again, you'll still get one more error because of the $y2 error as shown below.

```
C:\ >test.pl
Global symbol "$y2" requires explicit package name at C:\test.pl line 9.
Execution of C:\test.pl aborted due to compilation errors.

C:\ >
```

Rename $y2 to $y1 and rerun the script again. This time the expected results will be achieved. As you can see, the addition of use strict; made locating and correcting this error a snap.

Keep Things Simple

As important as good documentation and the implementation of strict variable declaration is, it is equally important to keep your Perl scripts as simple as possible. For starters, streamline your scripts as much as possible. As a general rule of thumb, you should favor simplicity over elegance. For example, instead of incrementing a variable as shown below

```
$x = $x + 1
```

you should use the following technique.

```
$x +=1
```

A big part of keeping things simple involves not reinventing the wheel whenever possible. In other words, don't write a subroutine to do something that has been already written and made available to use. Instead, take advantage of the modules shipped with Perl. Not only are they thoroughly tested and reliable, but they also allow you to reduce the size of your scripts, making them easier to maintain and less prone to error. In addition, you will find plenty of battle-tested modules ready for download at www.cpan.org, which you can use to tackle almost any programming situation.

Break Things Down into Subroutines

Another fundamental organizational tool for building Perl scripts is subroutines. Subroutines allow you to group related statements to make scripts easier to understand and maintain. Subroutines facilitate code reuse, thus allowing for smaller scripts. In addition, subroutines facilitate the scoping of variables, which provides you with tighter control over the data used in your scripts, thus reducing the possibility of error.

BACK TO THE TIC TAC TOE GAME

Now it is time to turn your attention back to this chapter's game project, the Tic Tac Toe game. This game displays an interactive game board that is automatically updated at the end of each player's turn. Even though the game is made entirely of text characters, it has a graphical look and feel. The game is designed to be played by two players and automatically keeps track of player turns.

The game board is organized into a logical series of squares, each of which is referenced via a coordinate system. Coordinates a1 through a3 represent squares that are located on the first row of the game board, b1 through b3 represent the middle squares, and c1 through c3 represent the lower row of squares.

Designing the Game

Following the same model used to develop the other scripts within this book, the Tic Tac Toe game is developed in a series of steps, as outlined below.

1. Creating a new script.
2. Developing MAIN Processing controlling logic.
3. Creating the reset_game subroutine.
4. Creating the main_menu subroutine.
5. Creating the play_the_game subroutine.
6. Creating the display_game_board subroutine.
7. Creating the validate_selection subroutine.
8. Creating the identify_selection subroutine.

9. Creating the `look_for_winner` subroutine.
10. Creating the `display_stats` subroutine.
11. Creating the `display_help` subroutine.
12. Creating the `display_about` subroutine.

Creating the Script File

Let's begin the development of the Tic Tac Toe game by creating a new Perl script file named TicTacToe.pl and adding the following code statements to it.

```perl
#!/usr/bin/perl
#
#The Tic Tac Toe Game (TicTacToe.pl)

use Clear_the_screen;

my $isvalid  = 0;
my $choice = "";

my $player  = "X";
my $winner  = "";
my $nomoves = 0;
my $message = "";

my $plays = 0;
my $xwins = 0;
my $owins = 0;
my $ties  = 0;


my $a1, $a2, $a3, $b1, $b2, $b3, $c1, $c2, $c3;
```

This script utilizes the `Clear_the_script` module's `clear` subroutine that you created back in Chapter 6, "Scope and Modules." The first statement after the opening comment statements loads the module. Next, a series of global variables used throughout the script are defined. In addition, a series of variables ($a1 through $c3) representing each square on the Tic Tac Toe board are declared.

Controlling Game Play

The next step in creating the Tic Tac Toe game is to develop the programming logic that provides high-level control over game execution. In the case of the Tic Tac Toe script, this means setting up a while loop that controls the display and interaction of the game's main menu, as shown below.

```perl
while (! $valid) {

  &reset_game();

  my $choice = "";

  $choice = &main_menu();

  if ($choice eq "play") {

      $plays += 1;
      &play_the_game();

  } elsif ($choice eq "stats") {

      &display_stats();

  } elsif ($choice eq "quit") {

      $isvalid = 1;

  } elsif ($choice eq "help") {

      &display_help();

  } elsif ($choice eq "about") {

      &display_about();

  }

}
```

As you can see, the first statement inside the while loop executes a subroutine named reset_game, which is responsible for resetting global variables in preparation for a new game.

Next, the `main_menu` subroutine is called. This subroutine collects user commands (e.g. Play, Stats, Quit, Help, About) and returns the results in a variable named $choice.

Next, an if…elsif conditional block executes, calling various subroutines based on the value of $choice. If $choice equals Play, the value of $play (which keeps count of the total number of games played) is incremented and the `play_the_game` subroutine is called. If $choice equals stats, the `display_stat` subroutine is called. If $choice equals Quit, the value of $valid is set equal to true, which causes the while loop to stop running, thus ending the game. Finally, the `display_help` and `display_about` subroutines are called if the player enters a Help or About command. If the player enters anything other than Play, Stats, Quit, Help, or About, the input is ignored and the while loop iterates, prompting the player to enter a command.

The Tic Tac Toe script consists of a number of other subroutines, which are called when necessary by the subroutines outlined in the sections that follow.

Preparing for a New Game

Before the start of any new game of Tic Tac Toe, it is necessary to ensure that the variables representing the squares on the game board are reset. In addition, a few other global variables used to control game play must also be reset. The code statements that perform this task are located in the `reset_game` subroutine, shown below.

```
sub reset_game {

    $a1 = " ";
    $a2 = " ";
    $a3 = " ";
    $b1 = " ";
    $b2 = " ";
    $b3 = " ";
    $c1 = " ";
    $c2 = " ";
    $c3 = " ";

    $player = "X";
    $winner = "";
    $nomoves = 0;
    $message = "";

}
```

By setting the value of $a1 through $c3 equal to "", you effectively clear off the game board. Setting $player equal to X makes Player X the default starting player for each new game. Setting $winner equal to "" erases any record of the previous game's winner. Setting $nomoves to zero readies the script to start tracking the number of moves made in the next game, and setting $message equal to "" removes any previously displayed message from the Tic Tac Toe game board.

Displaying the Game's Main Menu

The code to display the game's main menu is shown here. As you can see, it is contained in a subroutine named main_menu and begins by calling the Clear_the_screen module's clear subroutine.

```perl
sub main_menu {

  my $reply = "";

  Clear_the_screen::clear();

  print "                    Welcome to the  T I C   T A C    T O E    G A M E";
  print " \n\n\n\n\n\n\n\n\n\n\n\n";
  print " [Play] [Stats] [Quit] [Help] [About]\n\n";
  print " Enter command: ";

  chomp($reply = <STDIN>);

  return lc ($reply);

}
```

The subroutine displays a list of menu commands and returns the player's input after first converting it to lowercase.

Managing the Play of Individual Games

The play_the_game subroutine is responsible for controlling the play of individual Tic Tac Toe games. Because this subroutine is fairly complex, we'll put it together a few statements at a time. For starters, begin building the subroutine by writing the following statements.

```perl
sub play_the_game {

  my $isfinished = 0;
```

```
my $validmove = 0;
my $reply = "";
```

Here, three private variables are declared. $finished will be used to control the termination of the subroutine's loop, $validmove is used to keep track of whether a player's move is valid or invalid, and $reply will be used to store input provided by the player.

Now, append the following statement to the subroutine.

```
until ($isfinished) {

  if ($winner eq "X") {
    $xwins += 1;
    $message = "GAME OVER: Player X has won!";
    &display_game_board();
    print "\n Press Enter to continue: ";
    $reply = <STDIN>;
    return;
  }
```

The first statement sets up an until loop that will be used to control the execution of the game. Then an if block is set up that is responsible for determining when Player X has won the game, which it does by checking to see if the value of $winner has been set equal to X. If this is the case, $xwins is incremented by one in order to keep count of the number of games won by Player X. $message is then assigned a text string indicating that Player X has won the game. This string will be displayed when the game board is displayed, which occurs when the next statement executes. The subroutine then pauses, waiting for the player to press the Enter key. Once the Enter key has been pressed, the play_the_game subroutine is terminated by executing the return statement, passing control back to the while loop in the script's Main Processing Section.

Next, append the following statements to the play_the_game subroutine. As you can see, the statements check to see if Player O has won the game, replicating the same logic previously used to see if Player X had won the game.

```
  if ($winner eq "O") {
    $owins += 1;
    $message = "GAME OVER: Player O has won!";
    &display_game_board();
    print "\n Press Enter to continue: ";
    $reply = <STDIN>;
```

```
      return;
   }
```

Now append the following if block to the end of the subroutine. These statements check to see if the game has resulted in a tie, repeating the same basic logic used in the two previous code blocks.

```
   if ($winner eq "tie") {
      $ties += 1;
      $message = "GAME OVER: Tie!";
      &display_game_board();
      print "\n Press Enter to continue: ";
      $reply = <STDIN>;
      return;
   }
```

Next, append the following statements to the end of the subroutine.

```
   $message = "Player $player" . "'s move";
   &display_game_board();
   print " Select a square: ";
   chomp($reply = <STDIN>);
```

The first statement shown here assigns a string to $message that identifies whose turn it is. The message is displayed by the next statement, which calls the display_game_board subroutine. Next, the player is prompted to make a move by entering the coordinates representing a square on the game board. The player's input is then stored in a variable named $reply.

The next step is to validate player input, which is accomplished by appending the following code statements to the subroutine.

```
   $validmove = &validate_selection($reply);

   if ($validmove == 1) {
      $nomoves = $nomoves + 1;
      &identify_selection($reply);
   } else {
      Clear_the_screen::clear();
      print "Invalid move. Press Enter to try again.\n\n";
      $reply = <STDIN>;
   }
```

The first statement shown here calls the validate_selection subroutine, passing it $reply as an argument. The validate_selection subroutine determines whether the player's move is valid, passing its determination back to the calling statement, which assigns it to the variable named $validmove. Next, an if…else conditional code block executes, analyzing the value assigned to $validmove. If the variable is equal to true, the value of $nomoves is incremented and the identify_selection subroutine is called, thus denoting a specific square on the game board. If $validmove is not equal to true, the Clear_the_screen module's clear subroutine is called and an error message is displayed.

Not all games will end with a winner, so the next set of statements check to see if $nonames equals 9, in which case $winner is set equal to tie. Otherwise, the look_for_winner subroutine is called. This subroutine is responsible for determining if either player has won the game by selecting three squares in a row.

```
if ($nomoves == 9) {
   $winner = "tie";
} else {
   &look_for_winner();
}
```

Finally, you can finish up the play_the_game subroutine by appending the following statements to the end of the subroutine. As you can see, the value of $validmove is checked to see if it is equal to 1, meaning that the game is not over yet. Therefore, the value of $player is toggled between 0 and X at the end of every turn, thus controlling when each player gets a turn. The last two lines are closing curly braces, which match up against the until loop's and the subroutine's opening curly braces.

```
if ($validmove == 1) {
   if ($player eq "X") {
      $player = "O";
   } else {
      $player = "X";
   }
}


}


}
```

Displaying the Tic Tac Toe Game Board

The code statements that make up the `display_game_board` subroutine, shown below, are responsible for displaying the Tic Tac Toe game board when called.

```
sub display_game_board {

  Clear_the_screen::clear();

  print "                              Tic Tac Toe\n\n\n";
  print "                         1       2       3\n\n";
  print "                                 |       |\n";
  print "                     A     $a1   |  $a2  |    $a3\n";
  print "                                 |       |\n";
  print "                     -------|-------|-------\n";
  print "                                 |       |\n";
  print "                     B     $b1   |  $b2  |    $b3\n";
  print "                                 |       |\n";
  print "                     -------|-------|-------\n";
  print "                                 |       |\n";
  print "                     C     $c1   |  $c2  |    $c3\n";
  print "                                 |       |\n\n\n";
  print "                     $message\n\n"

}
```

To prepare the screen to display the game board, the `Clear_the_screen` module's `clear` subroutine is called first. Then a series of `print` statements execute, displaying the board. Note that embedded within certain `print` statements are global variables that represent each square on the game board. As players take turns making moves, these variables are assigned Xs and Os, allowing each move to be visually displayed each time the subroutine is called. You should also take note of the last `print` statement, which contains a reference to the `$message` variable, thus displaying any text string assigned to the variable.

Figure 8.12 shows how the game board looks when it is called for execution by the script.

Validating Player Moves

The `validate_selection` subroutine, shown below, is responsible for determining whether or not player moves are valid.

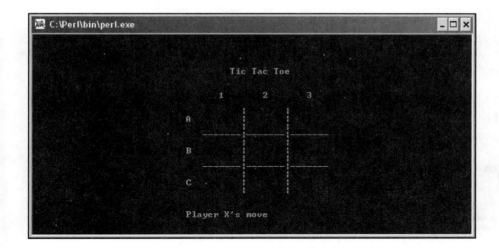

FIGURE 8.12

Building the Tic Tac Toe game's game board interface.

```perl
sub validate_selection {

  my $move = $_[0];

  CASE: {
    $move eq "a1" && do { if ($a1 ne " ") {return "false";} };
    $move eq "a2" && do { if ($a2 ne " ") {return "false";} };
    $move eq "a3" && do { if ($a3 ne " ") {return "false";} };
    $move eq "b1" && do { if ($b1 ne " ") {return "false";} };
    $move eq "b2" && do { if ($b2 ne " ") {return "false";} };
    $move eq "b3" && do { if ($b3 ne " ") {return "false";} };
    $move eq "c1" && do { if ($c1 ne " ") {return "false";} };
    $move eq "c2" && do { if ($c2 ne " ") {return "false";} };
    $move eq "c3" && do { if ($c3 ne " ") {return "false";} };

  }

  if ($move =~ /a1|a2|a3|b1|b2|b3|c1|c2|c3/) {
    return 1;
  } else {
    return 0;
  }

}
```

To be valid, a move (e.g. the selection of a square) must not be equal to a square that has been selected already. The custom CASE block shown above performs this validation check. In the event that the player's move matches an already selected square, a value of false is returned by the subroutine.

If the player input passes to the previous validation test, an if...else conditional code block is executed, which returns a value of true if the player's input was in the range of a1 through c3. Otherwise, a value of false is returned.

Associating Player Move with Game Board Squares

The code for the identify_selection subroutine, shown here, takes the player's move passed to it as an argument and assigns it to the appropriate square on the Tic Tac Toe game board.

```
sub identify_selection {

  my $move = $_[0];

  if ($move eq "a1") {$a1 = $player}
  if ($move eq "a2") {$a2 = $player}
  if ($move eq "a3") {$a3 = $player}
  if ($move eq "b1") {$b1 = $player}
  if ($move eq "b2") {$b2 = $player}
  if ($move eq "b3") {$b3 = $player}
  if ($move eq "c1") {$c1 = $player}
  if ($move eq "c2") {$c2 = $player}
  if ($move eq "c3") {$c3 = $player}


}
```

Determining when a Game Has Been Won

The look_for_winner subroutine, shown below, is responsible for determining whether the current player has won the game as a result of her last move.

```
sub look_for_winner {

  if ($a1 eq $player) {
    if ($a2 eq $player) {
      if ($a3 eq $player) {
        $winner = $player;
      }
```

```
    }
  }

  if ($b1 eq $player) {
    if ($b2 eq $player) {
      if ($b3 eq $player) {
        $winner = $player;
      }
    }
  }

  if ($c1 eq $player) {
    if ($c2 eq $player) {
      if ($c3 eq $player) {
        $winner = $player;
      }
    }
  }

  if ($a1 eq $player) {
    if ($b1 eq $player) {
      if ($c1 eq $player) {
        $winner = $player;
      }
    }
  }

  if ($a2 eq $player) {
    if ($b2 eq $player) {
      if ($c2 eq $player) {
        $winner = $player;
      }
    }
  }

  if ($a3 eq $player) {
    if ($b3 eq $player) {
      if ($c3 eq $player) {
```

```
            $winner = $player;
        }
      }
    }

  if ($a1 eq $player) {
    if ($b2 eq $player) {
      if ($c3 eq $player) {
        $winner = $player;
      }
    }
  }

  if ($c1 eq $player) {
    if ($b2 eq $player) {
      if ($a3 eq $player) {
        $winner = $player;
      }
    }
  }


}
```

As you can see, a total of eight separate evaluations are performed using a series of conditional code blocks. Each of the conditional code blocks includes additional embedded code blocks. Together the eight code blocks check for a winner by seeing if the current player has managed to line up three squares horizontally, vertically, or diagonally.

Displaying Game Statistics

The Tic Tac Toe game's main menu allows the player to view game statistics by entering the Stats command. When this command is issued, the display_stats subroutine shown below is executed.

```
sub display_stats {

  my $reply = "";
  my $row = "_" x 61;

  Clear_the_screen::clear();
```

```
print " Tic Tac Toe game Statistics\n\n";
print " $row\n\n";
print " Total number of games played: $plays\n\n";
print " Number of games won by player X: $xwins\n\n";
print " Number of games won by player O: $owins\n\n";
print " Number of games tied: $ties\n\n";
print " $row\n\n";
print "\n\n\n\n\n\n";

print " Press Enter to continue: ";
$reply = <STDIN>;


}
```

This subroutine begins by executing the Clear_the_screen module's clear subroutine and then displays a series of print statements that include embedded global variables representing various game statistics. The last two statements in the subroutine pause the script's execution until the player presses the Enter key.

Displaying the Help Screen

The display_help subroutine, shown here, is responsible for displaying instructions for playing the game. It is executed whenever the player enters the Help command at the game's main menu.

```
sub display_help {

  my $reply = 0;
  my $row = "_" x 61;

  Clear_the_screen::clear();

  print " TIC TAC TOE HELP:\n\n";
  print " $row\n\n";
  print " Type Play to begin the game or type Quit to exit. To view\n";
  print " game statistics type Stats. To get help type Help and to\n";
  print " learn more about the game and its developer type About.\n";
  print " $row\n\n";
  print "\n\n\n\n\n\n\n\n\n\n";
```

```perl
  print " Press Enter to continue: ";
  $reply = <STDIN>;

}
```

As you can see, this subroutine consists of a call to the Clear_the_screen module's clear subroutine followed by a number of print statements.

Displaying Additional Game Information

The code for the display_about subroutine is shown below. As you can see, it is basically identical to the display_help subroutine.

```perl
sub display_about {

  my $reply = 0;
  my $row = "_" x 61;

  Clear_the_screen::clear();

  print " ABOUT THE TIC TAC TOE GAME:\n\n";
  print " $row\n\n";
  print " The Tic Tac Toe Game - Copyright 2006.\n\n";
  print " Created by Jerry Lee Ford, Jr.\n";
  print " $row\n\n";
  print "\n\n\n\n\n\n\n\n\n\n\n";

  print " Press Enter to continue: ";
  $reply = <STDIN>;

}
```

The Final Result

That's it. You have everything that you need to assemble and execute the Tic Tac Toe game.
A complete copy of the TicTacToe.pl script is provided below. It has been enhanced through
the addition of an organizational script template and comments that document key functionality and make the script easier to read and understand.

```perl
#!/usr/bin/perl
#
#The Tic Tac Toe Game (TicTacToe.pl)
```

```perl
#-------------------------------------------------------------------------
# Initialization Section
#-------------------------------------------------------------------------

#Initialize external modules and script variables

use Clear_the_screen; #Load modules used to clear the screen

my $isvalid  = 0;  #Global variables used to control loop in Main Processing
                   #Section
my $choice = "";   #Global variable used to store player menu commands

my $player  = "X";    #Global variable used to keep track of player turns
my $winner  = "";     #Global variable used to identify who won the game
my $nomoves = 0;      #Global variables used to keep track of the number
                      #of moves made in a game
my $message = "";  #Global variables used to display status messages

my $plays = 0;  #Global variable used to count the number of games played
my $xwins = 0;  #Global variable used to count the games won by player X
my $owins = 0;  #Global variable used to count the games won by player 0
my $ties  = 0;  #Global variable used to count the number of tied games

#Global variables used to represent a square on the game board
my $a1, $a2, $a3, $b1, $b2, $b3, $c1, $c2, $c3;


#-------------------------------------------------------------------------
# MAIN Processing Section
#-------------------------------------------------------------------------

#This loop controls the game's main menu
while (! $valid) {

  &reset_game(); #Call subroutine that clears out the game board

  my $choice = ""; #Reset variable used to store player's menu selection
```

```perl
$choice = &main_menu();   #Call subroutine that displays the game's
                          #menu and collects player menu commands

if ($choice eq "play") {   #Process the Play menu command

    $plays += 1;   #Increment variable that keeps count of games played
    &play_the_game();  #Call subroutine that controls game play

} elsif ($choice eq "stats") {   #Process the Stats menu command

    &display_stats();  #Call subroutine that displays game statistics

} elsif ($choice eq "quit") {   #Process the Quit menu command

  $isvalid = 1;  #Set variable to true in order to terminate the loop

} elsif ($choice eq "help") {   #Process the Help menu command

  &display_help();  #Call subroutine to display the game's Help screen

} elsif ($choice eq "about") {  #Process the About menu command

  &display_about();  #Call subroutine to display the game's About screen

}

}


#-------------------------------------------------------------------------
# Subroutine Section
#-------------------------------------------------------------------------

#This subroutine is responsible for clearing the game board and for
#resetting default values for specific global variables
sub reset_game {

  #Reset each square on the game board to a blank space
```

```
$a1 = " ";
$a2 = " ";
$a3 = " ";
$b1 = " ";
$b2 = " ";
$b3 = " ";
$c1 = " ";
$c2 = " ";
$c3 = " ";

$player = "X"; #Reset default player
$winner = "";  #Reset global variable used to identify game winner
$nomoves = 0;  #Reset global variable used to keep count of player moves
$message = ""; #Reset variable used to display messages

}


#This subroutine is responsible for displaying the game's main menu and
#collecting player commands
sub main_menu {

  my $reply = "";  #Local variable used to store player commands

  Clear_the_screen::clear(); #Call module that clears the screen

  #Display the Welcome menu and prompt player to enter a command
  print "          Welcome to the  T I C   T A C    T O E    G A M E";
  print " \n\n\n\n\n\n\n\n\n\n\n\n";
  print " [Play] [Stats] [Quit] [Help] [About]\n\n";
  print " Enter command: ";

  chomp($reply = <STDIN>);  #Collect the player's command

  return lc ($reply); #Convert the player's command to lowercase and pass it
                  #back to the calling statement in the Main Processing
      #Section
```

```perl
}


#This subroutine controls the play of an individual game
sub play_the_game {

  my $isfinished = 0;  #Local variable used to control subroutine's loop
  my $validmove = 0;   #Local variable that identifies player moves as
                       #valid or invalid
  my $reply = "";  #Local variable used to store player commands


  until ($finished) {  #Each iteration provides the player with
                       #the opportunity to select a move

    #Check to see if player X has won the game
    if ($winner eq "X") {
      $xwins += 1;  #Increment the number of games won by player X
      $message = "GAME OVER: Player X has won!";  #Display winner
      &display_game_board();  #Call subroutine that displays the game board
      print "\n Press Enter to continue: ";
      $reply = <STDIN>;  #Pause to allow the player to read the screen
      return;  #The game is over so exit the subroutine
    }


    #Check to see if player O has won the game
    if ($winner eq "O") {
      $owins += 1;  #Increment the number of games won by player O
      $message = "GAME OVER: Player O has won!";  #Display winner
      &display_game_board();  #Call subroutine that displays the game board
      print "\n Press Enter to continue: ";
      $reply = <STDIN>;  #Pause to allow the player to read the screen
      return;  #The game is over so exit the subroutine
    }


    #Check to see if the players have tied
    if ($winner eq "tie") {
      $ties += 1;  #Increment the number of games that have been tied
      $message = "GAME OVER: Tie!";  #Display tie message
```

```perl
   &display_game_board();  #Call subroutine that displays the game board
   print "\n Press Enter to continue: ";
   $reply = <STDIN>; #Pause to allow the player to read the screen
   return;  #The game is over so exit the subroutine
}


#If we have gotten here the game is not over yet
$message = "Player $player" . "'s move"; #Set variable indicating
                                         #whose turn it is
&display_game_board();  #Call subroutine that displays the game board
print " Select a square: ";
chomp($reply = <STDIN>);  #Collect the player's move


#Call subroutine that validates player input and pass it the player's
#input as an argument
$validmove = &validate_selection($reply);


if ($validmove == 1) { #Process valid moves
  $nomoves = $nomoves + 1;  #Increment count
  &identify_selection($reply); #Call subroutine that associates
                               #the player's move with an actual
                               #square on the game board
} else {  #Notify the player of an invalid move
  Clear_the_screen::clear();  #Call module that clears the screen
  print "Invalid move. Press Enter to try again.\n\n";
  $reply = <STDIN>; #Pause to allow the player to read the screen
}


if ($nomoves == 9) { #if nine moves have been made with no winner
                     #being declared, the game ends in a tie
  $winner = "tie";  #Set variable to indicate a tied game
} else {
  &look_for_winner(); #Call subroutine that determines when the game
                      #has been won
}


#As long as the last move was valid, switch player turns
if ($validmove == 1) {
```

```perl
      if ($player eq "X") {
        $player = "O";
      } else {
        $player = "X";
      }
    }


  } #End loop

}



#This subroutine displays the game board using global variables to fill
#in player moves and a game status message
sub display_game_board {

  Clear_the_screen::clear();  #Call module that clears the screen

  #Layout the display of the Tic Tac Toe board
  print "                              Tic Tac Toe\n\n\n";
  print "                          1       2       3\n\n";
  print "                               |       |\n";
  print "                    A    $a1   |  $a2   |   $a3\n";
  print "                               |       |\n";
  print "                    -------|-------|-------\n";
  print "                               |       |\n";
  print "                    B    $b1   |  $b2   |   $b3\n";
  print "                               |       |\n";
  print "                    -------|-------|-------\n";
  print "                               |       |\n";
  print "                    C    $c1   |  $c2   |   $c3\n";
  print "                               |       |\n\n\n";
  print "                    $message\n\n"    #Include a place
                                              #to display
                                              #status messages

}
```

```
#This subroutine determines whether the player has made a valid move
sub validate_selection {

    my $move = $_[0];  #The Player's move is passed to the subroutine as an
                       #argument

    CASE: {  #Custom CASE statement used to process player moves. Players
             #cannot pick squares that have already been selected
        $move eq "a1" && do { if ($a1 ne " ") {return "false";} };
        $move eq "a2" && do { if ($a2 ne " ") {return "false";} };
        $move eq "a3" && do { if ($a3 ne " ") {return "false";} };
        $move eq "b1" && do { if ($b1 ne " ") {return "false";} };
        $move eq "b2" && do { if ($b2 ne " ") {return "false";} };
        $move eq "b3" && do { if ($b3 ne " ") {return "false";} };
        $move eq "c1" && do { if ($c1 ne " ") {return "false";} };
        $move eq "c2" && do { if ($c2 ne " ") {return "false";} };
        $move eq "c3" && do { if ($c3 ne " ") {return "false";} };


    }

    #There are only nine squares on the game board. Anything other than
    #these nine squares is invalid
    if ($move =~ /a1|a2|a3|b1|b2|b3|c1|c2|c3/) {
        return 1;  #Return true if the player entered a valid move
    } else {
        return 0;  #Return false for invalid moves
    }


}



#This subroutine associates the player's move with a specific square on
#the Tic Tac Toe game board
sub identify_selection {

    my $move = $_[0]; #The player's move is passed to the subroutine as an
                      #argument
```

```perl
    #Place an X or an O in the appropriate square
    if ($move eq "a1") {$a1 = $player} #$move contains a value representing
    if ($move eq "a2") {$a2 = $player} #a square on the game board
    if ($move eq "a3") {$a3 = $player}
    if ($move eq "b1") {$b1 = $player} #$player contains a value of
    if ($move eq "b2") {$b2 = $player} #either X or O depending on whose
    if ($move eq "b3") {$b3 = $player} #turn it is
    if ($move eq "c1") {$c1 = $player}
    if ($move eq "c2") {$c2 = $player}
    if ($move eq "c3") {$c3 = $player}

}


#This subroutine is responsible for determining if one of the players has
#won the game
sub look_for_winner {

  #Look for a winner in the first row
  if ($a1 eq $player) {
    if ($a2 eq $player) {
      if ($a3 eq $player) {
        $winner = $player;
      }
    }
  }

  #Look for a winner in the second row
  if ($b1 eq $player) {
    if ($b2 eq $player) {
      if ($b3 eq $player) {
        $winner = $player;
      }
    }
  }

  #Look for a winner in the third row
  if ($c1 eq $player) {
```

```
    if ($c2 eq $player) {
      if ($c3 eq $player) {
        $winner = $player;
      }
    }
  }

#Look for a winner in the first column
if ($a1 eq $player) {
  if ($b1 eq $player) {
    if ($c1 eq $player) {
      $winner = $player;
    }
  }
}

#Look for a winner in the second column
if ($a2 eq $player) {
  if ($b2 eq $player) {
    if ($c2 eq $player) {
      $winner = $player;
    }
  }
}

#Look for a winner in the third column
if ($a3 eq $player) {
  if ($b3 eq $player) {
    if ($c3 eq $player) {
      $winner = $player;
    }
  }
}

#Look for a winner diagonally from the top left corner to the bottom
#right corner
if ($a1 eq $player) {
  if ($b2 eq $player) {
```

```perl
      if ($c3 eq $player) {
        $winner = $player;
      }
    }
  }


  #Look for a winner diagonally from the bottom left corner to the top
  #right corner
  if ($c1 eq $player) {
    if ($b2 eq $player) {
      if ($a3 eq $player) {
        $winner = $player;
      }
    }
  }

}



#This subroutine displays statistics collected during game play
sub display_stats {

  my $reply = "";        #Local variable used to store player input
  my $row = "_" x 61;    #Local variable representing a line made up of
                         #sixty-one underscore characters

  Clear_the_screen::clear();   #Call module that clears the screen

  #Display game statistics stored in global variables
  print " Tic Tac Toe game Statistics\n\n";
  print " $row\n\n";
  print " Total number of games played: $plays\n\n";
  print " Number of games won by player X: $xwins\n\n";
  print " Number of games won by player O: $owins\n\n";
  print " Number of games tied: $ties\n\n";
  print " $row\n\n";
  print "\n\n\n\n\n\n";
```

```perl
   print " Press Enter to continue: ";
   $reply = <STDIN>;  #Pause to allow the player to read the screen


}



#This subroutine displays help information about the game
sub display_help {

   my $reply = 0;        #Local variable used to store player input
   my $row = "_" x 61;   #Local variable representing a line made up of
                         #sixty-one underscore characters


   Clear_the_screen::clear();  #Call module that clears the screen

   #Display help information
   print " TIC TAC TOE HELP:\n\n";
   print " $row\n\n";
   print " Type Play to begin the game or type Quit to exit. To view\n";
   print " game statistics type Stats. To get help type Help and to\n";
   print " learn more about the game and its developer type About.\n";
   print " $row\n\n";
   print "\n\n\n\n\n\n\n\n\n\n";

   print " Press Enter to continue: ";
   $reply = <STDIN>;  #Pause to allow the player to read the screen


}



#This subroutine displays additional information about the game
sub display_about {

   my $reply = 0;        #Local variable used to store player input
   my $row = "_" x 61;   #Local variable representing a line made up of
                         #sixty-one underscore characters


   Clear_the_screen::clear();  #Call module that clears the screen
```

```
#Display information about the game
print " ABOUT THE TIC TAC TOE GAME:\n\n";
print " $row\n\n";
print " The Tic Tac Toe Game - Copyright 2006.\n\n";
print " Created by Jerry Lee Ford, Jr.\n";
print " $row\n\n";
print "\n\n\n\n\n\n\n\n\n\n\n";

print " Press Enter to continue: ";
$reply = <STDIN>;  #Pause to allow the player to read the screen

}
```

Compared to the other scripts in this book, this game is the most complicated. Depending on how carefully you entered the code statements that make up this script, you may find that you run into a few errors. Hopefully, you will find that the information presented in this chapter will help to you quickly track down and correct any accidental errors you might make.

SUMMARY

In this chapter you learned how to debug your Perl scripts in order to track down and fix problems that prevent your scripts from running as you expect. You learned how to leverage the information provided in Perl error messages in order to locate and fix errors. You learned how to use the print statements as a tool for tracing the logical flow of your scripts and for keeping an eye on the values assigned to variables. You also learned how to work with the Perl debugger. This included learning how to set breakpoints, trace program flow, step through statements, and to monitor and modify variable values. You also learned how to use the Perl debugger as an interactive test environment. On top of all this, you developed the Tic Tac Toe game, tying together many of the concepts and programming techniques that you have learned throughout this book.

Before you put down this book, consider taking a few minutes to work on the following list of challenges to see if you can improve the Tic Tac Toe game and make it a little more fun.

CHALLENGES

1. Currently, the Tic Tac Toe game is set up such that Player X always goes first. Consider modifying the game to give players the choice of deciding whether Player X or Player O goes first.

2. As it is currently written, the Tic Tac Toe game displays a generic error message whenever a player makes an invalid move. Modify the script to provide more useful error messages. For example, make sure that error messages address the player responsible for making the error. In addition, explain exactly why the move was invalid (e.g. out of range, square already selected, etc).

3. Back in Chapter 6, "Scope and Modules," you were introduced to a CPAN module named Audio-Beep, which once installed provided you with the ability to add a beep sound to your Perl scripts. Consider downloading and installing this module and use it to generate a beep sound to indicate when a player makes an invalid move.

4. Rather than making game statistics available as a menu option on the game's main menu, consider modifying the game to display the statistics just to the right of the game board. This way players will be able to see a running total of each game won, lost, or tied without having to ask for this information.

Part

IV

Appendices

PERL SCRIPTING

EXAMPLES

As you have worked your way through this book, you have been learning how to program using Perl. In order to demonstrate the Perl programming techniques, this book has guided you through the development of an assortment of game scripts. A benefit of this approach is that you were able to focus on the ins and outs of Perl programming without also having to simultaneously focus on learning the requirements of a particular programming environment. Nothing beyond a cursory understanding of how to work with the operating system's Command Prompt was required. Hopefully, you found this streamlined approach to learning Perl both beneficial and entertaining.

It is important to understand that Perl is capable of a great many things besides computer game development. Perl has long been used as a programming language for supporting the development of professional websites. Using Perl, you can turn static websites into sites that provide visitors with dynamic content. When used in conjunction with other resources, such as databases, you can build full-featured websites capable of supporting services such as online shopping.

Computer administrators have long used Perl as a scripting tool in order to automate the administration of desktop, server, and network resources. By developing Perl scripts that automate desktop, server, and network tasks, Perl releases administrators from performing repetitive daily and weekly tasks, allowing them to focus their time and attention on other areas.

Perl has also been integrated into many enterprise automation applications purchased by large companies all around the world. The advantage of integrating Perl into these applications is that it allows software developers to build software applications for large numbers of customers, providing commonly required functionality. At the same time, by providing customers (e.g. corporate IT programmers) with the ability to develop Perl scripts, companies can fully customize the operation of the application to meet their specific needs.

In short, Perl has worked itself into virtually every aspect of modern-day programming and software development. The intent of this appendix is to demonstrate a few areas, beyond basic game development, where Perl can be applied. The examples provided in this appendix are not intended to serve as detailed working examples; rather, their purpose is to provide you with a glimpse into different ways that Perl can be applied to other types of programming tasks in different programming environments.

CGI Scripting

One of the most common uses for Perl has been to support the development and delivery of dynamic content on the World Wide Web in the form of *Perl CGI* scripting. *CGI* or the *Common Gateway Interface*, is a collection of programs and scripts that reside on web servers. By creating Perl CGI scripts, web programmers are able to process input provided by client browsers like Internet Explorer and then return appropriate content back to the client. For example, Perl CGI scripts can be used to retrieve information from databases facilitating online shopping. Perl CGI scripts can also be used to perform many other tasks, such as managing the display of web page banners, creating and retrieving cookies, and the generation of all sorts of dynamic content.

In order to use Perl to develop web content, you need access to a web server that supports Perl scripting. Usually, Perl scripts are stored in the *cgi-bin* directory on most web servers. You'll need the ability to copy or upload your Perl CGI scripts into this directory. If your web server does not have a cgi-bin directory or if you are unable to access it, you will need to speak to the web server administrator to find out where you should store your scripts. In addition, you'll need the ability to make your scripts executable. Again, if you are unfamiliar with how to do this, your web server administrator should be able to help.

Creating a Basic CGI File

In order to integrate Perl into your website, you need to create script files containing your Perl scripts. Depending on your web server, these files may need to be assigned a .pl or .cgi file extension. Consult with your system administrator to find out which file extensions are supported. As you would expect, there are subtle differences in the way Perl CGI scripts are written compared to the way other types of Perl scripts are written. As an example, take a look at the following script.

```
#!/usr/bin/perl -w

print "Content-type: text/html\n\n";
print "<html><head><title>Hello World</title></head>\n";
print "<body><h1>Hello World</h1></body></html>";
```

 HINT A basic understanding of HTML is also essential to understanding the material presented in this section. Unless you are interested in Perl CGI script development, you may not want to finish reading this section.

The first statement is the shebang, which should be quite familiar to you by now. The second statement is new. This statement tells Perl to print an *HTML header*. This statement tells Perl it should look to the client browser instead of the Command Prompt as the destination where output should be sent. Text/html represents one type of header. There are others. For example, there are headers that direct cookie output and that handle browser redirection.

As you can see, the remainder of the statements use print statements to print out the HTML tags required to build a web page, which the web servers send back to the user's browser when the Perl CGI script is executed.

Executing Perl CGI Scripts

There are a number of different ways that you can set up a Perl CGI script to execute. For starters, if you create and save the previous script as hello.cgi and store it as an executable file in you web server's cgi-bin directory, you can call upon it using the syntax provided below.

```
http://www.urlname.com/hello.cgi
```

When executed, the hello.cgi script displays the output shown in Figure A.1 in your web browser.

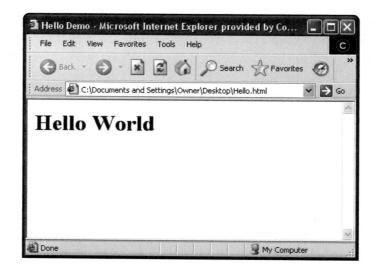

Viewing the HTML
page generated by
the sample Perl
CGI script.

Another option for setting up the execution of a Perl CGI script is to embed a reference to it in the Head or Body section of a web page, as demonstrated below.

```
<HTML>

  <HEAD>
    <TITLE>Hello Demo</TITLE>
  </HEAD>

  <BODY>
    <!--#include virtual="hello.cgi"-->
  </BODY>

</HTML>
```

When you embed a reference to a script in this manner, you must rename the web page that contains it by replacing its .html file extension with a .shtml file extension. As you can see, the actual reference to the Perl CGI script is located in a special tag located in the web page's Body section.

As you might have guessed, Perl's roots as a web programming language are quite deep. Entire books have been written that cover this aspect of Perl programming. If this is an area of programming that is of interest to you, you might want to check out the following titles:

- *CGI/PERL* (ISBN: 0619034408)
- *CGI Programming with Perl* (ISBN: 1565924193)
- *CGI Programming 101: Programming Perl for the World Wide Web* (ISBN: 0966942612)

Working with the CGI.pm Module

Rather than generating raw HTML tags by hand when developing Perl CGI scripts, you can take advantage of subroutines provided as part of the CGI.pm module, which is distributed as part of the standard Perl distribution. To use this module, all you have to do is import it into your Perl scripts as demonstrated below.

```
use CGI;
```

Once imported, you can use the CGI.pm module's subroutine to simplify the development of your Perl CGI scripts.

```
#!/usr/bin/perl -w
use CGI;
print header();
print start_html('Hello World');
print "<h1>Hello World</h1>";
print end_html;
```

The second line in this example imports the CGI module. The third line uses the CGI module's header function to print out an HTML header and is equivalent to Content-type: text/html. The next statement uses the CGI module's start_html function to generate the HTML tags required to build the beginning of the HTML page (e.g. <HTML>, <HEAD>, <TITLE>, and <BODY>). The statement that follows prints out a text string as a level 1 HTML header. The last statement uses the CGI module's end_html function to print out the HTML page's required closing HTML tags (e.g. </BODY> and </HTML>).

TRICK

As you learned in Chapter 6, "Scope and Modules," you can import entire modules or just portions of those modules. For example, in the previous example, you could replace the use CGI; statement with the following statement.

```
use CGI qw(:standard);
```

By importing only a portion of the CGI module, you limit the resources required to run your Perl scripts. In the previous example adding :standard instructs Perl to export a common subset of module subroutines into your script's namespace.

As you have seen, you can use either raw HTML or subroutines provided by the CGI module to generate required HTML tags. You can use any combination of these two approaches when developing your Perl CGI scripts, based on your personal preference.

Creating Reports and Documents

A very common use for Perl is to automate the generation and administration of text files, reports, and logs. Working with these types of resources requires the ability to create and open files. The basis for this type of interaction is through file handles.

Opening Files for Reading

In order to be able to read input from a file, you must first establish a file handle that represents the file. This is accomplished using Perl's open function. The open function readies a file for reading (or writing), allowing you to reference the file using its file handle.

The open function has the following syntax.

```
open(filehandle, 'filename')
```

The open function processes two arguments. *Filehandle* is the name assigned to the file handle that your script will use when working with the file. File handle names must start with a letter. By convention, you should use all uppercase characters and limit file handles to letters, numbers, and underscores. *Filename* is the complete path and filename for the file that you want to open. If no path information is specified, Perl will search the current directory for the specified file (e.g. the same directory where the Perl script is stored).

Be careful when developing scripts that need access files on different operating systems. On Windows, you typically specify the name and path of a file as demonstrated below.

```
open(LOGFILE, 'C:\Documents\MyScripts\InputFile.txt');
```

However, on Linux and Unix, the backward slashes are replaced with forward slashes as demonstrated here.

```
open(LOGFILE, '>/home/jerry/documents/myscripts/inputfile.txt');
```

Just to make things a little more confusing, things are done differently on Macintosh systems, where the colon character is used in place of the backward and forward slash to denote path structure.

```
open(LOGFILE, "HD:Jerry:Documents:MyScripts:InputFile.txt");
```

Reacting to Failures when Opening Files

Files are not always available when you want to access them. Files can be accidentally deleted, renamed, or moved to different locations. In addition, you might not have the security permission required to open the file. As a result, it's a good idea to provide for an alternate course of action. You can do this using the or operator and Perl's die function as demonstrated below.

```
open(LOGFILE, '>InputFile.txt') or die "Unable to open InputFile.txt";
```

Here, the statement attempts to open a file named InputFile.txt. In the event that the file cannot be opened, an error message is sent to STDERR and script execution is terminated.

TRICK

Perl also provides you with the ability to check and see if a file exists before you attempt to open it. This is accomplished using the following test.

```
if (-e 'inputFile.txt') {
  open(LOGFILE, '>InputFile.txt') or die "Unable to open
InputFile.txt";
}
```

Here, -e tells perl to check for the existence of the specified file before attempting to open it.

Reading File Contents

In order to read input from a file, it must first be opened. You can then use the <> input operator to read from it. For example, the follow statements open a text file and read the first line of text stored in it.

```
#!/usr/bin/perl

open(LOGFILE, 'InputFile.txt');
$x = <LOGFILE>;
```

You can easily read the contents of an entire input file using a loop. To see an example of how to accomplish this, let's work through a quick example. For starters, you'll need to generate a text file such as the log file shown in Figure A.2.

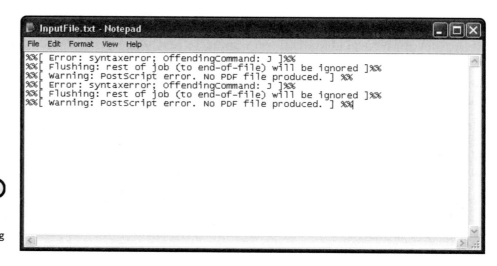

A small log file
found on a
computer running
Windows.

The following Perl scripts will read and process every line in this file, by placing the file handle representing the log file inside the <> operator and then using a while loop to iterate through every line in the log file.

```perl
#!/usr/bin/perl

open(LOGFILE, 'InputFile.txt');
while (<LOGFILE>) {
  print $_;
}


$reply = <STDIN>;
```

This script reads the log file in a scalar context a line at a time. Take note that the special $_ variable provides easy access to each line of text and that the loop automatically stops executing when the end of the file is reached. When executed, this script displays the output stored within the text file as demonstrated in Figure A.3.

Rather than process the contents of a text file in a scalar context, by processing each line in the input file one by one you can read a file in scalar context as demonstrated below.

```perl
#!/usr/bin/perl

open(LOGFILE, 'InputFile.txt');
@x = <LOGFILE>;
```

```
print @x;
```

```
$reply = <STDIN>;
```

Processing the
contents of the
log file.

Here, the contents of InputFile.txt are read into an array named @x. Each line within the text file is stored as an individual array element. The contents of the entire array can then be printed using a single statement without the need to set up a loop.

Opening Files for Writing

Reading data from files and writing data to them are separate operations. Therefore, you must set up separate file handles to perform these two different tasks. To open a file for writing, you must append the > special character to the beginning of the filename as demonstrated here.

```
open(LOGFILE, '>InputFile.txt');
```

When executed, this statement will create a new file named InputFile.txt in the current working directory. If a file with the same filename already exists, a new empty file replaces that file. If you want to preserve data already stored in an existing file, then you should open the file as demonstrated below.

```
open(LOGFILE, '>>InputFile.txt');
```

When opened using the >> special characters, any data you write to the file is appended to the end of the file.

Writing File Output

Writing output to a file is not much different than reading from it. First you must establish a file handle reference. You can then write output using the `print` function as demonstrated here.

```
#!/usr/bin/perl

open(LOGFILE, '>InputFile.txt');
print LOGFILE "Test script execution now beginning.\n";
```

When executed, this script creates a new file named InputFile.txt in the current working directory and writes a line of text to it. If a file of the same name already exists, its contents are replaced. If, on the other hand, you want to append to the end of the InputFile.txt instead of overwriting it, you could do so by modifying this example as shown below.

```
#!/usr/bin/perl

open(LOGFILE, '>>InputFile.txt');
print LOGFILE "Test script execution now beginning.\n";
```

Now the script creates InputFile.txt if it does not exist and then writes to it. Otherwise, it simply opens and appends its text string to the end of the text file.

TRAP   If you have not noticed, take a close look at the `print` statements in both of the previous examples and take note of the fact that there is no comma between the file handle and the text strings in either example. Strange as this may seem, this is the required syntax for this statement.

Closing Files when Done

Unless you close a file handle, Perl leaves it open. However, Perl automatically closes all file handles at script termination. Nevertheless, it is considered poor programming practice to leave file handles open after you are done working with them. Instead, you should execute the Perl `close` function at the appropriate location within your scripts as demonstrated below.

```
#!/usr/bin/perl

open(LOGFILE, 'InputFile.txt');
@x = <LOGFILE>;
close LOGFILE;
```

```
print @x;

$reply = <STDIN>;
```

MANAGING FILES AND DIRECTORIES

The administration of files and directories is an important task performed by desktop, server, and network administrators and can include performing many tasks, such as:

- Copying or moving log files from individual servers to a central location where they can be monitored and managed.
- Renaming daily log files at the end of each day in order to maintain an archive of backup log files.
- Deleting collections of temporary files that accumulate on workstations and servers in order to increase the amount of available disk space.
- The distribution of software files to network workstations and servers in preparation for later installation.

Rather than forcing you to use native operating systems' commands, Perl provides you with access to a number of operating system independent functions that support both file and directory administration. Where necessary, additional functionality is available in the form of external modules.

Managing Files

When it comes to the administration of files, there are a number of basic tasks that are commonly performed. These tasks include:

- Deletion
- Renaming
- Copying
- Moving

Perl provides built-in functions for performing the first two tasks. The last two tasks can be performed by taking advantage of subroutines provided by the `File::Copy` module, which is included as part of the standard Perl distribution.

HINT Before your can begin administering files and directories, you must first have the appropriate set of security permissions on the computer where the resources reside in order to perform the specified action.

Deleting Files

To delete one or more files on a computer running Windows, Linux, Unix, or MAC OS X, you can use the unlink function. Despite its name, this function provides your Perl scripts with the capability to delete one or more files passed as arguments as demonstrated below.

```
unlink ('x.log', 'InputFile.txt');
```

In this example, a log file and a text file located in the current working directory are deleted.

Renaming Files

Perl also has a function that provides you with the ability to rename files. This function is named rename and it takes two arguments, the name of the current file and the name that you want to rename it.

```
rename ('InputFile.txt', 'InputFile.old');
```

Be careful when using the rename function. If the file already exists with the same name as the file name that you are trying to rename another file to, the existing file will be overridden, assuming that you have permissions to do so.

Copying Files

Strangely, Perl does not provide functions for copying or moving files. However, Perl does come equipped with a module named File::Copy that you can import and use to perform either of these operations. Specifically, to copy a file from one directory to another, you can use the File::Copy method's copy subroutine, as demonstrated below.

```
#!/usr/bin/perl
use File::Copy;
copy('InputFile.txt', 'C:\Temp\InputFile.txt') or die "File copy failed";
```

In this example, the File::Copy module is imported into the script using the use function. Next, a file named InputFile.txt is copied from the current working directory on a Windows computer to the C:\Temp directory. However, if the file cannot be found, the die function is instead executed, sending a message to STDERR before terminating the script.

Moving Files

In order to move a script from one location to another, you can execute the File::Copy module's move subroutine as demonstrated below.

```
#!/usr/bin/perl
use File::Copy;
move('InputFile.txt', 'C:\Temp');
```

As with the module's `copy` subroutine, the `move` subroutine takes two arguments, the name and path of the file to be moved and the name and path of the location where the file is to be moved.

Managing Directories

The administration of directories is very similar to that of files. You just need to know which Perl functions and module subroutines to execute and what arguments these functions and modules require. Directory administration includes numerous tasks, including:

- Directory navigation
- Processing directory contents
- Creating new directories
- Deleting existing directories

The steps required to perform each of these tasks are outlined in the sections that follow.

Switching Directories

As has already been stated, when you pass a filename as an argument to a function or module subroutine without including any path information, Perl searches the current working directory. By default, the current working directory is the directory on which the Perl script resides. However, you can change the current working directory at any time using the `chdir` function. This function accepts one argument, the path and name of the directory that you want to make the new current working directory, as demonstrated in the following example.

```
chdir myscripts;
```

Here the current working directory is changed to the `myscripts` directory. Of course, for this example to work correctly, `myscripts` must be a directory and must also be a subroutine located in the current working directory.

If you find that you are developing Perl scripts that need to change the current working directory a number of times, it is easy to get confused as to what the current working directory is. To help in these situations, you can use the `Cwd` module's `cwd` function. The `Cwd` module is distributed as part of the standard Perl distribution and is therefore readily available. As an example of how to work with the `Cwd` module, consider the following example.

```
#!/usr/bin/perl

use Cwd;

print "Current Working Directory = " . cwd;
```

Here, the `Cwd` module's `cwd` subroutine is called from within a `print` statement. If run on a Windows system, you might see output similar to the following displayed.

```
Current Working Directory = C:/Documents and Settings/Owner/Desktop
```

Listing Directory Contents

Navigating from one directory to another is an interesting capability, but what do you do once you have established a new working directory? One useful task is to examine its contents, looking for a specific resource, such as a file or group of files. To do this you can use a scripting technique known as *globbling*. When globbling for files, you specify a pattern against which all the resources located in the specified directory are compared. To specify a pattern, you use the * character, which defines a pattern that contains zero or more characters. For example, *.txt would display all the files with a .txt file extension, whereas x*x would display any files beginning and ending with a x character.

There are different ways to glob for files, including the `glob` function, which is demonstrated below.

```
@filelist = glob '*.txt';
```

Here, a list of files in the current working directory with a .txt file extension are loaded into an array named `@filelist`. Once loaded, you can process the contents of the array and perform any required actions on the files that are listed (e.g. renaming, deleting, copying, and moving them).

Creating New Directories

If necessary, you can create new directories using Perl's `mkdir` function. This function works equally on Windows, MAC OS X, Linux, and Unix. The `mkdir` function processes two arguments, the name and path of the directory to be created and the permission attributes to be associated with the new directory. The permission attributes are required, even though they are only used on Linux and Unix systems. These permission attributes correspond to the permission attribute used by the Unix and Linux `chmod` operating system command.

A discussion of Linux and Unix permission attributes is beyond the scope of this book. However, you can learn just about anything you want to know about Linux and Unix security permissions on the Internet. For now, let's just assume that any new directory you'll be creating will not require tight security and that you are willing to allow public access to it, as demonstrated in the following example statement.

```
mkdir scriptdir, 0777;
```

Here a new directory named `scriptdir` is created in the current working directory.

Deleting Directories

In addition to creating new directories, you can also create Perl scripts that delete directories using Perl's built-in `rmdir` function. To use this function, pass it the name and path of the directory to be deleted as demonstrated below.

```
rmdir scriptdir;
```

Here the `scriptdir` directory, a subdirectory located inside the current working directory, is deleted, provided that you have the required security permissions to delete the directory. In addition, the specified directory must also be empty. The `rmdir` function will not delete a directory as long as it contains other resources.

PERLSCRIPT AND THE WSH

If you are going to be developing scripts specifically for Windows computers, you may want to look into PerlScript and *the Windows Script Host* or *WSH*. The WSH is a language independent scripting environment that runs on Windows computers. By default the WSH supports VBScripts and JScripts; however, if you install ActiveState's ActivePerl distribution, you are given the option of also configuring PerlScript, a WSH compatible version of Perl.

Using the WSH to run scripts on Windows computers gives you access to the WSH object model, which abstracts key Windows computer and network features, allowing you to programmatically access and manipulate these resources from within scripts. For example, the WSH object model provides scripts with access to the Windows registry, disk drives, networks, and the desktop. You may be thinking to yourself at this point that there must be a Perl module you can use to perform these same tasks, and you are correct. Once such module is `Win32`. However, the WSH also provides you with access to other Windows resources such as the *Active Directory* and *Windows Management Instrumentation* (*WMI*) and these are areas where PerlScript and the WSH provide you with greater access and easier control compared to working with regular Perl scripts.

In order to work with the WSH, you need to know how to program using a WSH compatible scripting language such as PerlScript. You also need to familiarize yourself with the WSH object model and learn how to use it to access and manipulate Windows resources. In addition, you need to know how to use the WSH to execute scripts.

 A full review of the WSH and its object model is beyond the scope of this book. In fact, it is such a large subject, entire books have been written about it. If this is an area of Perl scripting that interests you and you want to learn more about it, I suggest you read the following books.

- *Microsoft WSH and VBScript Programming for the Absolute Beginner, Second Edition* (ISBN: 1592007317)
- *Microsoft VBScript Professional Projects* (ISBN: 1592000568)
- *Windows Shell Scripting and WSH Administrator's Guide* (ISBN: 1931841268)
- *Learn Microsoft VBScript In a Weekend* (ISBN: 1931841705)

When you develop PerlScripts to be run by the WSH, you will generally want to assign these scripts a .pls file extension. When you do this, Windows automatically recognizes these scripts as WSH compatible. This means that you can execute them either from the Windows Command Prompt using the WScript or CScript execution hosts or from the Windows desktop by double-clicking on them. Depending on how you have written your PerlScripts, they may display output text at the command console or in graphical popup dialogs. To execute PerlScripts designed to run from the Command Prompt, you can start them by typing the CScript command followed by the script name as demonstrated below.

```
CScript test.pls
```

Alternatively, you can use the WScript execution host to run PerlScripts that display graphical output as demonstrated below.

```
WScript test.pls
```

In addition, you can double-click on any PerlScript from the Windows desktop to run it, regardless of whether it is designed to be run with the CScript or WScript execution hosts. As a quick demonstration of how to write a PerlScript, consider the following example.

```
#!/usr/bin/perl -w
#
# ScreenSvr.pl


#-------------------------------------------------------------------
# Initialization Section
```

```
#-------------------------------------------------------------------------

my $wshobject = $WScript->CreateObject("WScript.Shell");
my $screen = 'C:\Windows\System32\ssstars.scr';


#-------------------------------------------------------------------------
# MAIN Processing Section
#-------------------------------------------------------------------------

&make_registry_changes;

&display_popup_msg;

$WScript->Quit;


#-------------------------------------------------------------------------
# Subroutine Section
#-------------------------------------------------------------------------

sub make_registry_changes {

  $wshobject->RegWrite('HKCU\Control Panel\Desktop\ScreenSaveActive', 1);
  $wshobject->RegWrite('HKCU\Control Panel\Desktop\ScreenSaverIsSecure', 1);
  $wshobject->RegWrite('HKCU\Control Panel\Desktop\ScreenSaveTimeOut', 600);
  $wshobject->RegWrite('HKCU\Control Panel\Desktop\SCRNSAVE.EXE', $screen);

}


sub display_popup_msg {

  $WScript->Echo("Screen saver configuration complete.");

}
```

This script begins by declaring an instance of the WScript WshShell object, allowing the script to later execute the object's RegWrite method in order to modify registry values. Next, a scalar variable representing the name and path of the Starfield screen saver is declared. Next, two subroutines are called and then the script terminates its own execution by running the Quit method. Note that within the context of the WSH, a method is roughly equivalent to a function.

The call to the make_registry_changes subroutine results in the execution of the WshShell object's RegWrite method. This method is executed four times in order to modify registry keys that enable the Windows screen saver, turns on password protection, specifies a 10 minute screen saver time out, and assigns the Starfield screensaver. The display_popup_msg subroutine displays a text message that informs the user that the screen saver has been configured. When executed using the CScript execution host, this PerlScript makes the specified registry modifications and then displays its text message inside the Windows command console as demonstrated in Figure A.4.

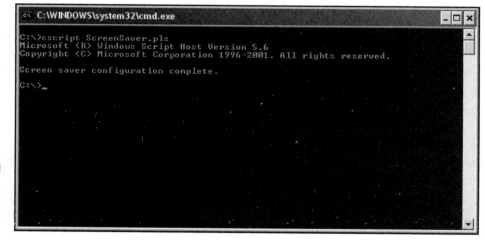

FIGURE A.4

Running a PerlScript using the WSH CScript execution host.

However, if run by the WScript execution host, the PerlScript instead displays its text message in a popup graphical dialog as demonstrated in Figure A.5.

FIGURE A.5

Running a PerlScript using the WSH WScript execution host.

TIP PerlScript can be used to develop scripts that run in any of a number of compatible execution environments. Such environments include the WSH, *Internet Information Server* or *IIS*, which is a Microsoft developed web server, and Internet Explorer. PerlScripts are run on IIS in the form of Active Server Pages, which are roughly equivalent to Perl CGI scripts, except that you can directly embed PerlScripts inside the HTML used in Active Server Pages. You can also directly embed PerlScripts inside regular HTML pages and they will execute just fine so long as the computers where the scripts are executed have ActiveState PerlScript installed. Of course this means that PerlScript is not well suited for use on the Internet where you cannot control the software installed on Internet surfer's computers. It may however be quite useful in corporate computer environments where ActiveState Perl's installation can be guaranteed.

Although it has not been covered in this book, you could write a script containing the same functionality as shown in the previous PerlScript using the Win32 module. The intent of the previous example was simply to demonstrate the mechanics involved in creating and running a PerlScript using the WSH. The real advantage of using the WSH comes when you need to access other components of its object module, which provide you with easy access to Windows resources such as the Active Directory and the WMI (Windows Management Instrumentation).

WHAT'S ON THE
COMPANION WEBSITE?

In order to become a proficient Perl programmer, you need to spend time working with the language and creating new Perl scripts. It helps to have access to sample scripts that you can study and learn. If you have created each of the Perl game scripts presented in the chapters of this book, then you already have access to a considerable amount of sample code with which you can experiment and learn. However, just in case you have not had the time to create each of the game scripts that have been presented, you'll find copies of the Perl scripts located on this book's companion website (www.courseptr.com/ downloads). This appendix provides a quick overview of each of these scripts.

Besides the book's Perl game scripts, you will also find a collection of links to shareware and freeware text editors and Perl editors on the website. This appendix provides a brief overview of each of these editors in order to assist you in evaluating them and determining if one of them suits your needs.

THE BOOK'S SOURCE CODE
This section provides an overview of the Perl scripts that you will find on this book's companion website.

TABLE B.1 PERL GAME SCRIPTS LOCATED ON THE COMPANION WEBSITE

Reference	Script	Description
Chapter 1	Perl Humor Script	This script demonstrates how to create an interactive Perl game that tells humorous jokes.
Chapter 2	Story of William the Great	This script demonstrates how to collect user input and then create a dynamic story that incorporates the information that has been collected.
Chapter 3	Perl Fortune Teller	This script demonstrates how to generate random numbers and apply conditional logic in order to create an automated fortune teller that answers player questions.
Chapter 4	Star Wars Jedi Master Quiz	This script demonstrates how to set up a loop in order to process a collection of answers to a game quiz where players are required to demonstrate their knowledge of *Star Wars* trivia.
Chapter 5	What's My Number Game	This script demonstrates how to better organize scripts using subroutines through the development of a number guessing game where the player attempts to guess a randomly generated number in the fewest possible number of guesses.
Chapter 6	Perl Lottery Number Picker	This script demonstrates how to set and control variable scope while creating a utility that players can use to generate a list of randomly selected lottery numbers.
Chapter 7	Rock, Paper, Scissors	This script demonstrates how to use regular expressions to process information collected by the user through the creation of a classic childhood game.
Chapter 8	Perl Tic Tac Toe	This script provides an opportunity to tie together all of the information presented in this book by developing a two-player version of the Tic Tac Toe game.

ADVANCED TEXT EDITORS

If you are a Windows or Linux user and are not terribly satisfied with the built-in text editors provided by your operating system, you may want to consider an upgrade. This book's companion website contains copies of two highly extensible text editors, JGsoft EditPad Lite and

JGsoft EditPad Pro. The Lite version is free for personal use but lacks some of the features of the Professional version.

JGsoft EditPad Lite

The JGsoft EditPad Lite script editor was originally designed as a replacement for Windows Notepad. However, a Linux version is now available. EditPad Lite lets you open more than one file at a time, which is especially helpful when you want to copy and paste code between Perl scripts.

Major product features include:

- Line and column numbering
- Automatic indent and outdent options
- Optional word wrapping
- A Goto line capability
- The ability to open any of the last 16 files using the Reopen menu
- The ability to perform lowercase, uppercase, and invert case operations
- Advanced search and replace for all open files
- A print preview capability

As shown in Figure B.1, you can learn more about EditPad Lite and download a free copy at www.editpadpro.com/editpadlite.html.

JGsoft EditPad Pro

JGsoft EditPad Pro provides access to all the features found in JGsoft EditPad Lite and a whole lot more. One of EditPad Pro's most notable features is its ability to define syntax color-coding schemes for specific file types, including Perl scripts. All that you have to do to set it up as a Perl editor is to visit www.editpadpro.com/cgi-bin/cscslist2.pl and download one of several predefined Perl color schemes.

Other major features provided by EditPad Pro include:

- The ability to create your own syntax color coding schemes
- Built-in spellchecking
- The ability to organize and manage multiple scripts into projects
- The ability to bookmark specific lines within a file

As shown in Figure B.2, you can learn more about JGsoft EditPad Pro and download an evaluation version at http://www.editpadpro.com.

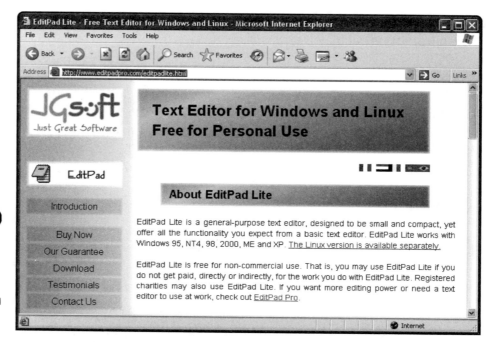

FIGURE B.1

The JGsoft EditPad Lite text editor represents a significant upgrade over Windows Notepad and most basic text editors.

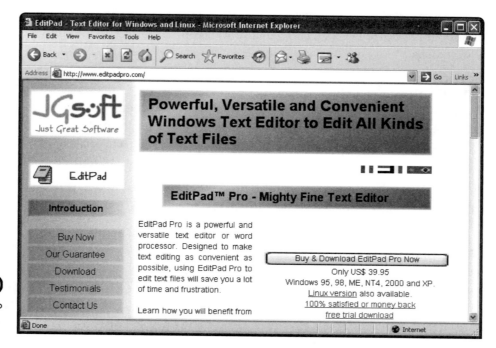

FIGURE B.2

JGsoft EditPad Pro is distributed as shareware.

Perl Editors

If you want more Perl-specific features than are provided by text editors available on your operating system or those listed previously in this appendix, then you might consider using a Perl editor. Of course, this will require you to take the time to learn how to work with the Perl editor in order to become proficient with it. In the sections that follow, you will learn about a number of very feature-rich Perl editors.

Perl Code Editor

Perl Code Editor runs on Microsoft Windows. Its major features include syntax color coding, automatic code indention, and line numbering. The Perl Code Editor is available online at www.perlvision.com/pce/, as shown in Figure B.3.

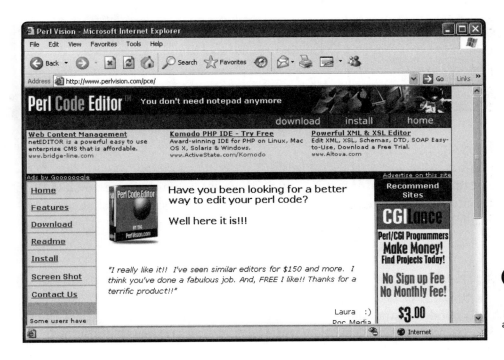

FIGURE B.3

Perl Code Editor runs on Windows and is available as a free download.

Perl Builder 2.0

Perl Builder 2.0 is a Perl editor that is made available in two versions, Standard and Professional. It runs on Microsoft Windows. It includes a CGI Wizard, which should be of benefit to beginner Perl programmers that are interested in Web development. You can download a trial copy of Perl Builder 2.0 at www.solutionsoft.com/perl.htm, as shown in Figure B.4.

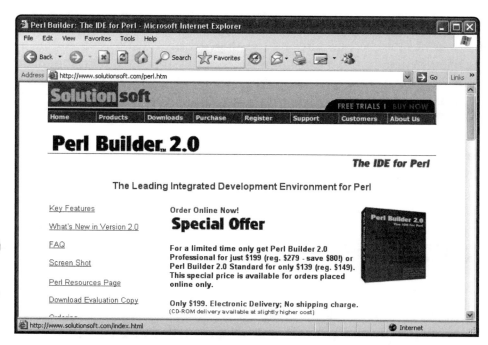

DzSoft Perl Editor

The DzSoft Perl Editor is designed to facilitate Perl/CGI script development. It runs on Windows and provides a number of helpful features, including syntax highlighting and a built-in collection of customizable code snippets. The DzSoft Perl Editor is distributed as shareware and can be downloaded at www.dzsoft.com/dzperl.htm, as shown in Figure B.5.

Komodo

Komodo is a full-featured integrated development environment (IDE) that supports the editing, testing, and debugging of multiple programming languages, including Perl. Komodo can be run on Linux, Windows, and Mac OS X. It can be downloaded as a 21-day trial from http://www.activestate.com/Products/Komodo/features/perl.plex, as shown in Figure B.6.

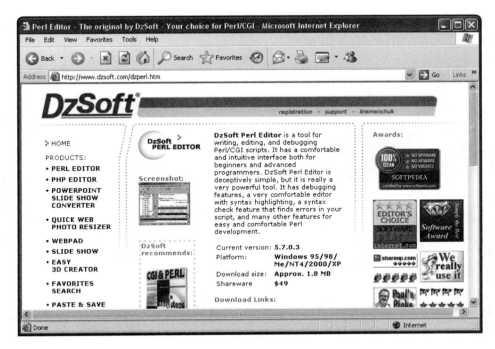

The DzSoft Perl Editor is a Perl editor designed to assist in the development of Perl/CGI scripts.

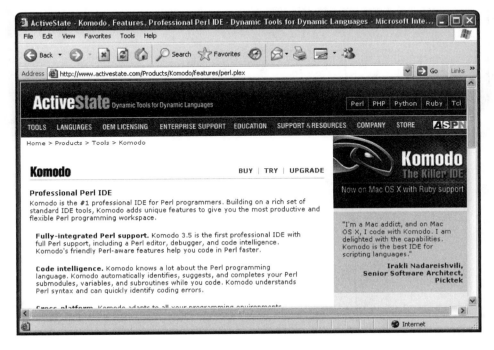

Komodo provides features that include statement color-coding, syntax checking, and code auto-completion.

PerlEdit

PerlEdit is a small Perl editor that runs on both Windows and Linux. Its features include color-coding and a visual debugger. In addition, PerlEdit provides a multi-document interface. You can download PerlEdit from http://www.indigostar.com/perledit.html, as shown in Figure B.7.

FIGURE B.7

PerlEdit is distributed as a 2MB download that is free for personal use.

WHAT NEXT?

Hopefully you have found this book to be a useful first step in your journey to become a Perl programmer. Don't look at this book as the end of your Perl programming education but rather as the beginning. Perl is an incredibly robust programming language that is constantly evolving and changing. To become a true Perl guru, you need to spend time writing Perl scripts and experimenting with the language to see how it works. You also need to keep reading and learning from other people's experiences. To that end, I have put together a list of resources that I think will help you to keep your momentum going. These resources include other books to read, Perl websites to visit, and mailing lists that you may want to join.

RECOMMENDED READING

This section provides a list of Perl programming books that you may want to look into as you continue your journey learning Perl.

Perl Fast and Easy Web Development

by Leslie Bate

ISBN 1931841179, Course Technology PTR, 2001

This book provides a gentle entry-level Perl primer and also serves as a guide to web programming, with a strong focus on using Perl with CGI.

Learning Perl, Fourth Edition

by Randal Schwartz, Tom Phoenix, and Brian Foy

ISBN 0596101058, O'Reilly Media, 2005

Despite its title, this book is best suited to programmers with previous hands-on Perl experience. However, even beginning Perl programmers will be able to gain insight from this book. If you stick with Perl, you'll eventually want to make this book part of your library.

Programming Perl, Third Edition

by Larry Wall, Tom Christiansen, and Jon Orwant

ISBN: 0596000278, O'Reilly Media, 2000

Don't let the publishing date of this book fool you. Even at six plus years of age, many Perl programmers still swear by this book. It is a bit of a challenging read, but the intermediate level Perl programmer will find it's well worth the time and effort.

Advanced Perl Programming, Second Edition

by Simon Cozens

ISBN: 0596004567, O'Reilly Media, 2005

As this title says, this book is targeted at advanced Perl programmers and requires a strong Perl programming background in order to be able to read and successfully follow along. While I would not rush out and buy this book today, it is probably one that you'll want to keep in mind for a year or two down the road.

Learn Perl In a Weekend

by Thomas Nowers

ISBN 193184177, Course Technology PTR, 2002

This book is designed to provide you with a complete Perl primer over the course of a weekend. It's a good source for beginning to learn how to use Perl and CGI to develop web scripts.

LOCATING PERL RESOURCES ONLINE

Of course, there are plenty of other good sources of information than just books. The Internet is filled with websites dedicated to Perl. I recommend spending some time surfing around to see what you can find. To help give you a head start, you might want to begin by visiting the websites listed below.

perl.com

perl.com, shown in Figure C.1, is sponsored by O'Reilly Media and has an obvious slant toward materials published by that organization. Still, there is a wealth of Perl information available at this website.

FIGURE C.1

perl.com provides easy access to Perl documentation, downloads, and articles.

The Perl Directory at Perl.org

The Perl Directory, shown in Figure C.2, is located at www.Perl.org. Here you will find links to tons of Perl resources, including documentation, users groups, modules, and information about Perl events and conferences.

Perlmonks

Perkmonks, shown in Figure C.3, is located at www.perlmonks.com. This website is a good source for finding just about anything you want to learn about Perl.

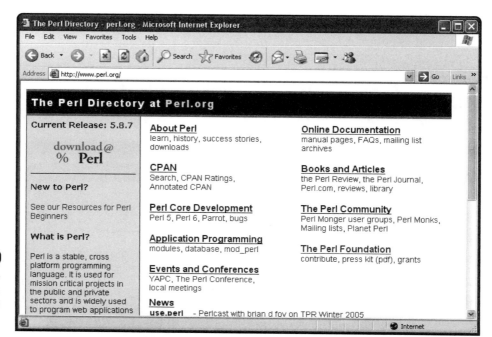

FIGURE C.2

The Perl Directory
provides you with
access to a wealth
of Perl related
information.

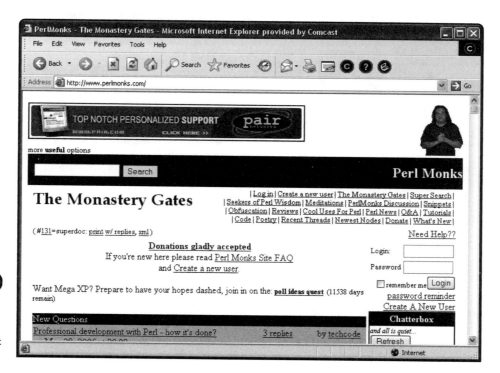

FIGURE C.3

Perlmonks is an
excellent source
for finding online
information about
Perl.

The Comprehensive Perl Archive Network

The Comprehensive Perl Archive Network, shown in Figure C.4, is located at www.cpan.org. This website provides access to a wide range of Perl resources, including documentation, Perl installation modules, sample scripts, and mailing lists.

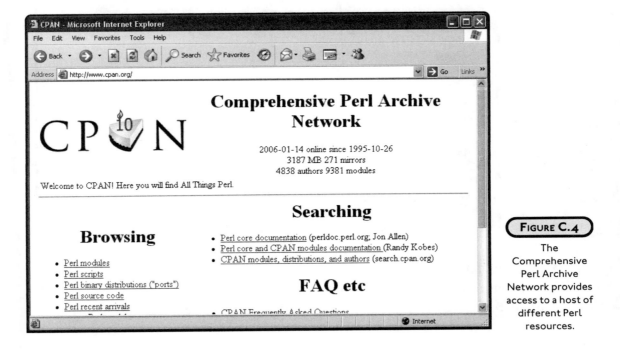

FIGURE C.4

The Comprehensive Perl Archive Network provides access to a host of different Perl resources.

The Perl Foundation

The Perl Foundation, shown in Figure C.5, can be found at http://perlfoundation.org. The mission of the Perl Foundation is to facilitate the development of Perl. It helps to accomplish this by coordinating the activities of different grassroots Perl groups. This is a great site for learning about the latest developments in Perl.

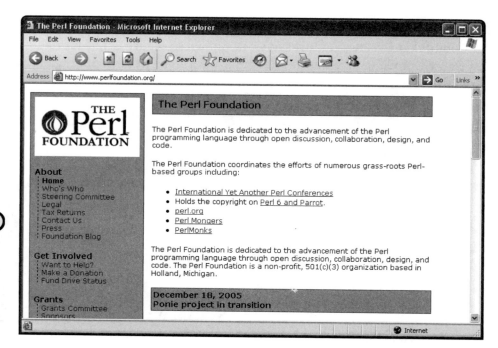

FIGURE C.5

The Perl
Foundation is a
non-profit
organization
dedicated to
furthering the
advancement of
Perl.

PERL MAILING LISTS

Sometimes the best source of new information is from other people in the same situation that you are in. By this I mean from other people trying to learn Perl. One way to introduce yourself to these people and to interact with them is to join a mailing list, or more specifically a Perl mailing list dedicated to beginning Perl programmers. While there is no shortage of Perl mailing lists that you can join, the sections that follow provide information about mailing lists that I think you may find particularly helpful.

perl.beginners

One mailing list dedicated strictly to beginner Perl programmers is perl.beginners, which you'll find at www.nntp.perl.org/group/perl.beginners/, as shown in Figure C.6.

Yahoo! Groups: perl.beginners

Another good mailing list that you should consider signing up with is the perl.beginners list sponsored by Yahoo! Groups, which you can register with at groups.yahoo.com/group/perl-beginner/, as shown in Figure C.7.

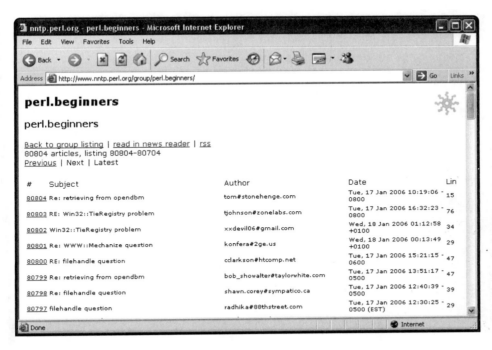

FIGURE C.6

perl.beginners advertises itself as a list where beginner Perl programmers can ask questions in a friendly atmosphere.

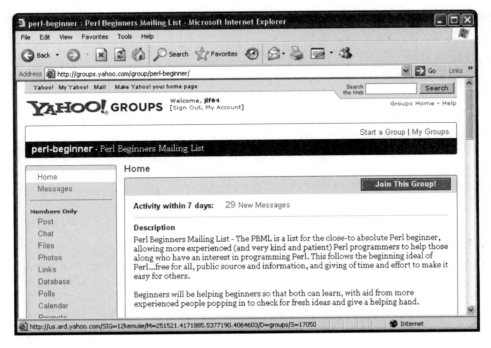

FIGURE C.7

The perl.beginners mailing list sponsored by Yahoo! allows thousands of registered beginning Perl programmers to share information.

GLOSSARY

Active Directory.   A service run on Microsoft Network that facilitates the administration and management of network security.

ActivePerl.   A Perl distribution provided by ActiveState that runs on a number of operating systems, including Windows, Linux, Mac OS X, AIX, and HP-UX.

Application Developer.   A term used to describe programmers.

Argument.   Data passed to a script or subroutine for use as input.

Array.   A collection of scalar data that is stored in an indexed list.

Array element.   An individual piece of information stored in an array.

Arithmetic operators.   Characters used to specify different mathematical operations in expressions (+, -, *, /, and %).

Assignment operators.   Characters used to assign values to numeric variables in expressions.

Awk.   A Unix-based programming language that is used to define text patterns in order to perform complex searches and the action to be taken when pattern matches occur.

Bare block.   A code block not associated with a conditional test or loop.

Bareword. A string defined without being enclosed inside quotes.

Boolean. A type of value that represents a true or false condition.

Breakpoint. A marker set by the Perl debugger that identifies points within a script where execution should be paused.

C. An extremely powerful and efficient general purpose programming language originally developed on Unix but now available on every major operating system. C is sometimes used as the programming language used to develop Perl modules.

C++. A programming language developed as an enhancement to the C programming language with strong support for object-oriented programming.

Call. The process of calling a function or subroutine within a Perl script.

Case sensitivity. A feature of Perl that differentiates between uppercase and lowercase spelling.

Code blocks. A group of statements enclosed within curly braces that are called and executed as a unit.

Command Prompt. A text-based interface that accepts commands and submits them for processing by the operating systems and then displays any results or errors that are returned.

Comment. A statement embedded inside a script that documents a portion of the script without affecting its execution. In Perl comment statements begin with the # character.

Comparison operators. Characters that are used to specify the type of tests to execute when formulating conditional statements.

Compiling. The process of converting a program into a format that can be executed by the operating system.

Concatenation. The process of joining two or more strings into a single string.

Conditional logic. The programmatic analysis of two or more conditions in order to determine the logical flow of the script.

Context. A Perl concept that means that things behave differently depending on the situation in which they are used.

CPAN (Comprehensive Perl Archive Network). The primary repository of Perl distributions, documentation, scripts, and modules.

cpan. A Perl utility that automates the process of finding, downloading, and installing Perl modules.

CScript.   A WSH execution host that supports the execution of command-line scripts.

Database Administrator.   An individual responsible for the administration of databases and for the development of automation that manages tasks such as database setup, backup, account administration, problem diagnosis, and performance tuning.

Databases.   A repository used to store and organize collections of data.

Debug.   The process of testing scripts and programs in order to identify and correct errors.

Decrement.   The process of decreasing the numeric value assigned to a scalar variable.

Delimiter.   A marker that separates different pieces of data passed to commands, procedures, or scripts.

Desktop Administrator.   An individual responsible for the administration of desktop computers and for the development of automation that performs tasks such as configuring network access, the synchronization of local and network files, software installation, and account management.

Element.   An individual piece of data stored in an array that is referenced using its indexed position.

Endless loop.   A loop that iterates forever preventing a script from completing its task.

Error.   A problem that occurs during the execution of a script.

Escaping.   A programming technique in which the \ character is appended to the beginning of a character in order to alter the default way Perl interprets the character.

Expression.   A programming statement that evaluates a statement and returns a value.

FAQs (Frequently Asked Questions).   A list of commonly asked questions and their associated answers.

File extensions.   A set of characters appended to the end of a filename that identifies a file type.

Floating point.   A real number containing a fractional part that may be rounded to based on a specified level of precision.

Function.   A collection of statements that are called and executed as a unit and which can return a result to the calling statement.

Global variables.   A variable that is accessible from any location within a script.

Globbing.   The process of searching directory contents based on simple pattern matches.

GUI (Graphical User Interface).   A point-and-click graphical interface that permits users to interact with the operating system using the mouse and keyboard.

Hashes.   A collection of data stored as a unit using key-value pairs.

Hexadecimal.   A numeric system with a base of 16 that uses the characters 0-9 and A-F to represent numeric values.

HTML (Hypertext Markup Language).   A markup language that is used to develop HTML pages.

IDE (Integrated Development Environment).   A script or program development environment that provides access to tools that assist in the development, testing, and debugging of scripts and programs.

Importing modules.   The process of loading a module into a Perl script.

Increment.   The process of increasing the numeric value assigned to a scalar variable.

Index.   A numeric value used to indicate the position of an element in an array.

Input.   Arguments passed to scripts and subroutines for use as data.

Iteration.   The process of repeating the execution of a loop.

Integer.   A whole number.

Internet.   A global public network made up of interconnected computer networks that communicate via TCP/IP, supporting global commerce and information sharing.

IIS (Internet Information Server).   A collection of services run on Windows servers that supports web hosting.

Interpolation.   The process by which Perl replaces a variable's name with its value.

Interpreted language.   A programming language used to develop scripts stored as plain text that must be interpreted at runtime.

Java.   An object-oriented programming language that facilitates the development of web-based applications. Java applications run within a Java virtual machine in an operating system independent environment.

JavaScript.   A popular scripting language that supports both client and server application development for web-based applications.

JScripts.   A Windows Script Host compatible scripting language used to develop administrative scripts on Windows computers.

Key-value pair.   An individual unit of data stored in a hash along with its associated label.

Komodo.   A graphical IDE developed by ActiveState with built-in script debugging features.

Linux.   An open source computer operating system derived from Unix that has grown in popularity in recent years and has made significant inroads in popularity in both corporate and home markets.

List.   A collection of scalar data that you can use to store and manage as a unit.

List data.   A collection of data stored as a list, array, or hash.

Load.   The process used to import variables and subroutines stored in modules into a Perl script.

Local Area Networks.   A computer network covering a small area such as a small business or home.

Local variable.   A variable that is similar to a private variable except that a local variable is accessible not just to the subroutine in which it is defined but also to any subroutines embedded within the subroutine.

Logical error.   An error created when a programmer instructs a script to do something other than what it was actually intended to do.

Logical operators.   Characters that are used to perform tests of other comparison operations.

Loop.   A collection of statements that are repeatedly executed until a specified condition is met or until a loop control statement executes, terminating loop execution.

Mac classic.   A computer operating system run on Apple computers prior to the Mac OS X operating system.

Macintosh.   A type of personal computer developed by Apple Computer. It was the first computer to feature a graphical user interface and mouse.

Mac OS X.   A proprietary operating system developed by Apple Computer for use on Macintosh computers, which is based on the Unix operating system.

MacPerl.   A Perl distribution developed for Macintosh computers that includes Mac-specific features and functionality.

Man pages.   Manual pages that store information about Perl commands on computers running Linux, Unix, and Mac OS X.

Metacharacter.   A character that changes the way pattern matching occurs.

Mathematical precision. The specification of the number of significant digits used to represent the fractional part of a number.

Module. An add-on component that provides capabilities not built in to Perl.

Network Administrator. An individual responsible for managing computer networks and for developing automation that helps to configure, diagnose, and administer network resources.

Object. A programming construct that consists of predefined properties and methods that can be used to control or manipulate the resources represented by the object.

Octal. A numeric system with a base of 8 that uses digits 0-7 to represent numeric values.

Initialize. The process of assigning a starting value to a variable.

OOP (object-oriented programming). A method of programming in which data and objects are stored and managed together along with the program code that manipulates them.

One-liners. A small Perl script executed on the fly from the Command Prompt.

Operator precedence. The process used by Perl to determine the order in which mathematic operations are executed.

Package. A means of organizing the variables and subroutines within Perl modules.

Parameter. One or more arguments passed to a command, utility, script, or application that is then processed as input.

Parse. The process of analyzing a string and breaking down its structure.

Pattern matching. The process of identifying matching values based on searches performed using patterns.

Perl (Practical Extraction and Reporting Language). A backcronym for a scripting language developed in 1987 by Larry Wall.

Perl CGI (Common Gateway Interface). A collection of programs and scripts residing on web servers that deliver web content to client browsers.

Perl Community. A term that refers to millions of Perl programmers around the world that interact and share information on Perl.

Perl Dev Kit. A collection of applications developed by ActiveState for the purpose of helping streamline the development and deployment of Perl scripts.

Perl interpreter. A tool used to parse Perl scripts, translating them into executable code that is then sent to the operating system for execution.

Perl library. The collection of modules, scripts, and files shipped as part of the Perl distribution.

Perldoc. A Perl utility that provides you the ability to search through Perl's documentation for specific topics.

Perl Package Module (PPM). A utility developed by ActiveState that automates the process of searching for, downloading, and installing Perl modules.

Permissions. Security settings that control access to computer resources.

Private variable. A variable that is not accessible outside of the control block, subroutine, module, or script in which it is defined.

Program. A collection of program statements that make up a script or application.

Prompt. A command-line interface that accepts text-based input which is passed on to the operating system for execution.

Pseudocode. A rough, English-like outline of the logic required to build all or part of a script or application.

Python. A scripting language named after the comedic troupe Monty Python that was made popular by the Linux operating system and later ported over to Windows.

Registry. A built-in Windows database where configuration information, including software, hardware, system, user, and application settings are stored.

RegExps. Another name used to refer to regular expressions.

Regular expression. A pattern used to describe or match a specified pattern.

Relational operators. An operator used to determine the state of equality between two values.

Reserved words. Keywords that make up the Perl programming language and that can only be used in accordance with the rules of Perl.

Runtime error. An error that occurs during the execution of a script that results when the script attempts to perform an illegal action.

Scalars. A single piece of data made up of a number or a string.

Scientific notation. A numeric system based on the power of 10.

Scope.   A term referring to the accessibility of a variable throughout a script.

Script.   A group of statements embedded inside a plain text file that is interpreted and executed.

Script editor.   A specialized text editor designed to facilitate script development with features such as color-coding and line numbering.

Script files.   A plain text file containing statements that make up a script.

Sed (Stream Editor).   A simple programming language originally developed on Unix that is used to programmatically read and process data stored in text files.

Server Administrator.   An individual responsible for the administration of computer servers and for automating maintenance tasks such as disk administration, service management, and performance tuning.

Shebang.   A special type of comment that is used to invoke the Perl interpreter.

Shell Script.   A script written for execution by the operating system's built-in command interpreter.

Slice.   The retrieval of a series of elements from an array.

Sort.   The process of arranging items in a particular sequence.

Special variables.   A collection of variables that is automatically created by Perl and accessible to statements within a Perl script.

Statement.   A executable line of code within a script or program.

STDERR (Standard Error).   The default location where Perl script error messages are sent.

STDIN (Standard Input).   The default location where Perl scripts look for input.

STDOUT (Standard Output).   The default location where Perl scripts send script output.

Step in.   The act of controlling the execution of a script during debugging where the debugger steps inside a subroutine, executing pausing at each statement within the subroutine.

Step over.   The action of controlling the execution of a script during debugging where the debugger steps silently through the execution of a subroutine, pausing at each statement that follows the subroutine.

String.   A group of text characters referenced as a unit.

Subroutine.   A custom collection of statements called and executed as a unit.

Symbol Table.   A collection of variable names and values defined within a package.

Syntax.   A set of rules outlining the format of commands.

Syntax error.   Errors that occur when you fail to follow the rules for formatting Perl code statements.

Template.   A predefined script outline that facilitates the development of structured scripts.

Terminal window.   A software application that provides access to an operating system Command Prompt.

Tracing.   The process of tracking script execution flow and variable values when debugging a script.

Troubleshooting.   The act of tracking down and eliminating errors when debugging a script.

Unix.   A computer operating system developed by AT&T Bell Labs in the 1960s which has since been ported to every major computing platform.

Validation.   The process of verifying that data input conforms to required specifications.

Value.   Data assigned to a variable.

Variable.   A reference to a piece of data stored in memory that is referenced based on an assigned name.

VBScript.   A Windows Script Host compatible scripting language used to develop administrative scripts on Windows computers.

Visual Basic.   An object-oriented programming language developed by Microsoft that is based on the BASIC (Beginner's All-Purpose Symbolic Instruction Code) programming language.

Warnings.   The enabling of additional error messages that help to identify potential errors in Perl scripts.

Web Developer.   A programmer that specializes in the development of scripts and applications that execute on the World Wide Web.

Whitespace.   The use of blank spacing and lines in order to improve the layout presentation of script statements.

Win32 Modules.   Perl modules designed to facilitate the development of scripts that run on Windows operating systems.

Win32::Registry.   A Perl module that facilitates the administration of the Windows registry.

Win32::Process. A Perl module that facilitates the creation and management of Windows processes.

Win32::Services. A Perl module that facilitates the administration of Windows services.

Windows. A proprietary operating system developed by Microsoft for use on personal computers.

WMI (Windows Management Instrumentation). An interface through which scripts and programs can access and administrate operating system resources on computers running Microsoft Windows.

WScript. A WSH execution host that supports the execution of desktop scripts capable of displaying graphical popup dialogs.

WSH (Windows Script Host). A language-independent scripting environment that runs on Microsoft Windows.

xterm. A terminal console found on many Unix and Linux systems.

INDEX

X

Y

Z